Perspectives on Supply Chain Management and Logistics

The Classic Group
3, Clanwilliam Terrace
Dublin 2
t: 01 642 4160

Perspectives on Supply Chain Management and Logistics

Creating Competitive Organisations in the 21st Century

Edited by
EDWARD SWEENEY

BLACKHALL
Publishing

This book was typeset by Ark Imaging for

Blackhall Publishing
33 Carysfort Avenue
Blackrock
Co. Dublin
Ireland

e-mail: info@blackhallpublishing.com
www.blackhallpublishing.com

© Edward Sweeney and the individual authors 2007

ISBN: 978-1-84218-129-4

A catalogue record for this book is available
from the British Library.

All rights reserved. No part of this publication may be reproduced, stored in a retrieval system or transmitted in any form or by any means, electronic, mechanical, photocopying, recording or otherwise, without the prior, written permission of the publisher.

This book is sold subject to the condition that it shall not, by way of trade or otherwise, be lent, resold, hired out, or otherwise circulated without the publisher's prior consent in any form of binding or cover other than that in which it is published and without a similar condition including this condition being imposed on the subsequent purchaser.

Note: every effort was made to contact the relevant parties for permission to reproduce copyright material in this book. If there are permissions outstanding, please contact Blackhall Publishing.

Printed in the UK by Athenaeum Press Ltd.

Contents

Preface		vii
Acknowledgements		xiii
About the Contributors		xv
Chapter 1	Introduction *Edward Sweeney*	1

SECTION 1 – SCM: CONTEXT, DEFINITION AND THE STRATEGIC AND FINANCIAL DIMENSIONS — 5

Chapter 2	The Evolving Supply Chain Management Context *Edward Sweeney*	7
Chapter 3	Understanding Supply Chain Management *Edward Sweeney*	27
Chapter 4	The Strategic Dimension of Supply Chain Management *Daniel Park*	73
Chapter 5	The Financial Dimension of Supply Chain Management *Des Lee and Edward Sweeney*	93

SECTION 2 – SCM: THE CUSTOMER PERSPECTIVE — 109

Chapter 6	Marketing and Supply Chain Integration: Substantiating Customer Care *Natalie Descheres*	111
Chapter 7	Understanding Customer Service *Liz Carroll*	131
Chapter 8	Customer Service and Supply Chain Design *Randal Faulkner*	159

SECTION 3 – SCM: THE SUPPLIER PERSPECTIVE — 169

Chapter 9	Outsourcing and its Role in the Supply Chain *Aoife O'Riordan and Edward Sweeney*	171

Chapter 10	Procurement and Purchasing in the Supply Chain *Micheal O'Fearghail*	191
Chapter 11	Purchasing Management: Elements of Good Operational Practice *Graham Heaslip*	209

SECTION 4 – ICT IN THE SUPPLY CHAIN — 233

Chapter 12	The Role of Information and Communications Technology in the Supply Chain *Ronan McDonnell, John Kenny and Edward Sweeney*	235
Chapter 13	Information and Communications Applications in Transportation and Logistics *Pietro Evangelista*	249
Chapter 14	E-Business and Supply Chain Management *Bernd Huber and Claudia Wagner*	265

SECTION 5 – THE FUTURE OF SCM: MAKING CHANGE HAPPEN — 281

Chapter 15	Supply Chain Benchmarking and Performance Measurement: Towards the Learning Supply Chain *Edward Sweeney*	283
Chapter 16	Re-engineering the Supply Chain: Making SCM Work for You *Edward Sweeney*	295
Chapter 17	Supply Chain Management: The Business Model of the 21st Century *Edward Sweeney and Randal Faulkner*	307

Glossary — 317

Index — 321

Preface

Like many people, I have been involved in logistics and supply chains for most of my life, without always necessarily being aware of it.

My first vacation job as a student was in the office of a ferry company in the Port of Rosslare in Ireland where my main responsibilities related to stock control. What was at the time a mechanical task of comparing closing stock of duty-free goods after a voyage to pre-voyage opening stock minus recorded sales, I now realise was an exercise in ensuring inventory data accuracy. I now also realise that inventory management is really a microcosm of the whole of supply chain management (SCM) in that it is essentially concerned with achieving the customer service levels demanded by the market, while at the same time optimising supply chain costs.

My second vacation job was in the post office in Wexford in the south-east of Ireland. During my time there I never heard the word 'logistics' used but the logistical and supply chain issues associated with mail collection and delivery continue to present challenges to staff in the postal service throughout the world. In many ways, the postal system is the most global supply chain of them all and it has been for centuries. The organisation, planning, implementation and control of the system is a complex task, now largely enabled by quite sophisticated information and communications technology (ICT) tools.

During my engineering undergraduate studies – largely focused on mechanical design aspects of the subject – the concept of a supply chain never really crossed my mind. My job as a designer would be to design products that were characterised by high levels of specification and performance. That parts for these products had to be sourced, components and sub-assemblies manufactured, finished products distributed, and that these products were to be sold to customers in a manner which contributed to shareholder value, were all of little or no concern to me as a design engineer. My first foray into the real world of manufacturing indicated to me that these issues were also of little or no concern to the numerous functional departments which comprised large manufacturing enterprises.

Preface

As a design engineer in industry, a peculiar *modus operandi* began to emerge before me. It went something like this. We – the designers – designed components, sub-assemblies and even complete products. We used all the latest ICT tools such as computer aided design (CAD) and finite element stress analysis. We typically ended up with a design of which we were very proud in terms of performance, functionality and aesthetics. The engineering manager then passed the design 'over the wall' to our colleagues in the manufacturing engineering department. Their job was to 'massage' the design so that it was capable of being manufactured, given the level of manufacturing process technology available. There usually followed a series of exchanges between 'us' – the engineering designers – and 'them' – the manufacturing engineers – with the design coming and going back and forward over the 'wall' many times until some form of agreement and compromise was reached. This typically involved 'us' making what were euphemistically referred to as 'concessions' to 'them'. A 'concession' was a recognition that a design change would not fundamentally interfere with the product's functionality. More often than not, product performance would be compromised but not its core functionality – it would still work! This process – which typically took several months – usually resulted in a final design with which we were not 100 per cent happy but which we knew would work, and which the manufacturing engineers knew they could make. A further series of similar interactions then took place involving purchasing and procurement personnel (and key suppliers), finance staff, and sales and marketing personnel. Eventually, a final specification was agreed (in most but by no means all cases) and the actual planning of purchasing, production, distribution and sales could begin. Several months, even years, would be consumed by this highly sequential process. The net result was often commercially disasterous, with products being introduced to markets much later than was really necessary. There must have been a better way!

Of course there was a better way. The better way was originally referred to as design for manufacture, where design and manufacturing engineers and managers worked together as a *team* to design new products. This was good insofar as it went but was subsequently expanded to include other functional departments within the organisation (e.g. purchasing, sales and marketing, distribution and logistics, finance, IT). This was the essence of what became known as simultaneous or concurrent engineering. It involved the replacement of the old approach, characterised by sequentiality and fragmentation, with a new one, characterised by parallelism and *integration*. I have italicised *team* and *integration* because these words, in my view, capture the essence of a supply chain approach to new product development (NPD) and new product introduction (NPI). At the time, the phrase 'supply chain' was not used to describe the approach but that's what it was in reality. *Teams* comprised designers, manufacturing engineers, production floor staff, purchasing and procurement professionals, sales and marketing personnel and finance and other specialist staff, as well as external stakeholders such as key suppliers and customers, and worked in an *integrated* manner with a shared vision and common goals. It really was 'design for total supply chain management'. This was my first real professional introduction to the potential of SCM but I still didn't realise it.

I began my academic career in Dublin in the 1980s – not a good time to begin an academic (or any other) career in Ireland. The economy of the nation was on the verge of collapse with mass unemployment and a Government running a recklessly high current budget deficit. In short, there was not a lot of time for the niceties of SCM. We struggled on as best we could, largely continuing to do things in the traditionally wasteful and fragmented ways to which we had become accustomed and with which we had become comfortable. Indeed, the educational system was accentuating the problem by teaching students about outmoded practices and by failing to recognise that innovative methods, emerging mainly from the Japanese automotive and consumer electronics sectors, existed and might offer some respite from the prevailing problems if understood and implemented appropriately.

In the late 1980s, I moved to the Warwick Manufacturing Group (WMG) – part of the University of Warwick. WMG was founded by Professor (now Lord) S.K. Bhattacharyya with a view to transforming UK industry through applied research, technology transfer and high quality vocational education and training. It worked with most leading technological and engineering companies in the UK and beyond, particularly in the automotive and aerospace sectors. It is easy to see in hindsight that there were many weaknesses in the practices being adopted by industry at the time. Nonetheless, I began to see, not just the potential of supply chain thinking, but also how it could make a real difference to the capability and performance of individuals, teams and organisations as a whole. Companies had by then largely come to realise the need for company-wide approaches to organisation design and redesign. The development of systems engineering approaches to manufacturing system redesign in the 1970s and 1980s was followed by the focus on organisational re-engineering, often based on business processes, in the late 1980s and early 1990s. A common feature of all of these approaches is a recognition that 'the whole is greater than the sum of the parts.' In other words, optimising subsystems (whether those subsystems are functional departments, production sites or individual processes in the manufacturing cycle) can result in a sub-optimised total system. Lack of efficiency and/or effectiveness is often a result of the poorly designed interfaces between subsystems rather than any inherent subsystem weaknesses. There are numerous examples of companies that have generated significant improvements in competitive advantage as a result of the application of this *integrated teamwork*-based 'total systems' thinking. We're back to *teams* and *integration* again.

By the time of my departure to the Far-East in the mid-1990s, SCM had become respectable in academic and commercial circles. It had grown out of a large number of traditional disciplines including logistics, purchasing, manufacturing systems engineering and operations management, but had a strong focus on multi-disciplinary *teams* working in an *integrated* manner throughout enterprises. By this time, several new dimensions were being added to the supply chain mix. Firstly, globalisation of business was becoming a reality, with the result that supply chain architectures had become more international in complexion. Secondly, many companies were beginning to realise that, without the right companies to work with up and down the supply chain, they could never realise their true competitive potential. Thirdly, ICT was developing at a rapid rate with the result that higher levels of integration within and between organisations was becoming a more realistic aspiration. These all combined to force SCM further up the list of strategic imperatives for organisations everywhere. Sectors such as mobile telecommunications and computers began to set new supply chain performance benchmarks. The rapidly growing 'tiger' economies of East Asia arguably saw these trends more starkly than anywhere else in the world. It was certainly an exciting place to be in the mid- to late 1990s.

I returned to Ireland to join the National Institute for Transport and Logistics (NITL) in 1998. There had been an incredible economic transformation since my departure, with the result that I ended up moving from one 'tiger' to another (see Appendix to Chapter 2). Indeed, it was this transformation which facilitated the return home of thousands of emigrants such as myself. NITL was established in 1998 by the Irish Government as Ireland's SCM 'Centre of Excellence', in recognition of the key role of SCM in creating competitive advantage for Irish business. NITL's mission was – and continues to be – to promote the development of supply chain excellence in Irish organisations, both private and public, for the benefit of the Irish economy. NITL offers a range of SCM services, including advice and consultancy, research, and training and education. NITL's mission reflects its strongly held belief that SCM is an increasingly important determinant of competitive advantage and is a key business process for companies. This is in line with NITL's 'Business Model of the 21st Century' (see Chapter 17), which recognises that world class companies are increasingly focusing their efforts and therefore their resources on new product introduction (with R&D and design management at its core), marketing (with brand management at its core) and SCM. Robust NPI and marketing processes ensure that good products with strong brands are introduced and maintained in markets in a timely and cost-effective manner. This can only bring competitive advantage if companies can consistently deliver high levels of customer service at the optimum total supply chain cost – this is where SCM plays a fundamental role. Again, the key lies in joined-up (i.e. *integrated*) thinking by *teams* across all parts of the supply chain.

Since its foundation in 1998, NITL has advised hundreds of organisations in its consultancy and advisory capacity, has delivered hundreds of training and education modules for thousands of individuals, and has contributed to the development of new leading edge thinking through its research programme. It has worked in all major sectors of the Irish economy, including food, biotechnology and pharmaceuticals, ICT and logistics service provision, as well as in many parts of the public sector. In the process, its staff have developed a unique and unrivalled experience of SCM and, in particular, its role in improving competitive capability in a rapidly changing economic and business environment. This book represents an attempt to share some of this experience.

Finally, those of you interested in music or sport (most of you and definitely me) will understand the essence of the core SCM concepts of integration and teamworking with reference to these pursuits. Take music as a case in point. If the various sections of a symphony orchestra were to play in isolation from each other, irrespective of the virtuosity of the individual players and section leaders, the result would likely be noise to most ears. However, with the aid of sheet music and a conductor, harmony can be added resulting in music to our ears[1] (see Figure 1). The sheet music is analogous to the supply chain plan, and the conductor to the supply chain manager. They ensure that the players operate as a *team* and perform in an *integrated* manner. Like all analogies, this one collapses if we try to extend it too far, but I hope that it reiterates the centrality of teams and integration to the SCM concept.

Similarly, the history of team sports is littered with examples of 'overachievers' – teams that perform better on the field of play than they apparently have any right to, based on the prowess of individual team members. A common feature of such teams is that they have strong leadership, a clear strategy based on competitor knowledge, tactics which they have the capability to implement in practice, a single-mindedness of purpose, and a strong work ethic. The corollary of this is, of course, that sports history is also full

---

[1] With acknowledgement to Benjamin Britten's *Young Person's Guide to the Orchestra* for this concept.

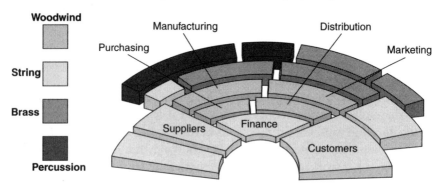

of examples of 'under-achievers' – teams full of prima donnas working in isolation from each other and with no clear purpose or strategy. I hope that the message is clear – it's all about individuals working as *teams* in an *integrated* and holistic manner.

This book is written by a mix of academics, consultants and practitioners, all of whom have significant theoretical and practical experience. They have tried to adopt the SCM approach and have worked as a *team* and in an *integrated* manner in the finalisation of the manuscript! Inevitably, there is some overlap between sections and chapters. This is a product of the fact that no individual link or element in a supply chain can be dealt with in isolation – it is the total supply chain performance which matters. The book was conceived with the many supply chain and logistics professionals, who are following formal learning programmes at all levels (certificate, diploma, degree and masters) in the subject, in mind. However, our intention is that it will be read equally profitably by students, researchers and practicing SCM and logistics professionals.

Edward Sweeney
Dublin, 2007

Acknowledgements

There are many people who have contributed, either directly or indirectly, to the publication of this book. They are too numerous to thank individually but the editor would like to express sincere gratitude to a number of people who played key roles in bringing this work to fruition. He would also like to apologise to those who, as a result of oversight on his part, he has not acknowledged specifically here.

To all contributors: Dan Park, Des Lee, Natalie Descheres, Liz Carroll, Randal Faulkner, Micheal O'Fearghail, Graham Heaslip, John Kenny, Ronan McDonnell, Pietro Evangelista, Bernd Huber and Claudia Wagner.

To the additional contributors to 'Volume 2': John Mee, Lorraine McGrath, Barbara Anderson, Gerry Glynn, Eoghan O'Grady and Cathal Heavey.

To NITL and DIT staff, past and present: Olivia Noone, Catherine FitzGerald, Pamela O'Brien, Stefan Bungart, Andy Maguire, Sinead Hennessy, Leon Browne, Margaret Whelan, Donal O'Malley, Leonora O'Donovan, Samir Shirin, Philip McCormack, Geraldine McHugh, Sam Reilly and Bernadette Bradley.

To other NITL module leaders and contributors: Walter Hunt, Rose McCarthy and, in particular, the late Stewart Dunlop.

To Gerard O'Connor, Elizabeth Brennan and all at Blackhall Publishing.

To the many supply chain academics from whom I have learned, including: Alan McKinnon, Martin Christopher, Richard Wilding, John Gattorna, David Bruce Grant, Richard Lamming and Kumar Bhattacharyya.

To the logistics research team at IRAT-CNR in Napoli who gave me the space to conceive this work: Alfonso Morvillo, Pietro Evangelista, Alessandra Marasco and all your colleagues.

To the many musicians, composers and other entertainers – too numerous to mention – who helped me to maintain my sanity during this project, particularly the latter stages.

Acknowledgements

To my family in Wexford: Madge, Sharon, Noel, Sinead, Olivia, Geraldine, John, Orla, Paul, James, Eoin, Sadhbh, Evan, Kay and Gwen.

There are no words which can express my appreciation to my wife, Joyce, for her apparently infinite patience, encouragement and love.

Finally, I want to thank my late father, Liam, for encouraging me in my education and in all aspects of my life, for unknowingly introducing me to supply chains at a very young age, and for adding the phrase 'chain link management' to the logistics/SCM lexicon. Royalties from this work will fund a scholarship scheme for promising young SCM students, named in his memory.

Edward Sweeney
Dublin, 2007

About the Contributors

Edward Sweeney is director of learning at the National Institute for Transport and Logistics (NITL), based at the Dublin Institute of Technology (DIT). At NITL he is responsible for the development and implementation of the integrated supply chain management (SCM) development programmes and he carries out research and consultancy work on behalf of NITL client companies. Edward has an engineering background and has worked and lectured in over 30 countries in Europe, North America and Asia. His work has been widely published and he is a regular contributor to business and academic conferences and seminars throughout the world. He enjoys travel and music.

Daniel Park qualified in Economics at the University of Glasgow. After an early career in marketing and logistics with Esso UK he joined Coopers & Lybrand (now Pricewaterhouse Coopers) in a senior managerial role in marketing and business strategy consultancy. Since 1984, he has been co-founder and partner in MASS Consulting Group, headquartered in Manchester UK and working worldwide on behalf of major international clients in the spheres of business strategy and organisational development. Shortly after the foundation of NITL, he was invited to act as module leader in Business Strategy for the M.Sc. and Executive programmes.

Des Lee runs his own consultancy company and lectures on many aspects of the supply chain, including financial management and organisation theory. He is a generalist by nature with an intense curiosity about organisations: how they work; why they don't work; and how to make them work better. Des spent fifteen years working in the electronics industry and has been involved in training and education for the past twenty years. He enjoys studying, wine (mostly French), music (mostly classical) and walking up mountains in Ireland every weekend and anywhere else on holidays.

About the Contributors

Natalie Descheres, having worked with a number of organisations (including Procter and Gamble, Motorola, Ernst and Young) in a supply chain context, has experience of the different dynamics in headquarters, manufacturing and distribution environments. Combining her tactical and strategic experience as a practitioner, manager and consultant, she has an overall appreciation of the holistic dimension of SCM. For the last five years, Natalie has developed a particular interest in the ethical and sustainable dimensions of growth-driven business management. She is now self-employed and is a regular contributor to NITL modules in the fields of marketing and supply chain partnerships.

Liz Carroll is training and development manager at ISME, the Irish Small and Medium Enterprises Association. She is a training and development professional with over twenty years experience specialising in the areas of customer service, communications, personal development and management development. Liz joined ISME from NITL where she was learning manager and lectured in a range of areas, including customer service, teamworking and problem solving. In addition to ISME and NITL, Liz has worked in training and education at the Institute of Public Administration, Rehab, the City of Dublin Vocational Education Committee, FÁS and the University of Bremen in Germany.

Randal Faulkner is an independent SCM consultant. He was previously director of consulting in NITL, which he joined from his previous position as managing director of the European Office of Cleveland Consulting Associates, the leading US logistics consultancy. He has practical understanding of transport and logistics through his previous role as general manager of Rainsford Logistics (a Guinness Ireland subsidiary). He has pioneered the introduction of SCM principles in Irish companies and his consulting clients have included many of the largest and best known companies in Ireland and abroad, including Unilever, Guinness Ireland, Becton Dickinson, Intel, BWG and the Irish National Lottery.

Aoife O'Riordan is currently working in Reckitt Benckiser (UK) as a supply chain executive. She is a graduate of Trinity College Dublin (TCD) with an honours degree in Manufacturing Engineering with Management Science. She has completed a M.Phil. thesis entitled *Outsourcing in Ireland: What is the Impact on Business Performance?* Aoife is also currently completing an M.Sc. in SCM at NITL. Her research has been presented at several academic and business conferences in Ireland and the UK in recent years.

In 2006, the paper she presented at the Irish Academy of Management conference was awarded the best postgraduate paper prize.

Michael O'Fearghail lectures in SCM at the Institute of Technology in Carlow, Ireland. His early career included a period of time as a computer programmer, and as a management accountant in the electronics industry. His experience as a financial controller in the healthcare and engineering sectors led him to conclude that the biggest challenge for manufacturing industry at that time was the need to adopt demand-driven materials management and purchasing systems. He joined IT Carlow – the first third-level institution in Ireland to introduce full-time undergraduate programmes in purchasing and materials management – in 1992. His current research interests lie in exploring the financial dimension of the supply chain.

Graham Heaslip is course director of the BBS (Hons) degree in SCM at IT Carlow. He is a member of the editing team for IT Carlow's *School of Business and Humanities, Postgraduate Studies Working Papers Review*. He is active in SCM research, supervising students pursuing MBS degrees from IT Carlow and conducting his own Ph.D. studies at the Logistics Institute of Hull University, UK. Graham has provided consultancy advice for many companies, notably Boston Scientific, Wyeth Pharmaceuticals and Lucent Technologies. He spent fourteen years working in the Irish Defence Forces, both at home and abroad, in a variety of logistical appointments, culminating in his being seconded to the World Special Olympics as deputy director for Logistics.

John Kenny has worked in the field of software development and consultancy for over 30 years, managing a software company for the last twenty. Specialising in the development of business solutions for varied enterprises, he has extensive knowledge of the business needs of SMEs and multinational organisations. His experience spanning this time period has given him a broad perspective on the software technologies in current usage and the ability to recognise truly innovative technologies from mere marketing hype. Over the last sixteen years he has lectured on a variety of postgraduate programmes in DIT and TCD.

Ronan McDonnell is a consultant specialising in distribution planning and modelling. His recent projects have involved developing distribution strategies for leading companies in the food sector that are facing the challenges of centralised distribution. He has worked on a number of research projects sponsored by public sector bodies, such as Forfás, Bord Bia and Enterprise Ireland. Ronan has considerable lecturing experience in the areas of logistics and operations management. He has published a number of articles on the topics of distribution planning and the role of information technology in the supply chain, and has compiled a directory of supply chain software for NITL.

Pietro Evangelista is a researcher in logistics and SCM at the Institute for Service Industry Research (IRAT) of the Italian National Research Council (CNR), based in Naples. His research interests include shipping and innovation in the logistics industry. This is reflected in several articles published in international journals, as well as chapters in books. His current research activity is focused on the impact of information and communications technology (ICT) on small logistics companies. He is a member of the editorial board of two international journals and acts as peer reviewer for other international journals. He lectures at the Faculty of Engineering of the University of Naples (Federico II).

Bernd Huber is a Senior Research Analyst at NITL. Bernd's research is based on ICT in the supply chain, in particular global e-business adoption drivers and their impact on key performance indicators. His Ph.D. focused on electronic purchasing consortia, highlighting ways organisations can co-operate electronically to aggregate purchasing volume and achieve both tangible and intangible benefits. Bernd is widely published, most recently in *Electronic Markets* and *Supply Chain Management: An International Journal*. He has also worked with Audi and various other multinational organisations on ICT implementation and SCM.

Claudia Wagner works as part of NITL's research and learning team. Her research expertise covers ICT strategies and implementation challenges, with particular emphasis on B2B e-marketplace diffusion in the airline industry and its impact on competitiveness and performance. Her research interests further include global procurement strategies in an SCM context, as well as air transport policy and regulation. Claudia has published articles in peer-reviewed logistics and transport journals, such as the *International Journal of Logistics: Research and Applications* and *Transportation Research Record*.

1

Introduction

EDWARD SWEENEY

BACKGROUND AND RATIONALE

The book's title *Perspectives on Supply Chain Management and Logistics: Creating Competitive Organisations in the 21st Century* reflects a number of important facts. Firstly, the focus of this book is on *competitiveness*. The fact that failing to implement appropriate change inevitably results in a decline in the relative competitive strength of organisations (i.e. that 'standing still' equals 'falling behind') underpins the focus of the constituent chapters. In a rapidly changing economic and business environment, innovation is the key to ensuring that competitive strength is sustained and built upon. The late 20th century saw significant changes in the structure of the world economy and brought with it new challenges in all aspects of business and operations management. The trend towards globalisation of enterprise is likely to continue into the 21st century and beyond. Supply chain management (SCM), with its focus on achieving the service levels demanded by markets and on optimising of total supply chain cost and investment, has a potentially pivotal role to play in addressing these challenges. For this reason this book focuses on the strategic role of SCM and logistics in building the capability necessary to succeed in today's challenging environment. The management of operational challenge and improvement is of course critical but cannot be meaningfully addressed in the absence of clarity in relation to the wider business environment and strategic dimension.[1] As noted in Chapter 4, against a background of increasingly rapid and at times discontinuous change, we need to consider

---

[1] A second book is currently under production. Its focus is on the achievement of operational excellence in SCM. It deals in detail with issues such as production and operations management, warehousing and inventory management, transport and distribution management, the people dimension of SCM and supply chain operations' improvement tools and methodologies.

the broader value of SCM in creating a *differentiated business model* that determines competitive advantage in the judgement of customers.

SCM: Context, Definition and the Strategic and Financial Dimensions

Section 1 (Chapters 2 to 5) sets out the overall strategic and financial context of SCM. The key question is: *How can organisations use SCM to build sustainable competitive capability in the evolving business environment?* To answer this question one must appreciate the major changes occurring in the competitive landscape. This is the focus of Chapter 2. In particular, the trend towards globalisation of business, vertical disintegration of enterprises and changing perspectives on the strategic role of SCM, form the basis of this analysis. This sets the context for the historical overview and detailed definitions of SCM which follow in Chapter 3 (Part A). A definition, known as the *Four Fundamentals* of SCM, which has been used as the basis for much of NITL's work in recent years, is detailed in Part B of Chapter 3. Part C goes on to discuss the role of logistics as an element of SCM, which is first and foremost a strategic issue. Chapter 4 sets out the essence of business strategy and strategic management, and the role of SCM in the development of a business. SCM is ultimately concerned with improving shareholder value. The financial dimension is, therefore, central to fully understanding the subject. Chapter 5 introduces financial management in the supply chain, with a particular focus on the role of SCM in improving enterprise profitability and cash flow performance.

The Customer Perspective

Section 2 (Chapters 6 to 8) recognises that SCM starts and finishes with the customer. Marketing, the subject of Chapter 6, is concerned with identifying and satisfying customer requirements profitably. Its role should be considered, therefore, as complementary to that of SCM. Traditionally, both in theory and practice, the two subjects have been dealt with separately. This is clearly untenable, given that they effectively represent two sides of the same coin. The focus of this chapter is very much on the interface between them. A detailed understanding of customer service requirements in different market segments effectively sets the specification for supply chain design. Chapter 7 builds on the introduction to customer service provided in Chapter 3. It examines all major aspects of the subject, while Chapter 8 demonstrates how this understanding can then be used as the basis for effective supply chain improvement.

The Supplier Perspective

Following the discussion of the customer dimension (the 'sell' end of the supply chain), Section 3 (Chapters 9 to 11) then goes on to examine the supplier dimension (the 'buy' end). Much of what is now referred to under the umbrella of SCM has its origins in this area. Paradoxically, there is a view that the more important purchasing and supply issues are seen to be, the less they can be managed solely within a tightly demarcated department. In this context, purchasing and supply matters become a wider supply chain concern and a critical component of effective SCM. Chapter 9 focuses on some of the strategic issues associated with the outsourcing of key elements of suply chain functionality. Chapter 10 examines outsourcing, procurement and purchasing in the wider supply chain context. Chapter 11 introduces some of the main elements of good operational practice in the arena of purchasing and supplier development and management.

Information and Communications Technology in the Supply Chain

It is clear that recent developments in information and communication technology (ICT) have facilitated significant changes in the manner in which organisations view SCM and, in particular, the key goal of supply chain integration. Section 4 (Chapters 12 to 14) explores these issues in some detail. The focus of Chapter 12 is on the overall role of ICT as a key integration enabler. It provides a taxonomy of the main categories of supply chain ICT applications. Chapter 13 examines the role of ICT more specifically in the transportation and logistics arena. In particular, the types of systems used in the third-party logistics (3PL) sector are considered. Supply chain integration is concerned with the extent to which all activities within an internal and/or external supply chain are linked together. Chapter 14, under the banner of 'e-business', looks at how the constituent parts of a supply chain are linked together via the flow of information and the effective implementation and integration of appropriate ICT tools.

The Future: Making Change Happen

The final section (Chapters 15 to 17) is concerned with bringing the various strategic supply chain elements together in manner which facilitates effective change and improvement. Chapter 15 is based on the notion that, 'What gets measured gets done!' It introduces supply chain performance measurement and the notion of *learning supply chains* – leveraging the supply chain as a mechanism to enable learning and competence development. Chapter 16 recognises that supply chain re-engineering must be carried out in a logical and systematic manner. It proposes a roadmap for supply chain re-engineering based on some of the key characteristics of SCM excellence. Finally, Chapter 17 looks to the future and outlines some of the likely challenges set to emerge over the coming years and examines some possible innovative supply chain architectures aimed at meeting these challenges.

OTHER OBSERVATIONS

As noted in the Preface, this book is intended to be read equally profitably by students, researchers and business managers. It is written by a mix of academics, consultants and practitioners, all of whom have significant theoretical and practical experience of the subject matter under discussion. Most are based in Ireland and the illustrative examples used, therefore, are often from Irish organisations or multinational corporations based in Ireland. Nonetheless, the book should be of value to readers in any part of the world. Indeed, the globalisation of supply chains means that the subject of SCM and logistics has become, by definition, a global one. Furthermore, the openness of the Irish economy also means that all contributors to this book have extensive international experience and arguably makes Ireland a good base from which to share SCM experience and knowledge. The word 'perspectives' has deliberately been included in the title to indicate that there are few 'rights' and 'wrongs' in relation to strategic SCM and logistics. Each contributor brings his or her own unique insights based on the nature of their experience. These insights are all of value, and the challenge for the reader is to relate the different emphases and priorities inherent in these perspectives to their own challenges and strategic imperatives.

Section 1

SCM: Context, Definition and the Strategic and Financial Dimensions

2

The Evolving Supply Chain Management Context

EDWARD SWEENEY

INTRODUCTION

A number of key issues are changing the strategic landscape of supply chain management (SCM) and logistics. Arguably, the three most significant such issues are:

1. Internationalisation (or globalisation) of supply chains.
2. Vertical disintegration.
3. The changing role of the supply chain as a source of strategic leverage.

Internationalisation is being driven by changing structures in the international economic and business environment. Vertical disintegration and the changing strategic view of the supply chain are both parts of the strategic response of firms to competitive pressures in the marketplace. The author recognises that these three issues are in many ways interrelated and interdependent.[1] Nonetheless, the following sections discuss each of these issues in detail. The Appendix to this chapter provides more detailed information regarding the issues raised specifically in an Irish context.

INTERNATIONALISATION

The structure of the international economic and business environment has changed significantly in recent years. The growth of trade blocs throughout the world has resulted in increasing global economic integration. This evolution, largely based on the reduction of barriers to the movement of capital, goods, services, people and information internationally, has

---

[1] For example, outsourcing of manufacturing to lower labour cost economies is facilitated by economic liberalisation in these countries.

facilitated increased international trade and foreign direct investment (FDI). The value of world merchandise trade reached about $6.07 trillion in 2002. In 1990 it was less than $2.85 trillion (UN 2004). According to the World Trade Organisation (WTO), international trade flows multiplied by a factor of 25 between 1950 and 2003 (WTO 2004). Annual foreign direct investment (FDI) expanded over 19-fold between 1973 and 2004, that is from $21.5 billion to over $410 billion (UNCTAD 2004). These trends have resulted in the increasing internationalisation of supply chains. This can be related to the 'buy–make–move–sell' model of product supply chains (NITL 2000).

Buy: Global sourcing of raw materials and other inputs has now become a reality for many organisations as the structure of the international economic and business environment has evolved (Fagan 1991; Trent and Monczka 2003). The WTO provides an interesting example in its 1998 annual report (WTO 1998). In the production of an 'American' car, 30 per cent of the car's value originates in Korea, 17.5 per cent in Japan, 7.5 per cent in Germany, 4 per cent in Taiwan and Singapore, 2.5 per cent in the United Kingdom and 1.5 per cent in Ireland and Barbados. That is, 'only 37 per cent of the production value ... is generated in the United States.' This phenomenon is large enough to be noticed in aggregate statistics. Feenstra and Hanson (1996) used US input–output tables to infer US imports of intermediate inputs. They found that the share of imported intermediates increased from 5.3 per cent of total US intermediate purchases in 1972 to 11.6 per cent in 1990. Campa and Goldberg (1997) found similar evidence for Canada and the UK.

Make: Access to lower cost manufacturing worldwide is now possible. For example, the expansion of China in recent years, based to a large extent on outsourcing (or 'offshoring') of labour-intensive manufacturing by companies from developed countries, is indicative of this (see Chapter 9). No other country has attracted as much FDI as China. In 2004, approximately $60 billion of FDI was absorbed; between 1979 and 2004, the total was approximately $560 billion (UNCTAD 2004). As a result, China is growing rapidly and attaining pre-eminence in global manufacturing in certain sectors. For example, the country already produces 50 per cent of the world's cameras, 30 per cent of air conditioners and televisions, 25 per cent of washing machines and 20 per cent of refrigerators (Pinto 2005). Similar trends have occurred in Eastern Europe. For example, *The Economist* (2001) has noted strong and growing FDI flows into the region.

Sell: Furthermore, as markets have opened up internationally for a range of products and services, international (and in some cases global) selling has become the reality. The cases of China and India are worthy of particular comment. As pointed out in a recent survey in *The Economist* (2005), the two countries are home to nearly two-fifths of the world's population and are two of the world's fastest-growing economies. A recent report by America's National Intelligence Council (2004) likened their emergence in the early 21st century to the rise of Germany in the 19th and America in the 20th century, with 'impacts potentially as dramatic'. The liberalisation of markets has sharpened the focus on the need for more robust approaches to international marketing strategy (Bradley 2004; Cateora and Graham 2004). For example, the term 'glocalisation' (from 'global' and 'localisation') has been used to refer to the creation of the local (country or regional) market presence of a global enterprise (Fan and Huang 2002).

Move: All of the above has implications for the logistics and distribution strategies of companies (Waters 2004). Increased trade volumes globally have created the need for new logistics pipelines. The growth in the international 3PL sector is a reflection of this. The large number of mergers and acquisitions in the sector has been driven significantly by the desire of companies to have a stronger global presence (Eyefortansport 2001). With specific reference to the European freight industry, Peters (2000) notes that growth in the 1990s has offered a lesson that 'the country-by-country model for logistics is no longer valid; companies have begun to reorganise themselves into continental operations based on integration and rationalisation.'

In short, as economic and business globalisation has happened so supply chain architectures have become more global. The resulting challenges in terms of SCM and supply chain design (SCD) have been the subject of significant research, debate and discussion (e.g. Arntzen *et al.* 1995; Gourdin 2000; Simchi-Levi *et al.* 2002; Bolstorff and Rosenbaum 2003; Ayers 2003).

Vertical Disintegration

Companies are increasing their focus on what they regard as their core activities or competencies. Oates (1998) defines core competencies as 'the central things that organisations do well'. The corollary of this is that activities regarded as 'non-core' are being outsourced. Greaver (1999) states that 'non-core competencies take up time, energy and workspace, and help management lose sight of what is important in an organisation.' Furthermore, the trend towards economic and business globalisation has facilitated the outsourcing of various activities to overseas locations (off-shoring – see above). Key supply chain activities are increasingly being outsourced to third-party organisations. This can again be related to the 'buy–make–move–sell' model of product supply chains.

Buy: Purchasing and procurement activities have generally not been outsourced in the traditional sense but the development of purchasing consortia has meant some sharing of responsibility for this activity between companies. Hendrick (1997) defines a purchasing consortium as:

> A formal or informal arrangement, where two or more organisations, who are separate legal entities, collaborate among themselves, or through a third party, to combine their individual needs for products from suppliers and to gain the increased pricing, quality and service advantages associated with volume buying.

Essig (1999) notes that a purchasing consortium is often just one element of an overall supply strategy.

Make: The classic 'make versus buy' decision has been a central theme in the field of manufacturing strategy for decades (e.g. Hayes and Wheelwright 1984). The traditional focus was largely on the financial and economic analysis of in-house versus outsourced options for particular processes within a manufacturing operation. Manufacturing outsourcing decision-making processes now tend to take a broader and more strategic view (e.g. Hill 1999). Many large manufacturers have outsourced significant parts of their production activity to third parties (e.g. Edwards and Edwards 2000; Hassey and Lai 2003). For example, in the electronics sector, the trend is one of original equipment manufacturers (OEMs) outsourcing significant amounts of manufacturing to contract manufacturing companies. Companies in the electronic manufacturing services (EMS) sector, such as Flextronics, Foxconn and Celestica,[2] have grown rapidly as a result.

Move: Transport and a range of other logistics activities are increasingly being outsourced by manufacturers and retailers (Scott and Westbrook 1991; McKinnon 1999). The 3PL sector has developed rapidly as it has responded to its customers' requirements for the supply of tailor-made services (Razzaque and Sheng 1998; Skjoett-Larsen 2000). The European Union

---

[2] See <http://www.flextronics.com>; <http://www.foxconn.com>; <http://www.celestica.com>.

PROTRANS project (PROTRANS 2003) developed a definition of 3PL based on a wide number of definitions which have appeared in the literature:

> Third-party logistics are activities carried out by an external company on behalf of a shipper and consisting of at least the provision of management of multiple logistics services. These activities are offered in an integrated way, not on a stand-alone basis. The co-operation between the shipper and the external company is an intended continuous relationship.

This definition reflects the manner in which shippers' requirements have evolved in recent years. The emphasis now is on the provision of integrated multiple services and the development of relationships.

Sell: Selling as a process has generally not been outsourced in the traditional sense. Nonetheless, many of the individual activities which comprise sales channels may be owned by other companies: the actual selling of products to consumers may be carried out by retailers, who may in turn obtain the products from wholesalers; third-party owned and managed call centres may be an integral part of the selling process; and third-party agents, franchisees or distributors may also have some responsibility (e.g. Friedman and Furey 1999).

The above has resulted in a shift away from the traditional model of 'control through ownership' towards models which are based on management and control through effective supply chain relationship management. The former is based on the strategic logic of vertical integration. Vertical integration is the degree to which a firm owns its upstream suppliers and its downstream buyers (Greaver 1999). Harrigan (1999)[3] provides a good description of the logic underpinning this approach to strategic development. The latter, effectively a process of vertical disintegration, has taken place as a result of the trends outlined above (Mpoyi 1999; Langlois 2001). Recent developments in ICT, in particular Internet technologies, have facilitated this process and laid the foundations for the 'network economy model' (Reddy and Reddy 2001). According to Hugos (2002), traditional supply chain models have 'given way to virtual integration of companies'. In short, as outsourcing of various elements of supply chain functionality takes place, supply chain architectures are becoming more virtual. The traditional *fully vertically integrated* approaches are being replaced by contemporary *fully virtually integrated* approaches – a new FVI is evolving.

---

[3] Prof. Harrigan of Columbia University presents a conceptual model based on four dimensions – breadth, stages, degree and form – based on analysis of data from sixteen industry sectors and the integration actions of 192 companies.

Strategic Leverage

Classically, in the field of strategic management, the generic approaches of cost leadership, differentiation and focus have been identified. Porter's classic text (1980) described these alternatives as follows:

- A cost leadership strategy requires a company to be a low-cost supplier, and to sell either at below average industry prices to gain market share, or at industry average prices to earn a profit higher than that of rivals.
- A differentiation strategy requires a product or service that offers unique attributes that are valued by customers, thereby allowing premium pricing.
- A focus strategy concentrates on a narrow segment and, within that segment, attempts to achieve advantage through either cost leadership or differentiation.

A significant proportion of the overall cost base of companies is in the supply chain. In the automotive industry, for example, A.T. Kearney (1999) reports that, typically, component costs (30 per cent), manufacturing and assembly costs (28 per cent) and distribution costs (four per cent) together represent 62 per cent of sales price. Hence, any worthwhile cost leadership approach needs to focus on the optimisation of total supply chain costs and the elimination of non-value-adding activities (NVAs). An NVA may be defined as: *any activity (or resource or asset) that adds cost (or time) to any supply chain process without adding value from a customer perspective.*[4] Much of this *lean* thinking has its origins in the Japanese automotive industry, in particular in the Toyota Production System (TPS) and the just-in-time (JIT) paradigm (Ohno 1988; Womack and Jones 2003). The main objective of this thinking was the elimination of waste (or *muda* in Japanese). Christopher and Gattorna (2005) present evidence that effective SCM provides 'opportunities for significant cost reduction and increased profits'.

Customer service is becoming a key source of differentiation or an order-winning criterion in many sectors (Christopher 2005). An order-winning criterion (or order winner) is a feature of the product or service offering which differentiates it from the competition and is, therefore, likely to be a source of increased market share. An order qualifier, on the other hand, is a feature which must exist to ensure that a product or service gets into the market in the first instance and stays there (Hill 1993). The latter tends to have order losing rather than order winning characteristics. In many sectors

---

[4] Author's definition based on Jones *et al.* (1997), Goldrat and Cox (1992), Womack and Jones (2003) and others.

the importance of customer service relative to product quality (now largely an order qualifier) and price (largely determined by the dynamics of supply and demand in the market and subject to downward pressure in many sectors) has increased (Sweeney 2004). Customer service is delivered by the supply chain. In this way, the supply chain itself has become a key factor in the development of a differentiation strategy.

As pointed out earlier, a focus strategy concentrates on a narrow segment and within that segment attempts to achieve advantage through either cost leadership or differentiation. The points made above in relation to the role of SCM in strategy formulation and implementation are, therefore, equally relevant in the context of a focus approach.

In short, a company pursuing a cost leadership, a differentiation or a focus strategy can leverage the supply chain as a fundamental element of their effort to improve competitive performance. The role of SCM in strategy formulation and implementation is given extensive treatment in the literature (e.g. Van Hoek and Harrison 2004; Simchi-Levi and Kaminsky 2003; Cohen and Roussel 2004). Two approaches are worthy of particular mention.

Firstly, Christopher and Ryals (1999) argue that SCM has a central position in the creation of shareholder value. In this context shareholder value is defined as the financial value created for shareholders in the companies in which they invest. The four basic drivers of enhanced shareholder value (i.e. revenue growth, operating cost reduction, fixed and working capital efficiency) are 'directly and indirectly affected by logistics management and supply chain strategy'. The framework of value-based management (VBM) plays a potentially important role in achieving these improvements in practice. The paper concludes by noting that, 'By seeking out opportunities for partnership in the supply chain combined with an emphasis on the reduction of non-value-adding time, the evidence suggests enduring improvement in shareholder value can be achieved.' The emphasis on time compression is important as it has the potential to reduce cost and improve customer service simultaneously.

A graphical representation of Gattorna's 'Strategic Alignment Model' is shown in Figure 2.1 (Gattorna *et al.* 2003). He argues that empirical evidence is mounting to suggest that, if organisations are to achieve sustained high levels of financial and operating performance, the four elements shown in the diagram must be dynamically aligned.
Alignment in this context means:

- an understanding of customers' buying behaviour;
- corresponding value propositions to align with the dominant buying behaviours;

Figure 2.1: The Strategic Alignment Model

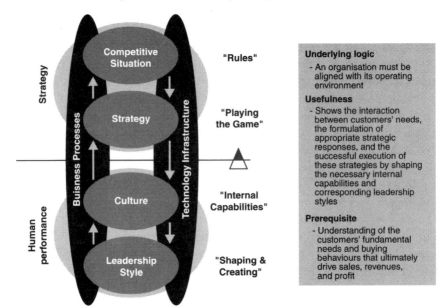

Source: Gattorna, J. et al. (2003), *Handbook of Supply Chain Management*, 5th edition, London: Gower.

- the appropriate capabilities (or cultural capability) embedded in the organisation to underpin the delivery of these specific value propositions;
- a composite leadership style at the executive level to ensure the appropriate sub-cultures are in place as required.

Organisations seeking superior performance must be both very aware of their customers' expectations and of their own internal capability. If these two dimensions are addressed adequately, then an organisation is fully aligned with its marketplace. This is in line with classical approaches to strategy formulation – Porter (1980) states that 'the essence of formulating a competitive strategy is relating the company to its environment' – but with a strong focus on the role of SCM in ensuring that strategic plans are realised in practice.

Concluding Comments

Economic and business globalisation is happening. Companies are increasing their focus on their core competencies and, as a result, vertical disintegration is happening. Finally, more and more companies are coming to regard the supply chain as a source of strategic leverage. In short, supply chains have become more global and more virtual (and, therefore, their management has become more complex) and SCM is becoming a more integral and integrated part of overall corporate strategy. Simultaneously, customers have become more discerning and are demanding better quality products, higher levels of service and reduced prices. This increasingly competitive business environment has sharpened the focus on the need for more robust approaches to supply chain design and management.

REFERENCES

Arntzen, B.C., Brown, G.G., Harrison, T.P. and Trafton, L.L. (1995), 'Global Supply Chain Management at the Digital Equipment Corporation', *Interfaces*, 25(1), 69–93.

Kearney, A.T. (1999), 'The Future of Automotive Distribution', report published by international consultants A.T. Kearney.

Ayers, J.B. (2003), *Supply Chain Project Management: A Structured Collaborative and Measurable Approach*, Los Angeles: CRC Press.

Bolstorff, P. and Rosenbaum, R. (2003), *Supply Chain Excellence: A Handbook for Dramatic Improvement Using the SCOR Model*, New York, American Management Association.

Bradley, F. (2004), *International Marketing Strategy*, 4th edition, London: Prentice Hall.

Campa, J.M. and Goldberg, L.S. (1997), 'The Evolving External Orientation of Manufacturing: A Profile of Four Countries', *Federal Reserve Bank of New York Economic Policy Review*, 3, 53–81.

Cateora, P.R. and Graham, J.L. (2004), *International Marketing*, 12th edition, New York: Irwin.

Christopher, M. (2005), *Logistics and Supply Chain Management: Creating Value-Adding Networks*, London: FT Prentice Hall.

Christopher, M. and Gattorna, J. (2005), 'Supply Chain Cost Management and Value-Based Pricing', *Industrial Marketing Management*, 34(2), 115–122.

Christopher, M. and Ryals, L. (1999), 'Supply Chain Strategy: Its Impact on Shareholder Value', *International Journal of Logistics Management*, 10(1), 1–11.

Cohen, S. and Roussel, J. (2004), *Strategic Supply Chain Management: The Five Disciplines for Top Performance*, New York: Higher Education.

Economist, The (2001), 'Investment in Eastern Europe', 15 November.

Economist, The (2005), 'Survey: India and China', 3 March.

Edwards, P. and Edwards S. (2000), 'What's Your Problem?', *Entrepreneur*, 28(7), 150.

Essig, M. (1999), 'Cooperative Sourcing as a New Strategic Supply Concept: Theoretical Framework and Empirical Findings', *Perspectives on Purchasing and Supply for the Millennium (Proceedings of the 8th International IPSERA Conference)*, March, 245–256.

Eyefortransport (2001), *Digital Logistics – Value Creation in the Freight Transport Industry* [online], Eyefortransport – First Conference. Available from: <http://www.eyefortransport.com> [accessed 15 March 2007].

Fagan, M.L. (1991), 'A Guide to Global Sourcing', *Journal of Business Strategy*, March–April, 21–25.

Fan, I.S. and Huang, C.P. (2002), 'Aligning Local Office Management Plan to Global Corporate Strategy', *Restructuring Global Manufacturing – Towards Global Collaborative Supply Networks (Proceedings of the 7th Annual International Manufacturing Symposium)*, 12–13 September, Institute for Manufacturing, Department of Engineering, University of Cambridge.

Feenstra, R.C. and Hanson, G.H. (1996), 'Globalization, Outsourcing, and Wage Inequality', *American Economic Review*, 86, 240–245.

Friedman, L. and Furey, T. (1999), *The Channel Advantage*, New York: Butterworth-Heinemann.

Gattorna, J., Ogulin, R. and Reynolds, M.W. (eds.) (2003), *Handbook of Supply Chain Management*, 5th edition, London: Gower.

Goldratt, E.M. and Cox, J. (1992), *The Goal: A Process of Ongoing Improvement*, New York: North River Books.

Gourdin, K.G. (2000), *Global Logistics Management: A Competitive Advantage for the New Millennium*, New York: Blackwell.

Greaver II, M.F. (1999), *Strategic Outsourcing – A Structured Approach to Outsourcing Decisions and Initiatives*, New York: Amacon.

Harrigan, K.R. (2003), *Vertical Integration, Outsourcing, and Corporate Strategy*, New York: Beard Books.

Hassey, P. and Lai, L. (2003), 'Outsourcing in the Manufacturing Sector – Where Is It At?', *IDC Research*, November.

Hayes, R.H. and Wheelwright, S.C. (1984), *Restoring Our Competitive Edge: Competing through Manufacturing*, New York: Wiley.

Hendrick, T.E. (1997), *Purchasing Consortiums: Horizontal Alliances among Firms Buying Common Goods and Services. What? Who? Why? How?* Tempe, AZ: Center for Advanced Purchasing Studies/National Association for Purchasing Management.

Hill, T.J. (1999), *Manufacturing Strategy: Text and Cases*, 3rd edition, London: McGraw-Hill/Irwin.

Hugos, M.H. (2002), *Essentials of Supply Chain Management*, New York: Wiley.

Jones, D.T., Hines, P. and Rich, N. (1997), 'Lean Logistics', *International Journal of Physical and Logistics Management*, 27(3/4), 153–173.

Langlois, R.N. (2001), 'The Vanishing Hand: The Changing Dynamics of Industrial Capitalism' [online], 14 September 2001, University of Connecticut Center for Institutions, Organizations and Markets Working Paper No. 01-1. Available from <http://ssrn.com/abstract=285972> [accessed 14 March 2007].

McKinnon, A. (1999), 'The outsourcing of logistical activities', in D. Waters (ed.), *Global Logistics and Distribution Planning: Strategies for Management*, 4th edition, London: Kogan Page, 215–234.

Mpoyi, R.T. (1999), 'Changing Corporate Strategies: Restoring Competitive Advantage through Vertical Disintegration', *Global Competitiveness*, 7(1), 26–34.

National Institute for Transport and Logistics (2000), 'Supply Chain Management Made Simple', Technical Fact Sheet Dublin: NITL.

National Intelligence Council (2004), 'Mapping the Global Future', Report of the National Intelligence Council's 2020 Project, NIC 2004-13.

Oates, D. (1998), *Outsourcing and Virtual Organisation – The Incredible Shrinking Company*, London: Century Business.

Ohno, T. (1988), *Toyota Production System: Beyond Large-Scale Production*, Portland: Productivity Press.

Porter, M. (1980), *Competitive Strategy*, New York: Free Press.

Peters, M. (2000), 'Europe's 3PL Industry Consolidates on the Road to Pan-European Services', *Achieving Supply Chain Excellence through Technology* (ASCET), Vol. 2, April.

Pinto, J. (2005), 'The China Manufacturing Syndrome', *Automation World*, January, 62–66.

PROTRANS (2003), *The Role of Third Party Logistics Service Providers and their Impact on Transport*, NEI Transport B.V., The Netherlands.

Razzaque, M.R. and Sheng, C.C. (1998), 'Outsourcing of Logistics Functions: A Literature Survey', *International Journal of Physical Distribution and Logistics Management*, 28(2), 89–107.

Reddy, R. and Reddy, S. (2001), *Supply Chains to Virtual Integration*, New York: McGraw-Hill.

Scott, C. and Westbrook, R. (1991), 'New Strategic Tools for Supply Chain Management', *International Journal of Physical Distribution & Logistics Management*, 21(1), 23–33.

Simchi-Levi, D. and Kaminsky, P. (2003), *Managing the Supply Chain: The Definitive Guide for the Business Professional*, New York: McGraw-Hill.

Simchi-Levi, D., Kaminsky, P. and Simchi-Levi, E. (2002), *Designing and Managing the Supply Chain*, 2nd edition, New York: McGraw-Hill/Irwin.

Skjoett-Larsen, T. (2000), 'Third Party Logistics – From an Inter-organizational Point of View', *International Journal of Physical Distribution and Logistics Management*, 30(2), 112–127.

Sweeney, E. (2004), 'Making Supply Chain Management Work for You!', *Logistics Solutions*, 7(4), 21–25.

Trent, R.J. and Monczka, R.M. (2003), 'Understanding Integrated Global Sourcing', *International Journal of Physical Distribution & Logistics Management*, 33(7), 607–629.

United Nations (2004), *World Economic and Social Survey*, New York: UN.

United Nations Conference on Trade and Development (2004), *Handbook of Statistics*, Geneva: UNCTAD.

Van Hoek, R. and Alan Harrison, A. (2004), *Logistics Management and Strategy*, London: FT Prentice Hall.

Waters, C.D.J. (ed.) (2004), *Global Logistics and Distribution Planning: Strategies for Management*, 4th edition, London: Kogan Page.

Womack, J.P. and Jones, D.T. (2003), *Lean Thinking: Banish Waste and Create Wealth in Your Corporation*, 2nd edition, London: Free Press.

World Trade Organisation (1998), *Annual Report*, Geneva: WTO.

World Trade Organisation (2004), *Annual Report*, Geneva: WTO.

APPENDIX: THE IRISH CONTEXT

Economic Overview[5]

Ireland has a small, open, trade-dependent economy and it has one of the fastest growing economies in the developed world. It currently constitutes around 1.8 per cent of the overall output in the euro area. In recent decades the Irish economy has been transformed from being agrarian and traditional manufacturing based to one increasingly based on the hi-tech and internationally traded services sectors. In 2003, the services sector accounted for 66 per cent of employment, industry for 28 per cent and agriculture for six per cent.

Over the last decade, unprecedented economic growth has seen the level of Irish real gross domestic product (GDP) almost double in size. This is reflected, for example, in headlines in *The Economist* such as: 'Ireland: Europe's Tiger Economy' and 'Ireland Shines' (*Economist, The* 1997); 'Tiger, Tiger, Burning Bright' and 'Lessons from the Irish Miracle' (*Economist, The* 2004). There have been many reasons advanced for Ireland's success, which in combination can help to explain the exceptionally strong growth rates experienced (e.g. Layte *et al.* 2005; *Economist, The* 2004). They include European Union (EU) membership and access to the single market; a high proportion of the population of working age; increased participation in the labour market especially by females; a reversal of the trend of emigration towards immigration; sustained investment in education and training; a relatively low corporation tax rate and a large multinational presence; coordinated social partnership agreements and a more stable public finance position.

In the context of SCM, the openness of the Irish economy is reflected both in the international mobility of its labour and capital and high levels of FDI. Ireland's share of global and EU FDI has risen sharply in recent years. From just under four per cent of the total in 2000, Ireland accounted for more than one-twelfth of total inflows to the EU-15 in 2003. On a global basis, the rate of increase was similar, reaching almost five per cent of total world inflows (Forfás 2005). The USA was the biggest source of FDI in 2003 with flows from that source estimated at approximately €8 billion or 25 per cent of the total. In terms of stocks of FDI, UNCTAD (2004) records a figure for Ireland equivalent to 127 per cent of GDP in 2003 ($193 billion). In absolute terms, this is the sixth highest level among the EU-15 and by far the largest in per capita terms.

---

[5] The economic data in this section is from the Economic and Social Research Institute (ESRI 2005).

Ireland's high level of external trade is reflected in the high ratio of combined exports and imports of goods to GDP which was just under 100 per cent in 2003. The global nature and profile of this trade can be seen from the data presented in Annex 1 (CSO 2006).

Outsourcing

It is evident from the previous section that, in recent years, Ireland has been a major destination for activities which have been 'offshored', particularly by US companies. Whilst there is much discussion about the outsourcing of supply chain activities by companies based in Ireland, there is limited published evidence about the extent of outsourcing of supply chain activities by companies in Ireland. In relation to manufacturing, there is evidence that significant amounts of (mainly labour-intensive) activity have migrated eastwards to lower labour cost locations, mainly in Eastern Europe and parts of Asia (ESG 2004). The growth in the logistics service sector is indicative of both increasing amounts of economic activity and of more outsourcing of transportation and warehousing activities to 3PL service providers. A large proportion of Ireland's total logistics expenditure is outsourced (Marketline International 1997) with a large proportion of manufacturing companies outsourcing some or all of their transport and logistics activities (NITL 1999).

Other Issues

A number of other issues combine to make logistics and SCM particularly critical from an Irish perspective. Firstly, the country's relatively peripheral location results in transportation costs for companies based in Ireland being higher than those in more favourable locations (Forfás 1995).[6] Furthermore, recent changes in the corporate taxation regime (in particular the introduction of a 12.5 per cent tax rate on service businesses) makes the option of companies establishing business units (profit centres) in Ireland with responsibility for the management of supply chain activities more attractive.[7]

---

[6] This Forfás report, which resulted in the establishment of NITL, suggested that, by adopting more integrated approaches to logistics management, companies based in Ireland could to some extent compensate for relatively high transportation costs.
[7] A number of examples of some of this thinking in practice now exist in Ireland, particularly in the technology sector.

REFERENCES

Central Statistics Office (2006), *External Trade 2005*, Dublin: CSO.

Economic and Social Research Institute (2005), *Annual Report and Review of Research for the Year ended 31 December 2003*, Dublin: ESRI.

Economist, The (1997), 'Survey: Ireland', 15 May.

Economist, The (2004), 'A Survey of Ireland', 14 October.

Enterprise Strategy Group (2004), *Ahead of the Curve, Ireland's Place in the Global Economy*, Dublin: Forfás.

Forfás (2005), *International Trade and Investment Report 2004*, Dublin: Forfás.

Forfás (1995), *World Class to Serve the World*, Dublin: Forfás.

Layte, R., O'Connell, P.J., Fahey, T. and McCoy, S. (2005), 'Ireland and Economic Globalization: The Experiences of a Small Open Economy', Chapter 16 in H. Blossfeld, E. Klijzing, K. Kurz and M. Mills (eds.), *Globalization, Uncertainty and Youth in Society*, New York: Routledge.

Marketline International (1997), *European Transport Monitoring: The Next Five Years in a Dynamic Marketplace*, London: Marketline.

National Institute for Transport and Logistics (1999), *The Logistics Requirements of Companies in Ireland*, Dublin: NITL.

United Nations Conference on Trade and Development (2004), *Handbook of Statistics*, Geneva: UNCTAD.

Annex 1: Republic of Ireland's External Trade 2005

Country	Imports				Exports			
	September 2005	September 2006	Jan–Sep 2005	Jan–Sep 2006	September 2005	September 2006	Jan–Sep 2005	Jan–Sep 2006
Great Britain	1,540.9	1,529.7	12,284.6	12,881.5	1,241.0	1,270.3	10,056.4	10,111.8
Northern Ireland	119.3	110.1	941.5	961.9	133.8	138.1	1,169.2	1,221.1
Austria	18.4	17.9	161.5	183.1	39.9	35.8	307.3	301.1
Belgium	92.0	95.1	802.7	890.0	1,423.1	1,418.7	9,885.3	10,825.6
Cyprus	0.9	0.9	15.3	18.0	2.1	2.2	21.2	23.2
Czech Republic	11.1	21.8	128.8	200.0	20.9	34.5	181.9	260.8
Denmark	81.9	31.8	600.3	489.8	46.3	47.9	418.4	426.2
Estonia	1.5	1.8	14.0	13.5	1.1	2.1	11.2	18.6
Finland	25.7	23.8	221.1	193.9	35.4	35.3	237.8	323.4
France	130.0	182.4	1,463.1	1,523.3	481.2	421.1	4,178.5	3,686.3
Germany	334.5	359.9	3,259.3	3,583.9	579.8	585.2	4,844.5	5,131.2
Greece	5.6	5.4	31.7	38.9	27.6	26.7	252.6	260.7
Italy	109.0	119.4	935.8	1,100.3	308.8	283.6	2,838.8	2,774.9
Latvia	11.0	3.4	40.0	49.5	0.5	0.4	3.9	4.0
Lithuania	1.3	1.3	15.5	16.0	1.3	2.6	10.3	13.0
Luxembourg	2.2	6.1	19.8	31.5	13.2	18.4	111.7	122.9
Hungary	12.8	34.3	128.1	247.3	12.5	20.5	93.3	181.0
Malta	0.2	0.3	2.6	2.3	0.9	1.0	9.2	9.0
Netherlands	155.9	175.9	1,682.8	1,822.1	269.2	272.4	2,625.8	2,475.7
Poland	11.9	17.9	96.6	123.7	22.5	35.2	189.5	265.7
Portugal	13.9	17.9	146.9	166.1	36.1	36.5	280.1	318.3
Slovakia	1.2	1.9	8.9	12.0	3.6	5.7	25.7	31.2
Slovenia	2.1	1.5	12.0	15.7	2.3	2.2	15.3	15.4

Annex 1 (continued)

Country	Imports				Exports			
	September 2005	September 2006	Jan–Sep 2005	Jan–Sep 2006	September 2005	September 2006	Jan–Sep 2005	Jan–Sep 2006
Spain	53.1	60.5	567.3	645.6	232.5	311.2	2,216.1	2,395.9
Sweden	39.6	57.3	396.7	471.2	96.5	93.0	770.2	789.1
EU Country not specified	36.8	47.9	374.3	518.7	5.6	4.6	56.2	48.7
Total EU	2,812.8	2,926.3	24,340.3	26,190.0	5,036.6	5,105.0	40,809.5	42,527.7
of which EU-15	2,758.8	2,841.2	23,878.5	25,491.9	4,968.9	4,998.8	40,247.9	41,214.8
Australia	12.3	12.8	90.7	110.5	85.2	60.1	528.8	584.6
Brazil	19.9	13.7	155.4	139.9	17.4	12.7	116.9	112.8
Canada	19.4	34.9	201.4	271.2	37.7	30.0	248.0	271.0
China	347.4	392.3	2,606.3	3,130.0	79.2	72.4	630.9	624.2
Hong Kong	45.2	28.9	342.5	236.5	54.8	73.5	407.9	430.8
India	17.1	17.5	178.6	171.0	12.7	16.2	97.4	117.7
Japan	151.4	160.6	1,616.2	1353.2	249.3	189.9	1,683.1	1,507.1
Malaysia	37.9	32.4	402.0	313.0	49.5	105.2	420.8	725.9
Mexico	10.8	12.6	88.6	112.8	41.7	33.8	348.8	411.8
Norway	235.3	152.7	1,084.9	1,469.5	77.1	58.0	441.8	437.6
Philippines	12.9	13.6	103.0	99.5	35.2	32.3	250.4	262.7
Russia	2.6	12.6	59.0	90.6	25.0	23.9	171.3	205.2
Singapore	68.7	81.5	572.9	985.4	142.7	45.8	583.7	474.3
South Africa	12.8	13.0	123.5	120.1	24.3	23.6	187.3	237.6

Annex 1 (continued)

Country	Imports				Exports			
	September 2005	September 2006	Jan–Sep 2005	Jan–Sep 2006	September 2005	September 2006	Jan–Sep 2005	Jan–Sep 2006
South Korea	73.0	53.9	706.5	644.2	58.2	41.5	370.6	381.6
Switzerland	54.5	68.5	398.9	306.6	138.6	163.9	2,456.7	1,691.9
Taiwan	78.4	93.3	677.3	712.5	28.8	24.5	236.8	221.5
Thailand	21.7	44.1	277.9	371.2	8.5	9.2	107.3	78.1
Turkey	19.5	35.0	302.2	375.0	32.8	30.6	239.9	279.4
USA	534.7	457.0	5,784.6	4,583.0	1,337.3	1,451.7	11,677.1	12,459.7
Other countries[1]	107.7	93.6	815.3	871.2	218.5	244.0	1,803.6	2,159.3
Country Unknown[2]	2.8	12.2	28.5	63.0	23.9	31.7	194.7	232.5
Unclassified estimates[3]	86.2	96.8	751.0	862.5	0.6	7.4	10.8	50.3
Total	**4,785.0**	**4,869.9**	**41,716.5**	**44,063.8**	**7,815.7**	**7,884.9**	**64,033.2**	**65,985.1**

[1] Other non-EU countries not listed individually
[2] Trade for which the country of origin or country of final destination is unknown
[3] Estimates not allocated by country

Source: Central Statistics Office (2006), *External Trade 2005*, Dublin: CSO.

3

Understanding Supply Chain Management

EDWARD SWEENEY

A plethora of supply chain management (SCM) definitions have been developed in recent years. There is evidence of differences in emphasis and approach between different industrial sectors, geographical areas and functional backgrounds. Furthermore, a variety of associated terminologies have also been developed which has added to the complexity. As noted by Ross (1998), this can limit management's understanding of the SCM concept and the practical effectiveness of its application. Nonetheless, SCM has risen to prominence in recent years in both academic and commercial circles. The number of professional bodies involved in the area is also a reflection of the growth in interest in the subject. However, there is still no universally accepted definition of what SCM is (and, indeed, is not). As pointed out in a seminal article by Mentzer *et al.* (2001):

> Despite the popularity of the term Supply Chain Management, both in academia and practice, there remains considerable confusion as to its meaning. Some authors describe SCM in operations terms involving flow of products and materials, some view it as a management philosophy, and some view it as a management process.

This chapter comprises three elements. Part A provides an overview of the historical evolution of SCM and of the various definitions which have been developed. Part B goes on to introduce the author's definition based on the *Four Fundamentals* of SCM. Finally, Part C explains the role within SCM of one of its principal antecedents, namely logistics.

PART A – SCM: EVOLUTION AND DEFINITION

HISTORICAL EVOLUTION OF SCM

The term SCM was originally introduced by management consultants in the early 1980s (Oliver and Webber 1982). Since then several attempts have been made to place contemporary SCM thinking in an historical context and/or to plot its historical development and evolution. The following sections provide an overview of three of the more useful and widely cited approaches. They also provide a framework for describing some key concepts and models which are now effectively constituent elements of the overall integrated SCM paradigm.

Fragmentation to Integration Model

Battaglia (1994) developed a model which indicates the way in which SCM has evolved from its main constituent functions from the 1960s to date (see Figure 3.1). It indicates that the evolution has involved a shift from highly fragmented to much more integrated approaches with the 1990s characterised as the decade of 'Total Integration'.

During the 'Evolving Integration' decade (the 1980s) various functional areas became integrated into *materials management* and *physical distribution* – these then became further integrated under the *logistics* umbrella. SCM extends this integration further by linking logistics with manufacturing, information technology (IT), marketing, sales and strategic planning. The model provides a useful visual representation of the way in which companies have attempted to move away from the functional stovepipe or silo approach to more integrated approaches, facilitated by IT. It is interesting to note that this model is analogous to two other 'three phase' approaches to logistics evolution.

Figure 3.1: SCM Evolution

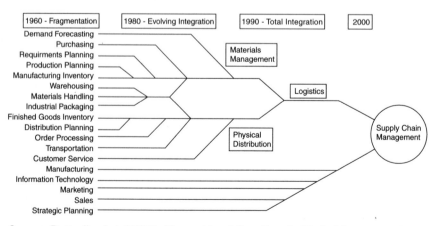

Source: Battaglia, A.J. (1994), 'Beyond Logistics: Supply Chain Management (Operations)', *Chief Executive (US)*, Nov.–Dec., 99, 48–50.

Masters and Pohlen (1994) describe the evolution of logistics management and the role of logistics managers in the following three phases:

1. Functional management (1960–1970): Functions such as purchasing, shipping and distribution are each managed separately.
2. Internal integration (1980s): The management of the supply chain functions of a single facility is unified and it becomes the responsibility of a single individual.
3. External integration (1990s): The management of supply chain functions throughout the chain is unified, requiring cooperation and coordination between links in the chain.

La Londe (1994) also describes the evolution of integrated logistics in three phases:

1. Physical distribution: The distribution of goods is all that needs to be managed by a logistics manager.
2. Internal linkages: It is important for the logistics manager to control both internal supply functions and physical distribution.
3. External linkages: Logistics management requires cooperation in management with upstream and downstream entities to maximise the benefits of the total logistics system.

The specific relationship between SCM and logistics will be discussed in Part C of this chapter.

Lean/Functional to Agile/Customised Migratory Model

Christopher and Towill (2000) use the personal computer (PC) supply chain to illustrate the migration from *lean*, functionally oriented approaches to *agile* and more customised supply chain architectures. They use a model originally developed by Murokoshi (1994) to highlight the four main stages in this evolutionary process (see Table 3.1).

As pointed out earlier, *lean* thinking has its origins in the Japanese automotive industry, in particular in the Toyota Production System (TPS) and the just in time (JIT) paradigm (Ohno 1988; Womack and Jones 2003). The main objective of this thinking was the identification and elimination of non-value-adding activities (NVAs) or waste (*muda* in Japanese). As noted in Chapter 2, an NVA may be defined as: *any activity (or resource or asset) that adds cost (or time) to any supply chain process without adding value from a customer perspective.*[1] In the early 1980s the focus was largely on cost

---

[1] Author's definition based on Jones *et al.* (1997), Goldrat and Cox (1992), Womack and Jones (2003) and others.

Table 3.1: Migration from Lean/Functional to Agile/Customised Supply Chains

Supply chain evolution phase	I	II	III	IV
Supply chain time marker	Early 1980s	Late 1980s	Early 1990s	Late 1990s
Supply chain philosophy	Product driven	Market orientated	Market driven	Customer driven
SC type	Lean functional silos	Lean supply chain	Leagile supply chain	Customised leagile supply chain
Market winner	Quality	Cost	Availability	Lead time
Market qualifiers	(a) Cost (b) Availability (c) Lead time	(a) Availability (b) Lead time (c) Quality	(a) Lead time (b) Quality (c) Cost	(a) Quality (b) Cost (c) Availability
Performance metrics	(a) Stock turns (b) Production cost	(a) Throughput time (b) Physical cost	(a) Market share (b) Total cost	(a) Customer satisfaction (b) Value added

Source: Christopher, M. and Towill, D.R. (2000), 'Supply Chain Migration from Lean and Functional to Agile and Customised', *Supply Chain Management: An International Journal*, 5(4), 206–213.

optimisation through improved efficiency, particularly in manufacturing processes.

As customer service issues such as product availability and lead time evolved from being order (or market) qualifiers to becoming market (or order) winners, the need emerged for not just lean functions and supply chains but for responsive and customer-oriented configurations. In other words, *agility* became a key concern. The agility concept is closely associated with Cranfield University in the UK and with Prof. Martin Christopher in particular (Christopher 2000; Christopher and Towill 2001). Christopher (2000) defines agility as 'a business-wide capability that embraces organisational structures, information systems, logistics processes and, in particular, mindsets'. Flexibility, with its origins as a business concept in flexible manufacturing systems (FMS), is a key characteristic of an agile organisation. In essence, the need for a shift from lean to agile paradigms has been driven by dynamic and increasingly competitive global markets. The concept of mass customisation (MC) is a key driver of this shift.

The MC concept was first coined by Davis (1989) and it promotes the ability to provide individually designed products and services to every customer. This contrasts starkly with the Henry Ford Model T paradigm. It is achieved through high process agility, flexibility and integration (Pine *et al.* 1993; Hart 1995; Eastwood 1996; Da Silveira *et al.* 2001). In short, as markets become more competitive and customers more discerning, there is a need to move towards the MC ideal, and supply chain agility is the route for making this happen. As Christopher (2000) notes, leanness may be an element of agility but it will not in itself provide the degree of organisational flexibility which is increasingly required to meet changing customer requirements.[2]

A final element of the Christopher and Towill Migratory Model worthy of comment is the *leagility* concept. The desirability of being both lean and agile has resulted in the rather contrived term, *leagile*, being coined. A leagile supply chain is defined as one which combines elements of both the lean and agile approaches. In technical terms, leagility involves the strategic use of a decoupling point (Naylor *et al.* 1999). This decoupling point aims to achieve responsiveness to volatile demand downstream (i.e. in the market) while providing level scheduling upstream from the decoupling point. In essence, it is an attempt to get the best of both worlds.

Lummus and Vokurka Historical Perspective

Lummus and Vokurka (1999) suggest that the origins of SCM can be traced to the quick response (QR) programme in the textile industry and later to the efficient consumer response (ECR) programme in the grocery industry.

The origins of QR are often traced back to Blackburn (1991) and a useful definition is provided by Fisher and Raman (1996). In the specific context of the textile sector they describe QR as:

> An initiative designed to cut manufacturing and distribution lead times through a variety of means including information technology such as electronic data interchange, point of sale scanners, and bar coding, logistics improvements such as automated warehousing and increased use of air freight, and improved manufacturing methods, ranging from laser fabric cutting to reorganisation of the sewing process into modular sewing cells.

---

[2]He actually makes the point that an industry may be very lean but not be sufficiently flexible or 'nimble' to consistently meet customer requirements profitably. He suggests that the automotive industry might be a case in point.

This definition recognises the central role of IT in the supply chain improvement process and that improving the speed of response to customer requirements demands a focus on both distribution and manufacturing issues. ECR originated from a grocery industry task force that was established in 1992 (Kurt Salmon Associates Inc. 1993) and focuses on the need for quick and accurate information flows in the supply chain as the key to supply/demand synchronisation and inventory reduction. The key common objective of QR and ECR is speed of response to customer requirements – both recognise this as an integral element of value creation. They also recognise the centrality of effective information management in the achievement of this objective.

Lummus and Vokurka (1999) go on to outline other early documented efforts at improving supply chain performance in companies across a range of sectors.[3] Their paper continues with a focus on collaborative efforts aimed at identifying 'best practices' (e.g. the SCOR model developed by the Supply Chain Council, see below) and on the need for a clear linkage between SCM and overall corporate strategy. It concludes by suggesting seven guidelines for companies beginning to manage across the entire supply chain. All seven relate, directly or indirectly, to the need for supply chain companies to work in a more coordinated and collaborative way.

The Supply Chain Council (SCC) was organised in 1996 and initially included 69 practitioner companies meeting in an informal consortium. By 2005, it had grown to approximately 800 members worldwide, across a range of sectors. The Supply Chain Operations Reference (SCOR) model is a product of the SCC and 'provides a unique framework that links business process, metrics, best practices and technology features into a unified structure to support communication among supply chain partners and to improve the effectiveness of supply chain management and related supply chain improvement activities' (Supply Chain Council 2005). Three key features of the model are important (illustrated in Figures 3A.1–3A.3 in Appendix A, respectively):

1. It integrates the concepts of business process re-engineering (BPR), benchmarking and process measurement into an integrated framework.
2. It is based on five distinct management processes:
    (i) Plan: Demand/supply planning and management.

---

[3]Hewlett-Packard, Whirlpool, Wal-Mart, West Co., Becton Dickinson, Baxter and Georgia-Pacific Corp.

(ii) Source: Sourcing stocked, make-to-order and engineer-to-order products.
(iii) Make: Make-to-stock, make-to-order and engineer-to-order production execution.
(iv) Deliver: Order, warehouse, transportation, and installation management for stocked, make-to-order and engineer-to-order products.
(v) Return: Return of raw materials and receipt of returns of finished goods.

3. It contains three levels of process detail:
    (i) Top level: Process types.
    (ii) Configuration level: Process categories.
    (iii) Process element level: Based on process decomposition.

Since its first introduction, a number of papers have appeared in the academic literature concerning the SCOR model (e.g. Stewart 1997; Huan *et al.* 2004).

Key Lessons from SCM Historical Evolution

The three approaches to SCM historical evolution outlined above highlight at least five key elements of contemporary thinking in the field:

1. There is a need to focus clearly on customer service issues, in particular the speed of response to customer requirements.
2. Markets have become more sophisticated and customers more discerning – this has resulted in the need to understand the relevance of MC (as opposed to traditional 'one size fits all' perspectives).
3. Intra-company integration of the constituent elements of supply chain functionality requires a strong management focus.
4. Effective information management, facilitated by recent developments in information and communications technology (ICT), is important in improving customer service performance.
5. Managing relationships with external parties which perform key supply chain roles has become more important.

Finally, the work of Gattorna *et al.* (2003), in particular the performance/capability continuum (see Figure 3.2), provides a useful conceptual overview which mirrors SCM historical evolution in many respects. Furthermore, most of the elements of contemporary SCM identified above are captured in this continuum. These will be returned to in more detail

Figure 3.2: Performance/Capability Continuum

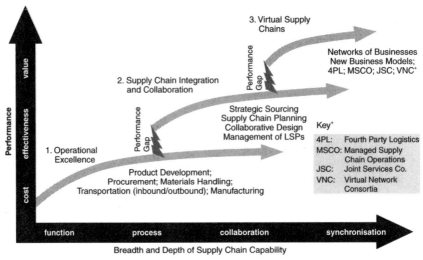

Source: Gattorna, J *et al.* (eds.), *Handbook of Supply Chain Management*, 5th edition, London: Gower. (2003).

later. The next section explores definitions of SCM in the literature with a view to synthesising the salient constituent elements of the field.

SCM DEFINITIONS

As noted earlier, a plethora of SCM definitions have been developed since the term was first introduced in the early 1980s. This section provides an overview of some of the important definitions and draws some conclusions from a synthesis of these definitions.

Defining SCM (Mentzer *et al.* 2001)

Mentzer *et al.* (2001) provide an excellent overview of the more important of these definitions (see Appendix B) and, based on their analysis, provide a definition of their own.

From the representative sample of SCM definitions in Appendix B, Mentzer *et al.* suggest that three definition categories can be identified. Firstly, many authors define SCM as a *management philosophy*. In this context, SCM adopts a systems approach to viewing the supply chain as a whole, from the supplier to the ultimate customer. A chain-wide collaborative approach, driven by a strong customer focus, aims to synchronise intra-firm and inter-firm capabilities. Secondly, many authors consider SCM as a *set of activities to implement a management philosophy*. Seven activities are proposed, based on the earlier research, which appear necessary in the successful implementation of the philosophy:

1. Integrated behaviour in customer and supplier firms.
2. Mutually sharing information.
3. Mutually sharing risks and rewards.
4. Cooperation among supply chain members.
5. The same goal and the same focus on serving customers.
6. Integration of processes.
7. Partnerships to build and maintain long-term relationships.

Thirdly, many authors have focussed on SCM as a *set of management processes*. In this context, a process is defined as, 'a specific ordering of work activities across time and place, with a beginning, an end, clearly defined inputs and outputs, and a structure for action.' This is very much in line with BPR thinking, as championed by Hammer (Hammer and Champy 1993). In essence, business processes take inputs and create outputs, and these outputs should be of value to a customer.

Some of the conclusions from the work of Mentzer *et al.* will be returned to later. A number of other approaches to defining SCM are worth considering beforehand.

CSCMP Definition

Founded in 1963, the Council of Supply Chain Management Professionals (CSCMP)[4] is a US-based association for individuals involved in SCM with over 10,000 members (CSCMP 2005). It defines SCM as follows:

> Supply chain management encompasses the planning and management of all activities involved in sourcing and procurement, conversion, and all logistics management activities. Importantly, it also includes coordination and collaboration with channel partners, which can be suppliers, intermediaries, third-party service providers, and customers. In essence, SCM integrates supply and demand management within and across companies.

CSCMP, in discussing boundaries and relationships, goes on to state that SCM is an 'integrating function', which 'drives coordination of processes

---

[4]CSCMP was known until 2005 as the Council of Logistics Management (CLM). It was known as the National Council of Physical Distribution Management (NCPDM) from its inception until 1985.

and activities with and across marketing, sales, product design, finance and information technology'. The approach represented by this definition reiterates some of the earlier points and again has a strong emphasis on internal and external coordination and collaboration. However, the final part of the definition provides a useful conceptual view of SCM and is noteworthy for its simplicity, with its focus on integration of supply and demand.

Christopher's Paradigm Shifts

Prof. Christopher was mentioned earlier in the context of supply chain agility. His various papers provide another valuable insight into the nature of SCM (see Christopher and Ryals 1999; Aitken et al. 2001; Christopher and Towill 2002; Christopher and Peck 2004). An important theme in his work is the move away from traditional approaches where companies viewed themselves as independent entities (or self-contained islands) to an apparently paradoxical recognition that companies may have to cooperate to be complete. This in turn requires a shift from traditional arms-length and often adversarial customer-supplier relationships towards relationships which are characterised by cooperation and trust. Arising from this thinking, Christopher and Ryals (1999) state that, 'SCM encompasses both the internal management of the logistics processes that support the flow of product and related information, as well as the upstream and downstream linkages with suppliers and customers.' This provides an insight into the concept of supply chain competition, with which Christopher is closely associated. He states that, 'leading edge companies have realised the real competition is not company against company, but rather supply chain against supply chain' (Christopher 1992). The adoption of this thinking has the potential to have a profound impact on the nature of strategic thinking in companies of all kinds. It challenges the conventional wisdom upon which the majority of traditional approaches to strategic thinking and strategy formulation are based. However, the extent to which this thinking has been adopted – or is even understood – in practice is unclear. 'Leading edge' companies may well have adopted this thinking to varying degrees but there is a need to understand its role and impact in the wider business community.

SCM and the Porter Model

One well-known approach to strategic thinking and strategy formulation, based on the concept of the value chain, was introduced almost a quarter of a century ago by Michael Porter (see Porter 1985). The idea of the value chain is based on the process view of organisations – the idea of seeing a manufacturing (or service) organisation as a system, made up of subsystems each with inputs, transformation processes and outputs. Inputs, transformation processes and outputs involve the acquisition and consumption of resources, such as money, labour, materials, equipment, buildings, land, administration and management. How value chain activities are carried out determines costs and affects profits.

Most organisations engage in hundreds, even thousands, of activities in the process of converting inputs to outputs. These activities can be classified generally as either primary or support activities that all businesses must undertake in some form. According to Porter (1985), the *primary* activities are:

1. **Inbound Logistics**, which involve relationships with suppliers and include all the activities required to receive, store and disseminate inputs.
2. **Operations** are all the activities required to transform inputs into outputs (products and services).
3. **Outbound Logistics**, which involve relationships with customers and include all the activities required to collect, store and distribute the output.
4. **Marketing and Sales** are activities that inform buyers about products and services, induce buyers to purchase them and facilitate their purchase.
5. **Service** includes all the activities required to keep the product or service working effectively for the buyer after it is sold and delivered.

The *support* activities are procurement, human resource management (HRM), technological development and infrastructure. A graphical representation of Porter's value chain is shown in Figure 3.3.

The relationship between this chain and SCM has been the subject of discussion in several papers (e.g. Barney 1997; Lazzarini *et al.* 2001). As noted earlier, supply chains are sets of activities representing successive stages of value creation. The literature on SCM suggests that vertical interdependencies require a systemic approach to the management of material and information flows between firms engaged in the chain. On the other hand, Porter's value chain analysis is primarily an approach that describes a set of sequential activities creating value *within* firms.[5]

---

[5] It is worth noting that attempts have been made to extend value chain analysis to activities between firms (e.g. Barney 1997).

Figure 3.3: Porter's Value Chain

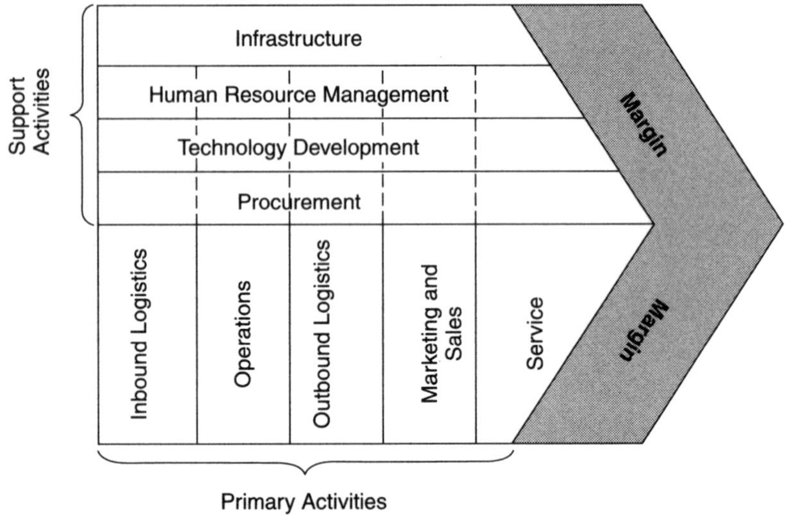

Support Activities	Infrastructure					Margin
	Human Resource Management					
	Technology Development					
	Procurement					
	Inbound Logistics	Operations	Outbound Logistics	Marketing and Sales	Service	Margin

Primary Activities

Source: Porter, M.E. (1985), *Competitive Advantage: Creating and Sustaining Superior Performance*, New York: Free Press.

Conclusions from SCM Definitions

This chapter began by making reference to Mentzer *et al.* (2001). It is appropriate to revert to this study once again, in particular to the two constructs proposed by the authors.

Firstly, they suggest that many definitions of SCM are trying to define two interdependent but different concepts in one term. The first is referred to as *supply chain orientation* (SCO) and is defined as 'the recognition by an organisation of the systemic, strategic implications of the tactical activities involved in managing the various flows in a supply chain'. However, SCM requires that SCO exists in several linked companies across a supply chain. In other words, SCO is a prerequisite for SCM.

Secondly, the definition of SCM proposed by the authors based on their analysis of the literature is:

> the systemic, strategic coordination of the traditional business functions and the tactics across these business functions within a particular company and across businesses within the supply chain, for the purposes of improving the long-term performance of the individual companies and the supply chain as a whole.

This definition amalgamates a variety of concepts and philosophies into a single sentence. Its authors claim that their work 'should help practitioners as well as researchers to understand SCM, to give guidance to what SCM is, its prerequisites, and its potential effects on business and supply chain performance'.

In conclusion, SCM is not new. The term may be relatively new but supply chains have existed for a very long time – in fact they have probably always existed! For example, Forrester's often cited article from the *Harvard Business Review* in 1958 states that:

> Management is on the verge of a major breakthrough in understanding how industrial company success depends on the interactions between the flows of information, materials, money, manpower, and capital equipment. The way these five flow systems interlock to amplify one another and to cause change and fluctuation will form the basis for anticipating the effects of decisions, policies, organisational forms, and investment choices.

His article introduced the demand amplification concept using a computer simulation model.[6] If, as Forrester suggested, management was on 'the verge of a major breakthrough' almost half a century ago, it seems pertinent to raise questions concerning how this breakthrough – mainly in relation to managing relationships between supply chain companies – has impacted on companies in reality. In fact, over 40 years after Forrester's article first appeared, Mentzer *et al.* (2001), in concluding their paper, ask the specific question: 'How prevalent is SCM?' This is a key question to which ongoing research needs provide some answers.

PART B – THE *FOUR FUNDAMENTALS* OF SCM

RATIONALE

A number of points are critically important from Part A of this chapter. Firstly, the very fact that many SCM definitions exist may, of itself, limit management's understanding of the SCM concept and the practical effectiveness of its application (as noted by Ross 1998). Furthermore, a range of – often quite complex – SCM language and terminology has evolved over

---

[6] More recent replications of this phenomenon include the 'Beer Game' simulation and research covering the 'Bullwhip Effect' (Lee *et al.* 1997).

the years. Given that there are many bodies of literature associated with SCM, this should not come as a major surprise. Croom *et al.* (2000), for example, identify eleven 'subject areas we consider to be core to any supply chain management literature survey as a discipline'.[7] Mentzer *et al.* (2001) refer to 'confusion', 'ambiguity' and 'a need to examine the phenomena of SCM more closely to define the term and concept'; Lambert of Ohio State University (Lambert 2004) states that, 'there is a great deal of confusion regarding exactly what SCM involves'; Croom *et al.* (2000) note that, despite the existence of SCM since the early 1980s, 'conceptually the management of supply chains is not particularly well understood.' Furthermore, many of the SCM definitions in the literature appear to attempt to provide a single-sentence definition (see above, in particular: CSCMP; Mentzer *et al.* 2001). In the author's view, the results are, almost inevitably, achievements in verbal and linguistic dexterity rather than definitions which are likely to add clarity from an SCM application perspective. The author's experience of using such definitions in recent years as part of post-experience education programmes in SCM has reinforced the validity of this viewpoint.

The *Four Fundamentals* represents an attempt to concisely, yet comprehensively, define the essence of SCM. It is aimed primarily at a practitioner audience and aims to bring clarity and understanding to the issue. The avoidance of jargon and complex language is an element of this. It seeks to describe the main constituent elements of SCM, as well as positioning SCM in the overall corporate strategic framework. Furthermore, it aims to provide a definition which is intelligible, irrespective of the functional background, business sector or geographical location of the practitioner. Finally, the *Four Fundamentals* needs to be relevant to supply chain professionals, irrespective of their level of experience and/or seniority in industry. It relates to:

1. Setting SCM objectives.
2. SCM philosophy.
3. Managing the flows.
4. Supply chain relationships.

The following sections describe each of the *fundamentals* in turn.

---

[7]Purchasing and supply; logistics and transportation; marketing; organisational behaviour; industrial organisation, transaction cost economics and contract view; contingency theory; institutional sociology; systems engineering; networks; 'best practices'; strategic management; and economic development.

FUNDAMENTAL ONE: SETTING SCM OBJECTIVES

The Role of Objectives

The concept of management by objectives (MBO) has been written about for many years (e.g. Albrecht 1979; Humble 1971) and continues to attract attention (Aggarwala 2002). The basic concept of MBO is that agreed objectives form the basis of the planning process. Setting objectives is of crucial importance for any planning activity and is central to the successful creation and implementation of any plan for several reasons, including the following:

- It focuses the attention of planners on the main targets to be achieved.
- It provides a sense of direction to those creating and implementing the plan.
- It provides a basis for *post hoc* evaluation of the plan.

For these and other reasons, the creation of business objectives continues to play a key role in lexicons of management training and education (Rouillard 2002).[8]

From an SCM perspective, the key objectives are:

- To meet or exceed the required or demanded customer service level in targeted markets/segments.
- To optimise total supply chain investment and cost.

This service/cost approach has long been regarded as central to SCM (Christopher 1992[9]).

Customer Service

Customer service has long been recognised as an integral component of a firm's marketing strategy to increase sales and profits (Lambert 1992; Lambert and Sterling 1993). Furthermore (and as noted earlier), customer service is becoming a key source of differentiation or an order winning criterion in many sectors (Christopher 2005). In many sectors, the importance of customer service relative to product quality (now largely an order qualifier) and price (largely determined by the dynamics of supply and demand

---

[8]Objective setting is often based on the **SMART** approach. Objectives should be **S**pecific, **M**easurable, **A**lligned, **R**ealistic and **T**ime-based.
[9]The title of this book *Logistics and Supply Chain Management: Strategies for Reducing Costs and Improving Service* reflects this.

in the market and subject to downward pressure in many sectors) has increased (Sweeney 2004). In other words, the importance of customer service as an element of the overall marketing mix of organisations has increased.

The key to the role of customer service in SCM lies in: (i) understanding customers' needs and requirements in targeted markets/segments; and then, (ii) meeting (or exceeding) these needs. To support this, the concept of an external and internal audit has been suggested (Sterling and Lambert 1989). The purpose of an external audit is primarily to understand customer expectations and competition service levels. An internal audit is used to assess the level of customer service provided and establish a benchmark against which changes in service can be appraised. In assessing prior research, Sterling and Lambert (1989) concluded that many of the past studies in this area narrowly defined customer service and failed to measure it from a customer's point of view. Similarly, the National Institute for Transport and Logistics (NITL) noted that: 'The first thing to ask is: "What do we mean by customer service?". To some organisations it means dealing with customer complaints; to others, it is about after-sales service; and, to yet others, it is the "have a nice day" attitude to customers.' They go on to suggest that, in an SCM context, customer service means 'something quite specific and includes all the factors involved in supporting and getting product to customers' (NITL 2001). Table 3.2 shows the suggested constituent elements of customer service.[10]

Table 3.2: Elements of Customer Service

Customer Service Elements
- Product Availability (can orders be filled?)
- Length of Order Cycle Time (time it takes from order to delivery, usually counted in days)
- Consistency of Order Cycle Time (always the same length of time from order to delivery)
- Invoice/Billing Procedures/Accuracy
- Information Request Responsiveness (how fast does company respond)
- Flexibility in Resolving Problems
- Distance to Suppliers Warehouse
- Special Customer Requests
- Frequency of Damaged Goods (do products get damaged on the way to the customer?)
- Quality of Order Department
- Emergency Coverage
- On-time Delivery

Source: NITL (2001), 'Customer Service', *Technical Fact Sheet*, Dublin NITL.

---

[10] These elements of customer service are discussed in more detail in Chapter 9.

These elements form the basis of both the external and the internal audit processes. Armed with the information yielded by these, companies can then develop market-driven customer service strategies, which 'deliver the level of service customers actually want and are willing to pay for, and exploit company strengths and competitor weaknesses' (NITL 2001). The title of the paper by Korpela *et al.* (2001), 'Customer Service Based Design of the Supply Chain', captures this approach very effectively.

Before concluding this overview of customer service in the supply chain, it is worth reiterating that increasing competition means that different market segments – and, indeed, different customers – will increasingly have different customer service requirements. This is in line with the MC concept discussed earlier. The original MC concept (Davis 1989) promoted the ability to provide individually designed products to every customer. As customer service becomes a more critical order winning criterion, the need to customise service levels to meet the requirements of different markets and customers is likely to become more important. In an SCM context, therefore, the author proposes an approach to MC which promotes *the ability to provide individually designed products, with individually incorporated service levels, to every customer*. In short, different customers may have different service requirements and these requirements are likely to change over time. The key challenge is to design supply chains which are sufficiently agile to meet these needs.

It is not just about *improving service* as the title of Christopher (1992) suggests. Rather, as pointed out earlier, the objective needs to be *to meet or exceed the required or demanded customer service level in targeted markets/segments*. This may result in a requirement to improve service but, as pointed out by NITL (2001) for example, 'it is quite common to find companies incurring significant costs to provide a speedy response to customers ... customers often indicate that speed is not the issue.' In other words, companies may be over-servicing customers in certain ways (e.g. length of order cycle time), while failing to meet their needs in other, more critical, ways (e.g. consistency of order cycle time). The key is to recognise that understanding customer service requirements is the starting point in the supply chain design process. In other words, as shown in Figure 3.4, a market-driven customer service strategy – based on clearly understood customer requirements – sets the specification for integrated SCM.

Total Supply Chain Investment and Costs

As noted earlier, a significant amount of the cost base of companies is in the supply chain and a key objective is to optimise this (and all other)

Figure 3.4: Customer Service in Integrated SCM Performance Specification

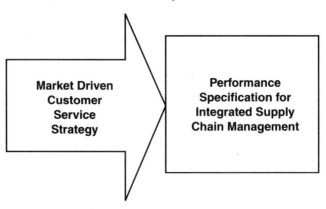

Source: Modified from Sweeney, E. (2004), 'Making Supply Chain Management Work for You!', *Logistics Solutions*, 7(4), 21–25.

expenditure. The emphasis must be on *total* supply chain costs. The key issue is that a reduction in expenditure in one part of the supply chain (e.g. purchasing) may result in an increase elsewhere (e.g. inventory holding costs). In line with overall SCM philosophy (see below) it is important to take a supply chain wide view and to recognise the inevitable trade-offs that need to be addressed. The trade-off approach to supply chain costing has been a feature of the literature for many years (Beckett 1967; Schiff 1972). Direct product profitability (DPP) represents an attempt to determine the costs of moving products through the entire supply chain. As the name suggests, DPP is essentially a technique for identifying the profit contribution of individual products by taking into account the specific supply chain costs incurred by particular items. As noted by Kurt Salmon Associates Inc. (1993) in the context of ECR in the grocery industry, the handling and storage costs attributable to specific products 'had virtually wiped out' apparently high gross profits. However, traditional DPP models ignored overhead and administrative costs, which resulted in inaccuracies in terms of determining real total costs. The development of activity-based costing (ABC) in the 1980s was an attempt to assign overhead costs more accurately within organisations (Cooper 1988).[11] However, as noted by La Londe and Pohlen (1996): 'Despite the advantages of ABC, the methodology does not provide a satisfactory solution to supply chain management.'

---

[11]Chapter 5 disucsses ABC and some of its weaknesses in more detail.

They note that the focus of ABC is on internal activities and go on to state that:

> These internal applications provide valuable information; however, they do not enable the supply chain participants to determine where non-value-added activities may exist in the supply chain, what high cost activities or processes to target for continuous improvement or re-engineering, what are the key factors driving supply chain costs, or how to incorporate the notion of functional shiftability – to strategically position logistics activities in the channel where the function can be best performed in terms of cost, time, or quality.

The total cost of ownership (TCO) approach addresses some of these weaknesses. As noted by Ellram (1995), this approach recognises that purchase price represents only a portion of the total cost of acquiring an item. It seeks to identify total acquisition price by including the costs of purchasing, stock holding, poor quality and delivery failure.

The previously cited paper by La Londe and Pohlen (1996) provides a useful supply chain costing model. The authors note that:

> Supply chain costing provides a mechanism for developing cost-based performance measures for the activities comprising the key processes within the supply chain. The capabilities provided by supply chain costing include the ability to: determine the overall effectiveness of the supply chain, identify opportunities for further improvement or re-engineering, measure performance of individual activities or processes, evaluate alternative supply chain structures or select supply chain partners, evaluate effects of technology improvements.

The six-step methodology[12] incorporates elements of trade-off analysis, DPP and ABC.

The foregoing relates to supply chain costs. Similar logic can be applied to the issue of investment in supply chain capability. In broad terms, such investment aims to improve service performance, reduce costs, or both. As noted by New (1996) the expenditure involved can be significant and needs to be subject to the usual investment appraisal processes to assess its value to the firm. Finally, it should be noted that the objective is not just about *reducing costs* as the title of Christopher (1992) suggests. Rather the

---

[12]The steps are: analysing supply chain processes, breaking processes down into activities, identifying the resources required to perform an activity, costing the activities, tracing activity costs to supply chain outputs, and analysis and simulation (see Chapter 5 for more detail).

Figure 3.5: Improved Financial Performance Measures the Effectiveness of SCM

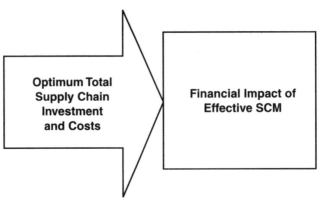

Source: Modified from Faulkner, R. (2002), 'You Need to Think Supply Chain Management', Presentation at European Union Asia ICT Workshop, Bangkok, Thailand, October.

objective needs to be, as pointed out earlier: *to optimise total supply chain investment and cost*. For example, it may be necessary to commit investment to supply chain improvement and/or to increase operating costs to meet (or exceed) customer service requirements. In any case, it is important that total supply chain investment and cost is assessed as fully and as accurately as possible. An understanding of the current situation provides a key input to the supply chain design process. It could also be argued that the effectiveness of SCM implementation is assessed by measuring its impact on financial performance, as shown in Figure 3.5.

The Service/Cost Conundrum

The foregoing raises the issue of how both customer service and financial improvements can be achieved simultaneously: that is, the *service/cost conundrum*. Conceptually, customer service improvements and cost reductions might appear to be mutually exclusive; that is, service improvements require investment in supply chain capability or increases in supply chain operating costs and reductions in expenditure cause service levels to be reduced. As noted by Stevens (1989), the objective is 'to effect a balance between what are often seen as conflicting goals of high customer service, low inventories and low unit cost.' Two simple equations (both cited in Christopher and Towill 2000) provide a useful illustration of this issue.

1. Supply chain total PDP costs = Physical PDP costs + Marketability costs.

PDP is *product delivery process*. 'Physical costs' include all production, distribution and storage costs. 'Marketability costs' include all obsolescence and stock-out costs (Fisher 1997).
2. Total value = (Quality × Service level)/(Costs × Lead time)
(Johansson *et al.* 1993).

The first equation indicates that costs associated with a failure to meet customer requirements are just as much a part of total cost as the, often more easily measurable, physical costs. To optimise total cost, therefore, customer service level demands need to be met and physical costs need to be optimised. As pointed out by Christopher and Towill (2000), the second equation is particularly helpful as 'it emphasises the futility of improving one performance measure at the expense of worsening another.' Furthermore, the equation re-introduces the concept of value. In the author's view this is the key to addressing the service/cost conundrum. The creation of value requires that all four elements in the equation are tackled simultaneously. One approach to this is through time-based SCM.

The concept of time compression in the supply chain is not new (Stalk and Hout 1990; Towill 1996; Mason-Jones and Towill 1998). Indeed, the JIT paradigm was based on the elimination of the seven forms of waste (or *muda*), one of which is specifically, 'waste of time in waiting' (Ohno 1988). Stalk and Hout (1990) claim that 95 per cent of the time consumed by business processes is wasted. Beesley (1996) states that the work of Warwick Manufacturing Group (WMG) in the mid-1990s substantiates this figure in a UK context.[13] He goes further by pointing out that 'in a total supply chain context, most UK examples are struggling to achieve one per cent value-adding time.' The key is that supply chain time compression has the potential to improve several of the elements of customer service (see Table 3.2) whilst simultaneously reducing cost (on the basis that 'time is money'). In this way the value creation process is significantly enhanced.

Summary and Some Concluding Points

Fundamental One recognises the importance of objectives and sets out clearly the two generic SCM objectives. Any attempt at improving supply

---

[13]Beesley (1996) notes that 'The Time Compression Programme (TCP) exists as a partnership between industrial and academic parties of the Warwick Manufacturing Group (WMG, part of the University of Warwick). The programme was launched as a club scheme within the [UK Department of Trade and Industry] DTI's Enterprise Initiative and is jointly funded by the DTI and industrial partners.'

Figure 3.6: Achieving Competitive Advantage through Integrated SCM

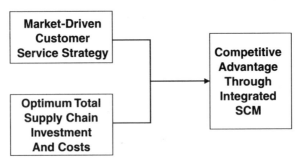

Source: Modified from Faulkner, R. (2002), 'You Need to Think Supply Chain Management', Presentation at European Union Asia ICT Workshop, Bangkok, Thailand, October.

chain capability needs to be based on improving performance in these two areas. Understanding customer requirements in the marketplace and current supply chain cost elements and drivers then becomes the starting point for the supply chain improvement/re-engineering process. As shown in Figure 3.4, the development of a market-driven customer service strategy sets the specification for SCM. Improved financial performance measures the effectiveness of SCM (see Figure 3.5). Figure 3.6 shows how achievement of the two objectives combines to create competitive advantage through integrated SCM.

Finally, it should be noted that there will inevitably be target markets (or segments or individual customers) which a company would like to service and where the cost of doing so provides the opportunity to capture profitable market share. Similarly, there will inevitably be others where the cost of doing so is prohibitive. This logic enables market segmentation and targeting to be based on 'cost-to-serve' models (Gebert *et al.* 1996). In this way SCM, and the setting of clear SCM objectives specifically, becomes a key element of corporate marketing planning.

FUNDAMENTAL TWO: SCM PHILOSOPHY

Supply Chain Integration

From the earlier discussion of both the historical evolution and the definitions of SCM it is evident that the concept of integration lies at the heart of SCM philosophy (see Christopher 1992; New 1996; Lambert 2004).

Cooper *et al.* (1997) specifically describes SCM as 'an integrative philosophy'. The work of Fawcett and Magnan (2002) identifies four levels of integration in practice:

1. Internal cross-functional integration.
2. Backward integration with valued first-tier suppliers.
3. Forward integration with valued first-tier customers.
4. Complete backward and forward integration ('from the supplier's supplier to the customer's customer').

The first of these relates to integration of activities and processes which are carried out within a single organisation (i.e. *internal* or *micro-* or *intra-firm* supply chain integration). The others describe varying degrees of integration of activities which span the boundaries of organisations (i.e. *external* or *macro-* or *inter-firm* supply chain integration), with the last one being viewed as the theoretical ideal. The following sections discuss internal and external integration in more detail.

Internal Chain Integration

The phrase 'internal supply chain' has appeared in the literature (Huin *et al.* 2002) to describe work aimed at breaking down the barriers between functions within organisations. To establish a framework for describing the key functions of a typical internal supply chain, New's comment (1997) that SCM 'revolves around the buying, making, moving and selling of "stuff"' is quite instructive. It is in line with the 'buy–make–move–sell' model of product supply chains (NITL 2000) introduced in Chapter 2. For the purposes of this section the author has added a fifth element, namely the 'store' activity. This has been done to ensure that all activities associated with the design and management of warehouses and other storage locations is given due recognition in the framework. Warehouse management has long been regarded as an integral element of the logistics activity of firms (see below) and a significant amount of specialist knowledge and expertise in this area has been developed over the years. Essentially, 'move' has been disaggregated into separate 'move' and 'store' elements, reflecting the specific characteristics of each of these activities.

Most businesses — certainly manufacturing-based businesses — can be described in terms of the five functions: buy, make, store, move and sell. This is what is referred to as the internal (or micro- or intra-firm) supply chain as shown in Figure 3.7.

Traditionally, these functions have been managed in isolation, often working at cross-purposes. SCM means thinking beyond the established boundaries, strengthening the linkages between the functions, and finding ways for them to pull together. A recognition that the 'whole is greater than the sum of the parts' calls for more effective integration between purchasing and procurement (buy), production planning and control (make), warehouse management (store), transport management (move) and customer relationship management (sell), as illustrated in Figure 3.8.

This shift, away from a functional orientation towards a more company-wide focus, is in line with the early stages of the various models of SCM historical evolution introduced previously. It is also analogous to the SCO approach of Mentzer *et al.* (2001) in the sense that SCO at firm level, as manifested in high levels of internal integration, could be regarded as a prerequisite for SCM, as manifested in high levels of external integration. Nonetheless, the desirability of achieving seamless integration is not something which is unique to SCM. As noted earlier, organisations have long realised the need for company-wide approaches to organisational design and redesign. The development of systems engineering approaches to manufacturing system redesign in the 1970s and 1980s (see Hitomi 1996) was followed by the focus on organisational re-engineering, often based on business processes, in the 1980s and 1990s (Hammer and Champy 1993). A common feature of these approaches was a recognition that 'the whole

Figure 3.7: The Internal Supply Chain

micro [internal]
supply chain

| buy | make | store | move | sell |

Figure 3.8: Integrating the Internal Supply Chain

micro [internal]
supply chain

is greater than the sum of the parts.' In other words, optimising subsystems (whether those subsystems are functional departments, production sites or individual processes in the manufacturing cycle) can result in a sub-optimised total system. Lack of efficiency and/or effectiveness is often a result of the poorly designed interfaces between subsystems rather than any inherent subsystem weaknesses. There are numerous examples of companies which have generated significant improvements in competitive advantage as a result of the application of this 'total systems' thinking (see Checkland and Scholes 1999[14]; Sweeney 1999).

Finally, elements of two earlier SCM definitions highlight some of the key organisational issues associated with internal integration. Monczka *et al.* (1998) state that, 'SCM requires traditionally separate materials functions to report to an executive responsible for coordinating the entire materials process.' In a similar vein, Houlihan (1988) notes that, in an SCM environment, 'responsibility for the various segments of the supply chain is not fragmented and relegated to functional areas such as manufacturing, purchasing, distribution and sales.'

External Chain Integration

Every product or service is delivered to the final consumer (the only source of 'real' money in the chain) through a series of often complex movements between companies which comprise the complete chain. An inefficiency anywhere in the chain will result in the chain as a whole failing to achieve its true competitive potential. In other words, supply chains are increasingly competing with other supply chains rather than, in the more traditional axiom, companies simply competing with other companies. The phrase 'supply chain' is used to indicate that the chain is only as strong as its weakest link.

The simplistic representation in Figure 3.9 of the external (or macro- or inter-firm) supply chain shows materials flowing from the raw material source through the various stages in the chain to the final consumer. Money (i.e. funds) then flows back down the chain. The point is that every link matters and that value is added, and profit generated, at each link along the way.

This aspect of *Fundamental Two* is central to most of the definitions of SCM introduced earlier. As Houlihan (1988) notes, 'the supply chain is viewed as a single process.' In other words, the various links in the chain

---

[14]Peter Checkland is particularly associated with 'Soft Systems Methodology' (SSM).

Figure 3.9: The External Supply Chain

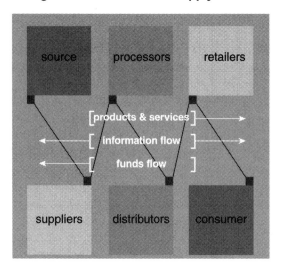

need to function in as seamless a manner as possible. Monczka *et al.* (1998) refer to the use of, 'a total systems perspective across multiple functions and multiple tiers of suppliers'. The reference to 'multiple functions' alludes to internal integration; extending this to 'multiple tiers of suppliers' introduces the external integration concept, albeit in the rather limited sense of backward integration with suppliers. As noted earlier, the theoretical ideal is complete backward and forward integration ('from the supplier's supplier to the customer's customer').

Summary and Some Concluding Points

Virtually all contemporary definitions place a strong emphasis on the need for a shift from traditional supply chain architectures, which were often characterised by fragmentation, to more effective configurations, which need to replace fragmentation with integration. This is true both in relation to internal and external chains. *Fundamental Two* recognises this fact. The achievement of high levels of internal integration has implications for the design of organisational structures. As noted earlier, 'leading edge' companies may well have adopted this philosophy to varying degrees but there is a need to understand its role and impact in the wider business community. Finally, moving from fragmented to more integrated approaches inevitably requires changes to the ways in which both internal and external customer and supplier relationships are created and managed (see *Fundamental Four*).

FUNDAMENTAL THREE: MANAGING THE FLOWS

Supply Chain Flows

Forrester's pioneering article from almost half a century ago (Forrester 1958) established a specific link between corporate success and the interactions between five flow systems:

1 Information.
2 Materials.
3 Money.
4 Manpower.
5 Capital equipment.

Since then, the concept of different flows interacting with each other, and the need to proactively manage these flows, is a theme which has been the subject of much research and discussion. For example, Jones and Riley (1985) suggest that 'SCM is concerned with the total flow of materials from suppliers through end users.' Stevens (1989) suggest that the objective of SCM is 'to synchronise the requirements of the customer with the flow of materials from suppliers'. Christopher and Ryals (1999) emphasise the importance of managing 'the flow of product and related information'.

In essence, for a supply chain to achieve its maximum level of effectiveness and efficiency, material flows, money flows and information flows throughout the entire chain must be managed in an integrated and holistic manner, driven by the overall service and financial objectives. The view of an external chain shown in Figure 3.9 indicates the way in which material, money (funds) and information flow between the companies that participate in the chain. Similar flows typically occur between the functions which comprise the internal chain. The following sections provide a overview of some of the issues involved in managing these material, money and information flows, with a particular emphasis on the latter.

Managing Material Flows

Figure 3.9 shows the flow of material ('products and services') from the source of materials forward (or upstream) to the final consumer in the external chain. It should be noted that there is also a backward (or downstream) flow of materials, mainly associated with product returns. The growing importance of reverse logistics in recent years has sharpened the focus on management of these flows. For example, 'Return' is the process most recently incorporated into the SCOR model.

Much SCM theory has its origins in the well-established field of materials management. The evolution of materials management in many ways mirrors the evolution of SCM as a whole. For example, the focus on manufacturing inventory reduction in the 1960s and 1970s (see Figure 3.1) became an integral part of the broader field of materials management in the 1980s and early 1990s (Battaglia 1994). The need for more integrated approaches to materials management across the supply chain became a strong focus in the 1990s (see Hines 1993). It could be argued that the whole field of logistics, with its origins in a military context, is fundamentally concerned with the efficient and effective management of the flow of materials through supply chains (see Part C of this chapter). In any event, ensuring that the right materials are in the right part of the supply chain at the right time remains an integral element of the SCM field.

Managing Money Flows

In a supply chain, money flows from the ultimate consumer of the product back down through the chain. The timing of these flows is critical to ensuring that supply chain companies maintain the ability to meet their ongoing operational expenditure commitments. The working capital cycle – a well-known construct in the field of financial management (see Keown *et al.* 2004) – provides a useful representation of financial flows in a supply chain (see Figure 3.10).

A performance metric used within the SCOR model is cash-to-cash cycle time. This is defined by adding the number of days worth of inventory held to the number of days of receivables outstanding and then subtracting

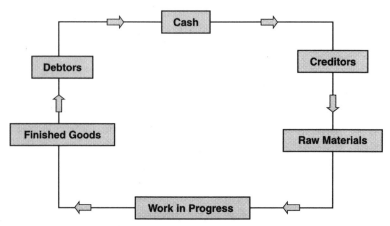

Figure 3.10: The Working Capital Cycle

the number of days of payables outstanding. The result is a measure of the number of days of working capital that are tied up in managing the supply chain.[15]

Managing Information Flows

As shown in Figure 3.9, information flows in the supply chain are bidirectional. From an SCM perspective, it can be argued that managing the information flows is the most critical of the activities described in this section. This is because the flow or movement of materials or money is usually triggered by an associated information movement. Effective management of material and money flows is, therefore, predicated upon the effective management of the related information flows. It is not surprising, therefore, that recent years have seen a huge interest in this area in the literature (see Evans *et al.* 1993; Mason-Jones and Towill 1998). The bullwhip effect to which Forrester's study (1958) referred is essentially the product of poor information management in the supply chain and leads to a requirement to hold excessive levels of inventory. The corollary of this is that if levels of demand visibility are high throughout the supply chain then inventory levels can be reduced. As Christopher (2005) notes, good information effectively becomes a substitute for high levels of inventory.

Recent years have also seen rapid developments in the ICT used to facilitate SCM. McDonnell *et al.* (2004) propose a taxonomy of supply chain ICT solutions which identifies four primary categories as follows:

1. **Point solutions**: Used to support the execution of one link (or point) in the chain (e.g. warehouse management systems or WMS).
2. **'Best of breed' solutions**: Where two or more existing stand-alone solutions are integrated, usually using middleware technology.
3. **Enterprise solutions**: Based on the logic of enterprise resource planning (ERP), these solutions attempt to integrate all departments and functions across a company into a single computer system that can serve all those different departments' particular needs.
4. **Extended enterprise solutions (XES)**: Refers to the collaborative sharing of information and processes between the partners along the supply chain using the technological underpinnings of ERP.

The move away from point towards enterprise solutions in many ways reflects the shift from internal and functional to external and process

---

[15] The financial dimension of SCM is explored in more detail in Chapter 5.

management orientations in recent years (as highlighted earlier). Other technologies, in particular electronic data interchange (EDI) and the Internet, have enabled supply chain partners to use common data. As noted by Christopher (2000), this facilitates supply chain agility as companies can act based on 'real demand, rather than be dependent upon the distorted and noisy picture that emerges when orders are transmitted from one step to another in an extended chain'.[16]

Summary and Some Concluding Points

Fundamental Three provides the key to putting the philosophy of SCM, as outlined in *Fundamental Two*, into operational practice. It highlights the specific activities that need to take place, and places a strong emphasis on the need for an integrated and holistic approach to their management. A stepwise decomposition of the buy–make–store–move–sell model, as carried out in the SCOR model, identifies in more detail what these activities are and how they interact. Indeed, most of the activities typically seen by companies as being part of SCM relate to the planning and control of these elements of supply chain functionality (Fawcett and Magnan 2002). In this context, 'planning and control' is concerned with material, money and information throughout the supply chain.

FUNDAMENTAL FOUR: RELATIONSHIP MANAGEMENT

Supply Chain Relationships

The need to replace fragmentation with integration (as advocated in *Fundamental Two*) and the holistic approach to flow management (as advocated in *Fundamental Three*) requires a re-appraisal of the way in which both internal and external customer/supplier relationships are created and managed. As noted by Sweeney (2005): 'SCM is not a 'zero-sum' game based on adversarial relationships. Rather, it needs to be a 'win–win' game based on partnership approaches.' This point is relevant to the interactions between the key 'internal' supply chain functions of buy, make, store, move and sell, as well as to relationships between an organisation and its external customers and suppliers. Several of the SCM definitions in the literature highlight the importance of relationship management. For example, Monczka *et al.* (1998) refer to the requirement for 'joint relationships with suppliers across multiple

---

[16]Information management issues are dealt with in some detail in Section 4 (Chapters 12 to 14).

tiers'. La Londe and Masters (1994) suggest that supply chain strategy includes, '...two or more firms in a supply chain entering into a long-term agreement; ...the development of trust and commitment to the relationship; ...the integration of logistics activities involving the sharing of demand and sales data.' The CSCMP definition specifically embraces the concept of 'co-ordination and collaboration with channel partners'. Finally, Lambert et al. (1998) go even further by suggesting that, 'Increasingly the management of relationships across the supply chain is being referred to as supply chain management (SCM).'

Types of Relationships

Lamming (1993) highlights the need to move: from 'zero-sum' to 'win–win' games; from competitive to collaborative approaches; and, from adversarial to partnership relationships (and beyond[17]). However, the reality is that many different possible relationship types exist. Quinn and Hilmer (1994) categorised relationships based on the trade-off between the need for flexibility and the need for control, as shown in Figure 3.11. Choosing the appropriate relationship model is a key issue in any given situation.

Figure 3.11: Categories of Customer/Supplier Relationship

Source: Modified from Quinn, J.B. and Hilmer, F.G. (1994), 'Strategic Outsourcing', *Sloan Management Review*, Summer, 43–55.

The Impact of Vertical Disintegration

As noted earlier, companies are increasingly focusing on what they regard as their core activities or competencies. The corollary of this is that activities

---

[17] As suggested in the title of his book – *Beyond Partnership: Strategies for Innovation and Lean Supply*.

regarded as 'non-core' are being outsourced. Key supply chain activities such as transportation, warehousing and manufacturing are increasingly being outsourced to third-party organisations. This has resulted in a shift away from the traditional model of 'control through ownership' towards models which are based on management and control through effective supply chain relationship management (Christopher 2005). In short, as this process of vertical disintegration has taken place, so supply chain architectures have become more virtual. For example, at the stage referred to by Gattorna *et al.* (2003) as 'Virtual Supply Chains' (see Figure 3.2), there is an emphasis on 'Networks of Businesses' and 'Virtual Network Consortia' (VNC). The traditional *fully vertically integrated* approaches are being replaced by contemporary *fully virtually integrated* approaches – a new FVI is evolving. This has sharpened the focus on the need for the creation of appropriate relationship forms throughout the supply chain, as well as on their effective management.

Strategic Partnering

Much of the literature presents the partnership approach as an ideal. For example, Harland *et al.* (1999) argue that: 'The search for closer co-operation and integration is evident not only with customers; suppliers are increasingly being viewed as partners, becoming more deeply involved in co-operative problem solving.' In a truly strategic partnership approach, according to Rothery and Robertson (1995), a number of features should be evident, as follows:

- Senior management from both firms meet regularly.
- Payments relate to specified business outcomes or pre-agreed levels of performance rather than fixed work volumes.
- Outsourcing contracts usually last for five years or longer.
- Disclosure takes the place of costs and margins between both parties.
- Each is involved in the other partner's strategic planning.
- Partner is not chosen on the basis of a competitive tendering process.
- Each partner searches for ways to reduce total costs of the partnership.
- Each partner must genuinely add value.

However, as noted by Stone (2002): 'In reality, few *partnerships* are arrangements between equal parties.' Fernie (1998) goes further by noting that, 'there is an impression that companies enter some form of partnership but in many cases lip service is being paid to the idea.' Lamming (1993) also refers to the 'lip service' trap in relation to customer/supplier partnerships by noting that, 'if companies talk about it for long enough, they begin to believe they are doing it.'

Summary and Some Concluding Points

Based on the foregoing, the creation and management of partnerships with all customers and suppliers (internally and externally) is not what *Fundamental Four* is about. As stated earlier, it is about recognising that putting SCM philosophy into practice requires a reappraisal of such relationships. There is no 'one size fits all' approach to this. There are many possible relationship forms and choosing the right ones in specific situations is the key. Nonetheless, one of the biggest manifestations of the application of SCM in recent years has involved the move away from adversarial relationships with key external suppliers towards relationships which are based on mutual trust and benefits, openness and shared goals and objectives. As noted by Harland *et al.* (1999), 'there has been an observed shift away from multi-sourced adversarial trading with suppliers, towards single or dual sourcing, resulting in a reduction (or 'rationalisation') of supplier bases used by firms.'

SUMMARY AND SOME CONCLUDING POINTS

The author believes that the *Four Fundamentals* concisely, yet comprehensively, defines the essence of SCM, as it has evolved from a variety of disciplines over time. In this regard, questions need to be raised regarding the extent to which an understanding of SCM, as contained in such a definition, is a prerequisite for effective implementation. As noted by Fawcett and Magnan (2002):

> SCM definitions vary widely from company to company and even from manager to manager within the same company. As a result, not only do SCM practices lack cohesion and visibility but supply chain strategies lack specificity and reach. Managers must be precise in their discussions of specific practices – this is true both within the firm and among channel members.

In a similar vein, Mentzer *et al.* (2001) made the point that 'without a clear understanding of SCM, we cannot expect wide application of SCM in practice'. Furthermore, and as noted earlier, Ross (1998) suggests that the complicated terminology often used in discussions of SCM can limit management's understanding and its effectiveness for practical application. The *Four Fundamentals* aids the development of such an understanding.

Part C – SCM: The Role of Logistics

Background

From the foregoing it is clear that one of the principal antecedents of SCM is the field of logistics. The CSCMP defines logistics management as:

> that part of Supply Chain Management that plans, implements, and controls the efficient, effective forward and reverse flow and storage of goods, services and related information between the point of origin and the point of consumption in order to meet customers' requirements.

Cavinato (1982) – quoted in Lummus *et al.* (2001) – has defined logistics as:

> the management of all inbound and outbound materials, parts, supplies, and finished goods. Logistics consists of the integrated management of purchasing, transportation, and storage on a functional basis. On a channel basis, logistics consists of the management of the pre-production, in-production, and post-production channels. The term logistics should be distinguished from physical distribution in that the latter normally applies to only the post-production channel.

A common feature of these two definitions of logistics is that they focus primarily on the management of material flows within a supply chain. Furthermore, they both regard logistics as one component element of the broader field of SCM. However, whilst this might be the most common approach to defining logistics and relating it to SCM, it is worth noting that there are a number of different schools of thought. As noted by Lummus *et al.* (2001), 'What is not always clear is how logistics differs from ... supply chain management'. Similarly, Larson and Halldorsson point out that, 'there is lack of agreement on how SCM is related to logistics' (2004).

Relating Logistics to SCM

Larson and Halldorsson (2004) identify four conceptual perspectives on SCM versus logistics:

1. Traditionalist.
2. Re-labelling.
3. Unionist.
4. Intersectionist.

Understanding Supply Chain Management

Figure 3.12: Perspectives on SCM versus Logistics

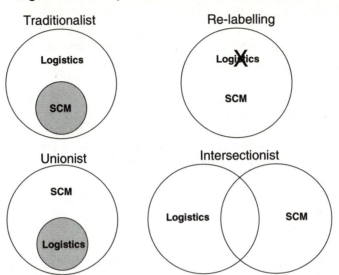

Source: Larson, P.D. and Halldorsson, A. (2004), 'Logistics Versus Supply Chain Management: An International Survey', *International Journal of Logistics: Research and Applications*, 7(1). Reprinted by permission of Taylor & Francis Ltd, (http://www.informaworld.com)

Their schematic representation of the perspectives contained in their paper is shown in Figure 3.12. The *traditionalist* school positions SCM in logistics: that is, SCM is just one small part of logistics. The *re-labelling* perspective simply renames logistics – what was logistics is now SCM!

The *unionist* perspective treats logistics as a part of SCM: SCM completely subsumes logistics. The logistics definitions cited in the previous section are examples of this school of thought. Finally, the *intersectionist* perspective is described as follows by Larson and Halldorsson (2004):

> The intersection concept suggests SCM is not the union of logistics, marketing, operations management, purchasing and other functional areas. Rather, it includes strategic, integrative elements from all of these disciplines. For instance, in the purchasing area, negotiating a long-term arrangement is a strategic element and transmitting a purchase order is tactical. The supply chain manager would be involved in the negotiations, but not the purchase order transmission. Similarly, in the logistics area, hiring a third-party logistics (3PL) provider is a strategic decision, while picking and packing in the warehouse are tactical. At the intersection, SCM co-ordinates crossfunctional efforts across multiple firms. SCM is strategic, not tactical.

Whilst each of these approaches is valid in its own way, the author's research indicates that the unionist view is the most widely adopted by scholars. The empirical evidence of Lummus *et al.* (2001) suggests a similar perspective amongst practitioners. Based on a small sample of manufacturers, retailers and 3PLs they conclude that:

> Logistics is generally viewed as within one company, although it manages flows between the company and its suppliers and customers. Supply chain management includes the logistical flows, the customer order management and production processes and the information flows necessary to monitor all the activities at the supply chain nodes.

In short, their evidence suggests that logistics is largely viewed as effectively a subset of SCM.

LOGISTICS AND THE *FOUR FUNDAMENTALS* OF SCM

The *Four Fundamentals* could be regarded as 'unionist intersectionist'. It is unionist in that it does view logistics as one element of the wider SCM field. Logistics, with its primary focus on the effective and efficient movement and storage of materials, plays a critcal role as part of *Fundamental Three*. Nonetheless, the strategic and integrative role assigned to SCM by the intersectionist perspective is in line with the *Four Fundamentals*, in particular *Fundamental Two*. The concept of using SCM as a source of strategic leverage, as discussed earlier, is in line with this view. This relates directly back to the need for clear SCM objectives – as articulated in *Fundamental One* – which link directly with the overall corporate mission and objectives of an organisation.

REFERENCES

Aggarwala, D.V. (2002), *Management by Objectives (MBO)*, New York: Deep & Deep Publications.

Aitken J., Christopher, M. and Towill, D. (2001), 'Understanding, Implementing and Exploiting Agility and Leanness', *International Journal of Logistics : Research and Application*, 5(1), 59–74.

Albrecht, K. (1979), *Successful Management by Objectives: An Action Manual*, London: Prentice Hall.

Barney, J.B. (1997), *Gaining and Sustaining Competitive Advantage*, Reading: Addison-Wesley.

Battaglia, A.J. (1994), 'Beyond Logistics: Supply Chain Management (Operations)', *Chief Executive (US)*, Nov.–Dec., 99, 48–50.

Beckett, G.A. (1967), 'Economics of Material Movement', *Transportation and Distribution Management*, March, 43–47.

Beesley, A. (1996), 'Time Compression in the Supply Chain', *Industrial Management and Data Systems*, 96(2), 12–16.

Blackburn, J.D. (1991), *Time-Based Competition: The Next Battleground in American Manufacturing*, The Business One/APICS Series in Production Management, US: McGraw-Hill, 246–269.

Cavinato, J.L. (1982), *The Traffic Service Corporation*, Washington, DC: The Traffic Service Corporation (cited in Lummus *et al.*, 2001).

Checkland, P. and Scholes, J. (1999), *Soft Systems Methodology in Action*, 2nd edition, Chichester: John Wiley & Sons.

Christopher, M. (1992), *Logistics and Supply Chain Management: Strategies for Reducing Costs and Improving Service*, London: Pitman.

Christopher, M. (2000), 'The Agile Supply Chain Competing in Volatile Markets', *Industrial Marketing Management*, 29(1), 37–44.

Christopher, M. (2005), *Logistics and Supply Chain Management: Creating Value-Adding Networks*, London: FT Prentice Hall.

Christopher, M. and Peck, H. (2004), 'Building the Resilient Supply Chain', *International Journal of Logistics Management*, 15(2), 1–14.

Christopher, M. and Ryals, L. (1999), 'Supply Chain Strategy: Its Impact on Shareholder Value', *International Journal of Logistics Management*, 10(1), 1–11.

Christopher, M. and Towill, D.R. (2000), 'Supply Chain Migration from Lean and Functional to Agile and Customised', *Supply Chain Management: An International Journal*, 5(4), 206–213.

Christopher, M. and Towill, D. (2001), 'An Integrated Model for the Design of Agile Supply Chains', *International Journal of Physical Distribution and Logistics Management*, 31(4), 235–246.

Christopher, M. and Towill, D. (2002), 'Developing Market Specific Supply Chain Strategies', *International Journal of Logistics Management*, 13(1), 1–14.

Cooper, M.C., Ellram, L.M., Gardner, J.T., and Hanks, A.M. (1997), 'Meshing Multiple Alliances', *Journal of Business Logistics*, 18(1), 67–89

Cooper, R. (1988), 'The Rise of Activity-Based Costing – Part One: What Is an Activity-Based Cost System?' *Journal of Cost Management*, Summer, 45–54.

Croom, S., Romano, P. and Giannakis, M. (2000), 'Supply Chain Management: An Analytical Framework for Critical Literature Review', *European Journal of Purchasing and Supply Management*, 6(1), 67–83.

Da Silveira, G., Borenstein, D. and Fogliatto, F.S. (2001), 'Mass customization: Literature Review and Research Directions', *International Journal of Production Economics*, 72(1), 1–13.

Davis, S. (1989), 'From Future Perfect: Mass Customizing', *Planning Review*, 17(2), 16–21.

Eastwood, M. (1996), 'Implementing Mass Customization', *Computers in Industry*, 30(3), 171–174.

Ellram, L.M. (1995), 'Activity-Based Costing and Total Cost of Ownership: A Critical Linkage', *Journal of Cost Management*, Winter, 22–30.

Evans, G.N., Naim, M.M. and Towill, D.R. (1993), 'Dynamic Supply Chain Performance: Assessing the Impact of Information Systems', *Logistics Information Management*, 6(4), 15–25.

Faulkner, R. (2002), 'You Need to Think Supply Chain Management', Presentation at European Union Asia ICT Workshop, Bangkok, Thailand, October.

Fawcett, S.E. and Magnan, G.M. (2002), 'The Rhetoric and Reality of Supply Chain Integration', *International Journal of Physical Distribution and Logistics Management*, 32(5), 339–361.

Fernie, J. (1998), 'Outsourcing Distribution in UK Retailing', *Research Paper 9801*, Institute of Retail Studies, University of Stirling.

Fisher, M. (1997), 'What is the Right Supply Chain for Your Product?' *Harvard Business Review*, March/April.

Fisher, M. and Raman, A. (1996), 'Reducing the Cost of Demand Uncertainty through Accurate Response to Early Sales' *Operations Research*, 44(1), 87–99.

Forrester, J.W. (1958), 'Industrial Dynamics: A Major Breakthrough for Decision Makers', *Harvard Business Review*, 38 (Jul.–Aug.), 37–66.

Gattorna, J., Ogulin, R. and Reynolds, M.W. (eds.) (2003), *Handbook of Supply Chain Management*, 5th edition, London: Gower.

Gebert, P., Goldenberg, C.B. and Peters, D. (1996), 'Managing Customers through Cost-to-Serve', *CMA Magazine*, 70(7), 22–23.

Goldratt, E.M. and Cox, J. (1992), *The Goal: A Process of Ongoing Improvement*, New York: North River Books.

Hammer, M. and Champy, J. (1993), *Re-engineering the Corporation: A Manifesto for Business Revolution*, New York: HarperCollins.

Harland, C.M., Lamming, R.C. and Cousins, P.D. (1999), 'Developing the Concept of Supply Strategy', *International Journal of Operations and Production Management*, 19(7), 650–673.

Hart, C. (1995), 'Mass Customization: Conceptual Underpinnings, Opportunities and Limits', *International Journal of Service Industry Management*, 6(2), 36–45.

Hines, P. (1993), 'Integrated Materials Management: The Value Chain Redefined', *International Journal of Logistics Management*, 4(1), 13–22.

Hitomi, K. (1996), *Manufacturing Systems Engineering: A Unified Approach to Manufacturing Technology and Production Management*, 2nd edition, London: Taylor and Francis.

Houlihan, J.B. (1988), 'International Supply Chains: A New Approach', *Management Decision*, 26(3), 13–19.

Huan, S.H., Sheoran, S.K. and Wang, G. (2004) 'A Review and Analysis of Supply Chain Operations Reference (SCOR) Model', *Supply Chain Management* 9(1), 23–29.

Huin, S.F., Luong, L.H.S. and Abhary, K. (2002), 'Internal Supply Chain Planning Determinants in Small and Medium-Sized Manufacturers', *International Journal of Physical Distribution and Logistics Management*, 32(9), 771–782.

Humble, J.W. (1971), *Management by Objectives in Action*, London: McGraw-Hill (European Series in Management and Marketing).

Johansson, H.J., McHugh, P., Pendlebury, A.J. and Wheeler, W.A. (1993), *Business Process Reengineering: Breakpoint Strategies for Market Dominance*, Chichester: John Wiley & Sons.

Jones, T. and Riley, D.W. (1985), 'Using Inventory for Competitive Advantage through Supply Chain Management', *International Journal of Physical Distribution and Materials Management*, 15(5), 16–26.

Jones, D.T., Hines, P. and Rich, N. (1997), 'Lean Logistics', *International Journal of Physical and Logistics Management*, 27(3–4), 153–173.

Keown, A.J., Martin, J.D., Petty, J.W. and Scott, D.F. (2004), *Financial Management: Principles and Applications*, 10th edition, New York: Prentice Hall.

Korpela, J., Lehmusvaara, A. and Tuominen, M. (2001), 'Customer Service Based Design of the Supply Chain', *International Journal of Production Economics*, 69(2), 193–204.

Kurt Salmon Associates Inc. (1993), *Efficient Consumer Response: Enhancing Consumer Value in the Grocery Industry*, Food Marketing Institute, Washington, DC.

La Londe, B.J. (1994), 'Evolution of the Integrated Logistics Concept', in Robeson, J. and Capacino, W. (eds), *The Logistics Handbook*, New York: Free Press.

La Londe, B.J. and Masters, J.M. (1994), 'Emerging Logistics Strategies: Blueprints for the Next Century', *International Journal of Physical Distribution and Logistics Management*, 24(7), 35–47.

La Londe, B.J. and Pohlen, T.P. (1996), 'Issues in Supply Chain Costing', *International Journal of Logistics Management*, 7(1), 1–12.

Lambert, D. (1992), 'Developing a Customer-Focused Logistics Strategy', *International Journal of Physical Distribution and Logistics Management*, 22(6), 12–19.

Lambert, D.M. (2004), 'Supply Chain Management', Chapter 1 in D.M. Lambert (ed.), *Supply Chain Management: Processes, Partnerships, Performance*, Sarasota, FL: Supply Chain Management Institute.

Lambert, D. and Sterling, J. (1993), 'Customer Service', Chapter 3 in J. Hopkins, D. Harmelink (eds.), *Distribution Management Handbook*, New York: McGraw-Hill.

Lambert, D.M., Cooper, M.C. and Pagh, J.D. (1998), 'Supply Chain Management: Implementation Issues and Research Opportunities', *International Journal of Logistics Management*, 9(2), 1–19.

Lamming, R. (1993), *Beyond Partnership: Strategies for Innovation and Lean Supply*, London: Prentice Hall.

Larson, P.D. and Halldorsson, A. (2004), 'Logistics Versus Supply Chain Management: An International Survey', *International Journal of Logistics: Research and Applications*, 7(1).

Lazzarini, S.C., Chaddad, F.R. and Cook, M.L. (2001), 'Integrating Supply Chain and Network Analysis: The Study of Netchains', *Journal of Chain and Network Science*, 1, 7–22.

Lee, H.L., Padmanabhan, V. and Whang, S. (1997), 'Information Distortion in a Supply Chain: The Bullwhip Effect', *Management Science*, 43(4), 546–558.

Lummus, R.R. and Vokura, R.J. (1999), 'Defining Supply Chain Management: A Historical Perspective and Practical Guidelines', *Industrial Management and Data Systems*, 99(1), 11–17.

Lummus, R.R., Krumwiede, D.W. and Vokurka, R.J. (2001), 'The Relationship of Logistics to Supply Chain Management: Developing a

Common Industry Definition', *Industrial Management and Data Systems*, 101(8), 426–432.

McDonnell, R., Sweeney, E. and Kenny, J. (2004), 'The Role of Information Technology in the Supply Chain', *Logistics Solutions*, 7(1), 13–16.

Mason-Jones, R. and Towill, D.R. (1998), 'Time Compression in the Supply Chain: Information Management is the Vital Ingredient', *Journal of Enterprise Information Management*, 11(2), 93–104.

Masters, J.M. and Pohlen, T.L. (1994), 'Evolution of the Logistics Profession', in Robeson, J. and Capacino, W. (eds), *The Logistics Handbook*, New York: Free Press.

Mentzer, J.T., DeWitt, W., Keebler, J.S., Min, S., Nix, N.W., Smith, C.D. and Zacharia Z.G. (2001), 'Defining Supply Chain Management', *Journal of Business Logistics*, 22(2).

Monczka, R., Trent, R. and Handfield, R. (1998), *Purchasing and Supply Chain Management*, Cincinnati: South-Western College Publishing.

Murakoshi, T. (1994), 'Customer Driven Manufacturing in Japan', *International Journal of Production Economics*, 37, 63–72.

National Institute for Transport and Logistics (2000), 'Supply Chain Management Made Simple', *Technical Fact Sheet*, Dublin: NITL.

National Institute for Transport and Logistics (2001), 'Customer Service', *Technical Fact Sheet*, Dublin: NITL.

Naylor, J.B, Naim, M.M. and Berry, D. (1999), 'Leagility: Integrating the Lean and Agile Manufacturing Paradigms in the Total Supply Chain', *International Journal of Production Economics*, 62(1/2), 107–118.

New, S.J. (1996), 'A Framework for Analysing Supply Chain Improvement', *International Journal of Operations and Production Management*, 16(4), 19–34.

New, S. (1997), 'The Scope Of Supply Chain Management Research', *Supply Chain Management*, 2(1), 15–22.

Ohno, T. (1988), *Toyota Production System: Beyond Large-Scale Production*, Portland: Productivity Press.

Oliver, R.K. and Webber, M.D. (1982), 'Supply-Chain Management: Logistics Catches Up with Strategy', *Outlook* 31 (reprinted in: M. Christopher (ed.) (1992), *Logistics: The Strategic Issues*, US: Chapman and Hall, 63–75).

Pine, J., Victor, B. and Boyton, A. (1993), 'Making Mass Customization Work', *Harvard Business Review*, 71(5), 108–111.

Porter, M.E. (1985), *Competitive Advantage: Creating and Sustaining Superior Performance*, New York: Free Press.

Quinn, J.B. and Hilmer, F.G. (1994), 'Strategic Outsourcing', *Sloan Management Review*, Summer, 43–55.

Ross, D.F. (1998), *Competing Through Supply Chain Management*, New York: Chapman and Hall.

Rothery, B. and Robertson, I. (1995), *The Truth about Outsourcing*, Aldershot: Gower.

Rouillard, L. (2002), *Goals and Goal Setting: Achieving Measured Objectives*, 3rd edition, Fifty Minute Series, US: Crisp Publications.

Schiff, M. (1972), *Accounting and Control in Physical Distribution Management*, Chicago: National Council of Physical Distribution Management.

Stalk, G. and Hout, T.M. (1990), *Competing Against Time*, New York: Free Press.

Sterling, J. and Lambert, D. (1989), 'Customer Service Research: Past, Present and Future', *International Journal of Physical Distribution and Materials Management*, 19(2), 1–23.

Stevens, G.C. (1989), 'Integrating the Supply Chains', *International Journal of Physical Distribution and Logistics Management*, 8(8), 3–8.

Stewart, G.(1997), 'Supply-Chain Operations Reference Model (SCOR): The First Cross-Industry Framework for Integrated Supply Chain Management, *Logistics Information Management*, 10(2), 62–67.

Stone, T. (2002), 'Critical Appraisal of Implications of Partnership Arrangements on Employees and Companies', *Logistics Solutions*, 5(2), 24–28.

Sweeney, E. (1999), 'The Systems Approach to Analysing Supply Chains and Improving their Performance' in Cox A. *et al.* (eds.), *Perspectives on Purchasing for the New Millennium, Proceedings of the 8th International Purchasing and Supply Education and Research Association (IPSERA) Conference*, Belfast, March, 739–744.

Sweeney, E. (2004), 'Making Supply Chain Management Work for You!', *Logistics Solutions*, 7(4), 21–25.

Sweeney, E. (2005), 'Managing the Supply Chain: The Role of Information and Communications Technology (ICT) as a Key Enabler of the Process', *Business Ireland*, Summer Issue, 105–109.

Towill, D.R. (1996), 'Time Compression and Supply Chain Management – A Guided Tour', *Journal of Enterprise Information Management*, 9(6), 41–53.

Womack, J.P. and Jones, D.T. (2003), *Lean Thinking: Banish Waste and Create Wealth in Your Corporation*, 2nd edition, London: Free Press.

Appendix A: SCOR Model

Figure 3A.1: SCOR Process Reference Model Elements

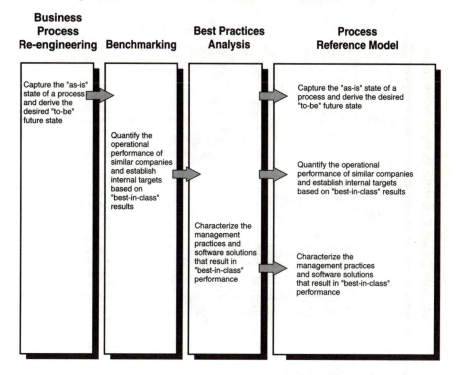

Figure 3A.2: SCOR Management Processes

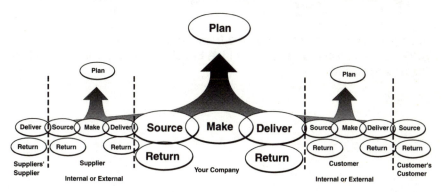

Figure 3A.3: SCOR Levels of Process Detail

#	Description	Schematic	Comments
1	Top Level (Process Types)	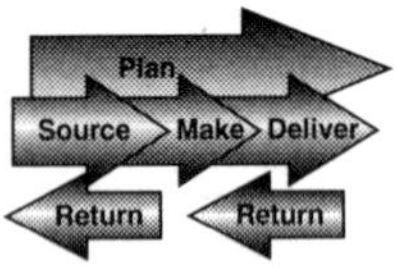 Plan; Source, Make, Deliver; Return, Return	Level 1 defines the scope and content for the Supply Chain Operations Reference-model. Here basis of competition performance targets are set.
2	Configuration Level (Process Categories)	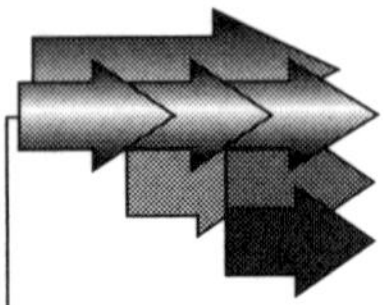	A company's supply chain can be "configured-to-order" at Level 2 from 30 core "process categories." Companies implement their operations strategy through the configuration they choose for the supply chain.
3	Process Element Level (Decompose Processes)	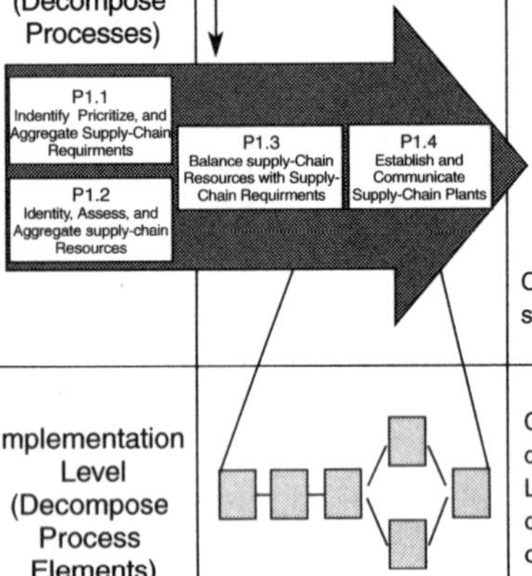 P1.1 Identify, Prioritize, and Aggregate Supply-Chain Requirements; P1.2 Identify, Assess, and Aggregate supply-chain Resources; P1.3 Balance supply-Chain Resources with Supply-Chain Requirements; P1.4 Establish and Communicate Supply-Chain Plans	Level 3 defines a company's ability to compete successfully in these chosen markets and consists of: • Process element definitions • Process element information inputs and outputs • Process performance metrics • Best practices, where applicable • System capabilities required to support best practices • Systems/tools Companies "fine tune" their operations strategy at Level 3.
4	Implementation Level (Decompose Process Elements) — Not in Scope		Companies implement specific supply chain management practices at this level. Level 4 defines practices to achieve competitive advantage and to adapt to changing business conditions.

Supply-Chain Operations Reference-model

Source: Figures 3A.1, 3A.2 and 3A.3 from the Supply-Chain Council, Inc. SCOR® is a registered trademark of the Supply-Chain Council in the United States and Canada.

APPENDIX B: SCM DEFINITIONS

Monczka, Trent, and Handfield (1998)	SCM requires traditionally separate materials functions to report to an executive responsible for coordinating the entire materials process, and also requires joint relationships with suppliers across multiple tiers. SCM is a concept, 'whose primary objectives is to integrate and manage the sourcing, flow, and control of materials using a total systems perspective across multiple functions and multiple tiers of suppliers.'
La Londe and Masters (1994)	Supply chain strategy includes: '...two more firms in a supply chain entering into a long-term agreement;...the development of trust and commitment to the relationship; ... the integration of logistics activities involving the sharing of demand and sales data; ... the potential for a shift in the locus of control of the logistics process.'
Stevens (1989)	'The objective of managing the supply chain is to synchronize the requirements of the customer with the flow of materials from suppliers in order to effect a balance between what are often seen as conflicting goals of high customer service, low inventory management, and low unit cost.'
Houlihan (1988)	Differences between supply chain management and classical materials and manufacturing control: '1) The supply chain is viewed as a single process. Responsibility for the various segments in the chain is not fragmented and relegated to functional areas such as manufacturing, purchasing, distribution, and sales. 2) Supply chain management calls for, and in the end depends on, strategic decision making. "Supply" is a shared objective of practically every function in the chain and is of particular strategic significance because of its impact on overall costs and market share. 3) Supply chain management calls for a different perspective on inventories which are used as a balancing mechanism of last, not first resort. 4) A new app-

	roach to systems is required—integration rather than interfacing.'
Jones and Riley (1985)	'Supply chain management deals with the total flow of materials from suppliers though end users...'
Cooper *et al.* (1997)	Supply chain management is '... an integrative philosophy to manage the total flow of a distribution channel from supplier to the ultimate user.'

Source: Mentzer, J.T. *et al.* (2001), 'Defining Supply Chain Management', *Journal of Business Logistics*, 22(2). Courtesy of the Council of Supply Chain Management Professionals.

4

The Strategic Dimension of Supply Chain Management

DANIEL PARK

INTRODUCTION

Where does supply chain management (SCM) make its impact in the development of a business?

SCM is probably most often thought of as a set of tools and techniques aimed at improving operations and business processes, resulting in unit cost reduction, faster times in completing activities and processes, optimal utilisation of materials, minimising of waste, consistency in product and process quality, and other similar operational objectives and activities. These are commonsense and necessary objectives. Indeed, if an organisation is unable to perform well in all or most of these spheres, it is unlikely to remain in existence very long. However, as Porter (1996) has pointed out in a seminal article, 'Operational effectiveness and strategy are both essential to superior performance. . . . But they work in very different ways.' He continues, 'Operational effectiveness means performing similar activities better than rivals perform them. . . . In contrast strategic positioning means performing different activities from rivals or performing similar activities in different ways.'

The concept of **business strategy** is central to the long-term success of any enterprise, and SCM is emerging as a potentially powerful contributor to the strategic health of an operation.

Let us begin by defining business strategy. Concepts such as competitiveness, differentiation, gaining customer preference and long-term planning, are encountered in the multiplicity of definitions found in standard textbooks on the subject of strategy. I have synthesised the 'conceptual capital' of **business strategy** into a single definition, as follows:

> A business strategy is a cohesive entity of programmes, projects and policies that concentrate corporate resources to enable an organization to establish, sustain and enhance its competitiveness and capabilities for self-renewal. (Park 2000)

To this I add my definition of **_strategic management_**, which is the practical activity. It is as follows:

> Strategic management is the planning and delivery of the programmes and projects by harnessing resources that will enable an organization to fulfil its business objectives within a measured timespan and in accordance with agreed performance criteria.

It will be seen that there is no reference in my definitions to a 'long-term' dimension. This is because we should question whether long-termism is relevant in all cases. Business strategy is just as relevant to companies that are forced to take a short-term time horizon, whether through intrinsically short product life-cycles or because of their need to recover urgently from competitive weakness. This raises another point worth emphasising: business strategy is just as important for companies that start from a position of competitive weakness as it is for companies that are doing relatively well. The same principles apply, but the priorities, activity content, time-scales of action, performance objectives and measurement criteria are likely to be very different.

In an age in which knowledge and technologies of product design, creation and distribution are becoming more widely diffused internationally, the quest for sustainable advantage has begun to acquire new characteristics. First, the traditional choice between price-based and differentiation-based competition is a lot less clearly drawn than in the past. Many companies, including an increasing number located in Asia, are beginning to demonstrate that there is not always a trade-off between price and differentiated product quality. We are beginning to see the emergence of world-class operations located in Asia and the Indian subcontinent offering (physical and service) products to demanding international customers at world-class standards with extraordinary price-competitiveness. Second (as noted in Chapter 2), the globalisation of capital, commodity, materials and product markets is blurring the boundaries that have traditionally defined such concepts as 'country of origin'. Third, the World Trade Organisation (WTO) is gradually removing tariff, quota and other barriers to trade so that, not only have industrialised countries acquired greater freedom to enter more markets than in the past, but also the newly industrialising countries are becoming better placed to compete in developed markets of the world.

Inevitably, as the playing field gradually becomes more level, the factors determining international competitiveness change. Sometimes the change is encountered in the factors themselves, sometimes in the content of the factors. An example of the former is the increase in collaboration and joint ventures. The latter is illustrated in the trend towards developing the capability to reach niche segments of markets with highly specific product and service elements within a focused and creatively differentiated product offering. This is where SCM can make a strategic impact.

If a company can differentiate itself by achieving cost-competitiveness in getting high-quality, highly-specified products to the best-margin customer and can renew such competitiveness faster than competitors can emulate it, then that company sustains a competitive advantage that should be reflected in above-average profitability in relation to its sector average. If a company's final products are becoming increasingly difficult to differentiate, then the effectiveness of the supply chain and the ability of the organisation to reconfigure that supply chain rapidly, as competitive conditions change, may become the sole critical factor underpinning its business strategy. This ability is often termed 'agility' or 'resilience', and it enables a company to outweigh the growing problem of commoditisation of product and service and the consequent price convergence between competing suppliers by giving the agile/resilient company compensating access to value (and hence profit) elsewhere in the chain of value-adding transformations from raw material to finished product and beyond. Such an approach looks at value and the reasons why customers assign value between various elements of the supply chain. The phenomenon of customer-driven migration of value, as analysed by Slywotzky, needs to be understood, indeed anticipated, in a continuous quest for meeting customer expectations profitably as well as meeting them to the extent necessary to outweigh the actions of competitors (Slywotzky 1995). There is, after all, no point is exceeding a customer's expectations to a competitively unnecessary extent and incurring a loss in so doing!

There are, moreover, a number of supply chains at work: (i) the product supply chain, (ii) the financial supply chain and (iii) the information supply chain. The managerial challenge is to harness each of these supply chains to create and sustain superior performance, so that (a) strategy and objectives are realistic and (b) operational activities are concentrated on achieving the objectives for the business. Achieving and sustaining a consistent balance between the direction set for the company (or business unit within a company) and the actions and resources needed in execution is what Gattorna has termed 'strategic alignment' (2003, 2006). Therefore let us look at the opportunities presented by the application of tools and techniques of SCM for creating robust business strategies against a background of the growing internationalisation of business.

The Product Supply Chain

First, let us consider a full supply chain. It starts with materials management leading to product creation, but the concept must go beyond the point at which the product is manufactured and made available for consumption if a company is to derive as much added value as possible from the business. This can be summarised as shown in Figure 4.1.

Sustained customer satisfaction is the significant goal, because it is both the driver of cost-effective operations and also a potentially powerful contributor to anticipating future market needs. The constant search for products that meet, and preferably anticipate, changing customer demand is carried out in the 21st century against a background of shortening product lifecycles, more open markets and more creative and collaborative relationships in the process of product creation itself.

Consider the complexities of many contemporary products and one central question emerges. Is it possible, let alone desirable, for any company to have world-leading competencies in every aspect of product creation? The answer to this question is illustrated very powerfully in civil aircraft manufacture, where the business has at the moment concentrated itself into two major manufacturers – Boeing and Airbus – plus several niche manufacturers. If we consider all the activities and products, components and sub-assemblies that go to make up the modern civil aircraft, it is unthinkable that a single company could have excellence in all. Neither would it be economically efficient to try and get into this position. The investment cost of achieving competitive excellence in all the activities, technologies, products and skills that go to

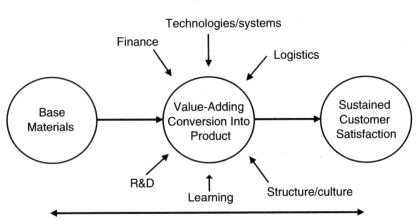

Figure 4.1: Doing Business via the Concept, Tools and Techniques of SCM

make the modern civil aircraft would be prohibitive to any organisation. Therefore the essence of civil aircraft manufacture is the ability to set up and coordinate multiple supply chains to enable the airplane manufacturer to offer a competitive final product that not only meets customer expectations but also makes sufficient profit to satisfy shareholders in the business and to finance future development.

SCM therefore impacts on airplane manufacturers at two levels. Competence in configuring and re-configuring supply chains (i) creates the value-adding differentiation that sustains competitive advantage **and** (ii) ensures operational effectiveness in execution. It is not a question of attempting to define whether SCM is a set of operational management tools and techniques or a strategic framework: *in an increasing number of business sectors SCM makes its impact at **both** levels.* The aircraft industry has been working in this way for a very long time and other sectors are now learning how to do so.

It therefore follows that effective collaboration is becoming increasingly significant in achieving and sustaining competitive advantage in many sectors of business. It follows that, if competition is moving from product-versus-product towards supply chain-versus-supply chain, then the effectiveness of all links in the chain must be assured, otherwise the strength of the chain is, quite simply, that of its weakest link. This is in line with *Fundamental Two* of SCM, as introduced in Chapter 3.

Against a background of greater internationalisation and ultimately globalisation of business on both the output (marketing) and input (procurement) sides, the issue becomes even more challenging. It becomes not only an issue of supplier selection, but of customer selection too. For example, if a highly competitive supplier of an engineering sub-assembly is dependent on customers who are competitively weak in their part of the total business, the weakness of such customers has strategic impact on the supplier. It is not enough to be competitive in your own business as classically defined (product market/product segment): business strategy must take into account the need to create internationally competitive supply chains within the broader process of value-addition (total accessible value within the business domain). The new element to add to the concept of competitive advantage is the contribution made by a business to supporting the competitive advantage of the potentially most attractive players in other parts of the full value chain (strategically a proxy for 'supply chain'). Putting it more directly, top-performing suppliers should aim to work with top-performing customers.

To take one example, the collapse of the British car manufacturer MG Rover in 2005 has brought about significant damage to a number of supply chain partners who failed to foresee MG Rover's demise and take the decisions necessary to prevent one large, weak customer ruining their own business. Many of these supply chain partners functioned at a high standard at the operational level. However, as Hamel and Valinkangas have pointed out (2003), 'a company can be operationally efficient and strategically inefficient'. In contrast, those supply chain partners of MG Rover, who took the trouble to meet the often very exacting standards of other motor vehicle manufacturers in the UK and internationally, and to reduce their dependence on MG Rover, have prospered. The starting point of their strategic thinking was the (correct) view that there is nothing unattractive or problematic about world demand for automobiles. The strategic issues are that (a) the geography of demand is shifting and (b) the competitive performance and relative positions of rival automobile manufacturers are shifting too. This reinforces Slywotzky's analysis of value migration on a global scale.

So we are faced with greater fluidity in business/market structures as a result of increasing internationalisation, more collaborative approaches to satisfying customer requirements and tightening criteria in terms of cost, speed and product/process quality. Improvements in operational effectiveness are necessary, but the advantage that they deliver may be short lived unless they are either technically difficult or prohibitively expensive for competitors to emulate – which, increasingly, they rarely are. We are prompted to re-focus our attention on the nature of competitiveness, and this is moving from product to business model.

Therefore any organisation must concentrate, not only on achieving improvements to product and service against criteria that matter to customers, but also on the way in which each customer engages with the organisation. It is here that the major opportunities for differentiation are increasingly found and these opportunities are derived increasingly from the interdependent activities of (a) time compression, (b) utilisation of shared facilities and (c) leveraging the advantages of production specialisation. Let us look at these in turn.

Effective SCM can reduce time-to-market from initial product concept to final delivery. Time compression is emerging as a potential source of competitive advantage because it is a powerful differentiator between rival suppliers. SCM gives a holistic dimension to this. In an increasing number of business spheres, where it is becoming increasingly difficult to differentiate on the basis of product specification and cost, time compression can be harnessed to create value through acceleration of the delivery of value to the customer. There are benefits in faster financial cycle time and quicker recoupment of costs, but these are measures of operational effectiveness.

The strategic dimension is that, the quicker a company can deliver value to a customer, the more likely it is to be selected and retained. This involves optimal design of internal logistics integrated with the supporting processes of outsourced operations.

However, time compression is not about activities such as 'time and motion study' or 'time management', which are about getting people to work faster. Time compression is about designing a differentiated process that maximises the amount of time in which value is being added to a product during its creation. As Gregory and Rawling (1997) argue, most analyses of value chains and value migration within value chains ignore the economic and strategic implications of opportunities and deficiencies associated with time-cycles in the total process of value creation and value capture that is illustrated at the beginning of this section. SCM facilitates value creation and value capture, and it is a powerful means of *accelerating* both these activities and achieving differentiation in the view of the customer, via the dimension of time.

Exploitation of shared facilities is also becoming strategically significant. As a direct result of the development of affordable computing capacity, a whole new range of organisational forms has become available. We are observing a shift from the fixed, asset-based organisational form to more activity being completed on the basis of 'molecular' or 'network' organisational structures. These have been more commonly termed 'virtual' or 'extended' companies, and are often referred to as 'agile corporations'.

In most manufacturing sectors of the world's developed economies, there is one issue above all others that concentrates the mind of management: the erosion of unit prices and the decline in control of manufacturers over pricing. Each year, manufacturers of many industrial products are facing the need to reduce product prices, or offer more features for the same price. In recent years, producer prices have, quite simply, been eroding throughout the developed world and, most notably, in economies that have been noted for their manufacturing leadership in the whole of the post-World War II period – the USA, UK, Germany and Japan. In contrast, prices for services have hardened. In response to this phenomenon, most manufacturers in the developed world have changed the way in which manufacturing is managed. The first phase of this response was termed 'lean manufacture', which was pioneered in Japan.

However, even by the late 1980s the concept was already mature. Lean manufacture may be cost-effective in simple accounting terms; it can, however, be somewhat inflexible. Individual lean manufacturing operations do not always respond well to fluctuations in demand. Therefore, a concept of 'agile manufacturing' developed initially in the USA for defence-related manufacturing operations and emerged under the support of the US government in the early 1990s. This concept is one of 'stitching together' alliances of lean manufacturing operations. If one operation experiences a sudden surge or drop in demand, it can call on other members of the alliance to provide or accept products from any member of the alliance. Taking one example, if we look at the dispatch area of electronics or consumer durable goods factories we will see products boxed under another manufacturer's brand name, almost certainly a competitor's.

The principle here is that agile manufacturing enables participants to undertake effective 'operational smoothing' activity. However, it does not guarantee profitability. Manufacturers of television sets have seen profits erode year over year, whilst the features of the product at a given price level have increased and product reliability has improved to the point where demand for chargeable after-sales service has fallen. In contrast, General Electric has experienced considerable price erosion in its mainstream products and yet has improved profitability consistently, partly as a result of improvements in the basic operations of the company but mainly by selling related high-value services (such as customer financing, consultancy in product utilisation) along with the products themselves.

Manufacturing efficiency still matters. Nowadays, however, manufacturing is not always the main source of added value in the total supply chain. Much value has migrated elsewhere. SCM is the critical approach to identifying and accessing this value.

Related to sharing and optimising use of facilities is the question of production specialisation. SCM enables participants to identify and intensively develop the elements of the value-adding process in which they enjoy distinguishing and differentiating competencies. It is not possible, let alone desirable, to be top-class in every element. The investment cost would be excessive and could not be recouped. Hence, in 'tiered' supply structures, the Tier 1/Tier 2 and other tiers are mutually dependent and each participant in the value chain contributes according to his core competencies.

This is quite different from (operational) outsourcing. Outsourcing is a subcontracted operation and its impact is operational and based on elementary economics – the law of comparative advantage. What is meant here by shared facilities is a *collaborative* and *integrated* process based on **competencies** that are bound together into a competitive whole through the technologies of SCM. Optimisation of facilities takes advantage of multiple levels of differentiation, thereby gaining and sustaining competitive advantage on the basis of supply chain-versus-supply chain rather than on the basis of individual product. This does not mean that individual products could in some cases not be best-in-class, since this would result in the strength of the chain being determined by its weakest link.

The essence of this approach, with SCM at its heart, is that members of the tiered supply chain are able to **concentrate** their efforts on the activities in which they excel and are individually differentiated. As stated earlier, **concentration** and **differentiation** are the essence of effective business strategy.

The Financial Supply Chain

Banks and other financial institutions are suppliers. They operate in a highly competitive market and, given that nowadays most transactions are undertaken electronically rather than by means of physical (usually paper) instruments, global reach is not so difficult to develop. The constraints and forces for deceleration of this trend are legal and political, not technological.

The concept of being a 'supplier', let alone a 'supply chain partner', has not been easy for the financial institutions to accept. It ought not to be so difficult. Capital is one resource needed in the development and operation of a business, along with labour, materials, technology and any other resource. Quite simply, it is *supplied* under internationally competitive conditions.

The managerial dimension of corporate finance is about identifying and harnessing a specific resource – capital – in the development of a business on the best available terms in the market. However, imperfect markets and asymmetrical information give rise to differentiated resource costs and potential competitive advantage can be gained through the mechanisms via which this resource is accessed and harnessed. Put at its simplest, the average cost of capital paid by a company (input) can be just as significant strategically in creating cost-effective differentiation as any differentiation that might be achievable at the level of product/service (output) and that might consequently enable a company either to charge a premium price or to reduce costs.

Financial SCM is in essence no different from the competitive advantage derived from SCM applied in sourcing steel, plastic, audit services or any resource needed by a business. It is just like sourcing in a low labour-cost country to take advantage of different wage rates. There is a similar balance between the 'price' of the commodity denominated in its own currency (in this case the interest rate) and the possible volatility of the exchange rate of that currency against the user's currency of accounting.

This is very significant in that the relationships found in 21st-century corporate finance are increasingly cross-border. The input may be commoditised; but the relationship is not. Engaging a financial supply chain partner that is expert in, for example, arbitrage and currency hedging can be strategically significant. Securing a two-way information flow between supplier and customer can form the base for taking major cost out of a business in the procurement of a vital resource.

This is best illustrated by a theoretical example. Suppose the interest rate in Singapore is more attractive than in Ireland. There is no technical reason why funding cannot be set up in Singapore dollars or in any other currency that a Singapore bank is in a position to provide. So what about the exchange rate risk? Hedging is one approach to minimising the risk. Take a trading example. Suppose you expect to receive payment in Singapore dollars in six months time and you are concerned that the Singapore dollar may weaken against the euro in this period. You can buy an equivalent amount of euros at the current exchange rate in the international market. This capability and corresponding set of competencies are becoming more significant strategically as businesses globalise. In these circumstances, a key element of the decision would be the balance between the professional fees that a Singapore bank would charge for setting up and possibly contract-managing the facility, and the turn on the interest rates. An alternative approach would be to raise funding, without hedging in the purely technical sense, in a 'cocktail' of several currencies whose projected exchange rate movements have a high probability of counterbalancing each other over the time-frame of the organisation's exposure. This may be more appropriate in major capital project funding than in short-term trade financing, since the time-scale outflows of capital are normally staged over an extended period.

The base discipline here is the anticipation and management of forward markets and, for many organisations, this activity is left to the banks, from which they make some of their profit. The supply chain view is that an organisation can become more actively involved in this activity and form a partnership with banks just like any other supplier and take a joint view of the accessible risk and reward.

Supply/uptake of finance is one of the business activities that has globalised most quickly into operating across national and regional boundaries twenty-four hours per day. This is perhaps not surprising when one considers that the transactions are to all intents and purposes computer-based nowadays. The underlying point for our purposes is this: finance is a resource with its own supply chain, and the outputs that can be generated from this supply chain can be identified and harnessed in the pursuit of strategic advantage.

The view of finance as a resource and bank relationships as a supply chain underpins a strategically important point that is often missed. Cost-efficiency is not restricted to the operational processes of end-product creation and product movement: it can be found in any processes concerned with selection and utilisation of resources. Corporate and development finance constitutes one such example. Calculate the cost of supply chain (in)efficiency as a percentage of total operating cost – particularly in increasingly international operations – and one finds out how bank profits have risen by externalising costs and transferring them to the customer, whilst keeping to themselves activities into which value has migrated as markets have globalised. This is certainly not a criticism of the financial community: financial institutions have made a strategically rational move to protect the benefits of an arm's length relationship for as long as these can be protected. However, in an era of sophisticated computer-based transactions, any organisation gradually faces fewer entry barriers (mainly skill related) to some of the activities that have traditionally been the exclusive domain of the financial sector. An SCM approach on the part of the customers of the financial institutions has initiated a value migration. This has affected not only banking but also insurance and risk management – customers are internalising some parts of the supply chain, originally the protected preserve of these specialist professionals. SCM has enabled many organisations to evaluate more critically the 'existence value' of suppliers of financial services to address the value migration from physical product (price erosion trend) to service product (price hardening trend).

Many organisations are therefore finding that they can counter the financial community's practice of externalising costs and passing these onto the customer by internalising some of the true value-adding functions that the financial community has traditionally been able to keep to itself. Customer–supplier relationships are changing in terms of their content and are becoming increasingly international. The response of many banks and venture capital institutions is evidenced in international merger and acquisition, not only to serve major multinational customers at the day-to-day operational and transactional level, but to collaborate strategically with customers of any size and scope who have decided to acquire skills in cost-effective cross-border commodity sourcing – and finance is a commodity resource – for the purpose of reducing the average cost of capital.

We have considered earlier the concept of the agile corporation, and our thinking has been focused on product creation. The same thinking on agility, SCM and their dual impact at operational and strategic levels applies in managing the financial supply chain.

THE INFORMATION SUPPLY CHAIN

Information has become part of the 'body tissue' of modern business.

We are becoming accustomed to phrases such as 'the information revolution', 'the learning organisation' and 'the knowledge economy'. Like most buzzwords and buzzphrases they are founded on a base of truth. There has never been so much information so readily available. Strategically, the importance of managing the information supply chain, consisting of both acquisition and diffusion, is growing.

The SCM issue, as it relates to the impact of information on securing and sustaining competitive advantage, is to do with identifying content and process. Information that impacts on business strategy is that which enables decision-makers to anticipate the potential for change and form a view as to a balance of risk-minimising and profit-maximising activities that will enable the company to construct and develop a business strategy (the cohesive entity of programmes and projects) that provides for profitable growth in a changing business environment. Above all, it is management of the supply of relevant information for analysis that enables the necessary trade-offs to be made as robustly as possible. Successful business strategy can depend as much on decisions on what not to do as on choice of the preferred course of action and its content. Managing the information supply chain facilitates this.

Against a background of growing international competition and increasingly easy access to information on markets, customers and competitors, more accurate and lower-risk decisions can be made, thereby enabling better concentration of resources to be achieved. Continuous research is needed to distinguish 'signals' from 'background noise'.

Information can be acquired externally (commercial and technical trends in markets, and competitive moves and potential of rivals) and internally (performance relative to competitors against factors that matter to customers now and in the future).

At a high level of aggregation, the major factors affecting the business environment require continuous critical analysis. This information includes major movements in political, economic, social and technological spheres, most often termed by the acronym 'PEST' analysis. It moves through analysis of the specific business environment – the factors affecting current and future value available in the business. This is affected by changes in the relative balance of inter-company rivalry within the business plus the effects of bargaining power of suppliers and buyers, and the threats of new entrants to the business and/or substitute products. These factors are summarised by Porter (1985) in his well-known 'Five Forces Analysis'.

This results in two analytical frameworks that are basic to business strategy, and these are now set out diagrammatically. The PEST analysis is illustrated in Figure 4.2, this example being a much-simplified framework. In international strategy the content of this analysis would be very detailed. Porter's five forces framework is as shown in Figure 4.3.

Figure 4.2: PEST Analysis

VARIABLE	ELEMENTS OF ANALYSIS
Political	Ruling party and political climate Government policy International policy Legal controls, trade legislation, etc. Health and safety, employment law Wage and price controls
Economic	Economic growth, disposable income Inflation, interest rates Taxation policy – direct and indirect Balance of payments – exchange rates
Social	Changing trends in lifestyle Demography and population Environmental aspects
Technological	Industry-wide R&D and innovation Communications infrastructure Information technology

Figure 4.3: Five Forces Analysis

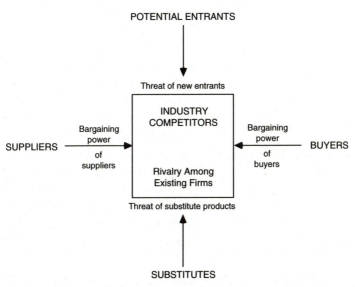

Source: Porter, M.E. (1985), *Competitive Advantage: Creating and Sustaining Superior Performance*, New York: Free Press.

The 'Porter Model' recognises many factors already discussed, but also that buyers and suppliers have an influence on the business and market environment that is sometimes underestimated. Companies have to consider the balance of forces in the market and formulate an appropriate strategy. For example, a small company operating in a highly concentrated market would have neither the economies of scale nor the purchasing power to enable it to compete on price alone. A strategy of non-price factors (such as quality, delivery) would potentially be more useful. We now consider the content of each the above elements.

Element	**Significant Content**
Intensity of rivalry	Number of firms, balance between firms, growth available, fixed cost structure, extent of differentiation, switching costs, similar/diverse strategies, low/high exit barriers.
Threat of new entrants	Economies of scale, product differentiation, capital requirements, switching costs, cost disadvantages irrespective of scale, government policy.
Substitutes	Product packaging, bundling, systems, solutions rather than products, new technologies.
Bargaining power of buyers	Buyers have power: when concentrated or when buying large proportion of company's output, when purchase represents significant per cent of buyer's costs, if product is undifferentiated, if there is threat of backward integration.
Bargaining power of suppliers	Suppliers have power: when selling to fragmented buyers, when buyer is not a significant customer, if supplier's product is vital to company, where high switching costs have built up, if there is threat of forward integration.

The PEST and Five Forces Analyses give an overview of the external framework within which the business operates. The other side of the coin is the internal perspective, specifically how the organisation performs against

Strategic Dimension of SCM

Figure 4.4: The 'Spider' Diagram

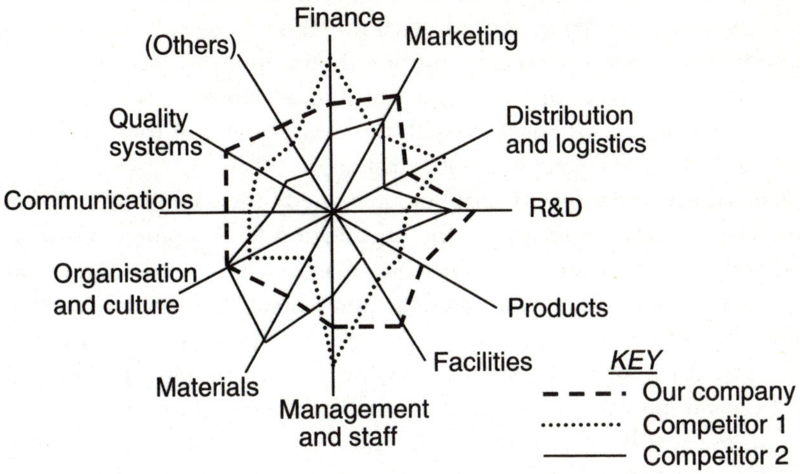

(Diagram showing axes: Finance, Marketing, Distribution and logistics, R&D, Products, Facilities, Management and staff, Materials, Organisation and culture, Communications, Quality systems, (Others))

KEY
– – – Our company
·········· Competitor 1
——— Competitor 2

competitors in meeting customer requirements. This could typically be represented in a 'spider' diagram (see Figure 4.4), bearing in mind the need to identify the critical factors and also to assign a weighting to them. This analysis identifies where advantage should be reinforced (or gained/regained). It prevents the direction of finite resources into performance improvement in areas of lesser importance to customers when remedial action is needed in areas of high significance in the buying decision. Alternatively, it identifies where an organisation can press home advantage already held against criteria that carry most weight in a customer's selection decision. The theoretical example in Figure 4.4 illustrates how this analysis works. The criteria will of course differ by business sector, and the criteria can be set out in descending order of importance clockwise from the top.

These analyses do not, however, constitute a once-for-all exercise. Constant revision of the information base on which decisions are made is vital. The process of information management and the detail and accuracy of the information can in itself constitute a contribution to differentiation and competitive advantage in that, done effectively, it enables an organisation to compress the time taken in reaching more robust decisions in comparison with rivals.

SCM, as applied to acquisition and diffusion of information, is relevant to our concept of the 'learning organisation'. Leveraging of information is at the heart of this process. The concept of learning as a contributor to business strategy is fundamental. Effective learning should be strategy focused; it should ensure, not only that current strategy is as robust as possible for the period of its duration, but also that there is sufficient knowledge-based foresight to build the organisation's next competitive platform. In order for an organisation to remain ahead of competition (if already strongly positioned) or (if currently weakly positioned) to close the gap and catch up with best-in class, the supply and quality of information on which decisions are made is significant, together with the development of tools, techniques and capabilities of leveraging that learning.

Unfortunately, the type of analyses mentioned earlier are often undertaken only in circumstances in which the organisation faces a problem – such as cost creep, deterioration in sales revenue/margin, customer defections, quality problems and other value-eroding phenomena. Sustained advantage is gained by organisations that undertake these analyses as a continuous activity and then disseminate the results into the specific learning processes that develop and integrate the component parts of the organisation.

This is a supply chain for learning, and it lends itself to the principles of SCM just as any other process in the central operational dimension of buy–make–move–store–sell. Figure 4.5 illustrates how this supply chain works and makes its strategic impact.

This leads to strategy-based organisational development in which there is concentration on the factors that enable the organisation to implement programmes and projects that deliver competitive advantage in product and

Figure 4.5: The Supply Chain for Learning

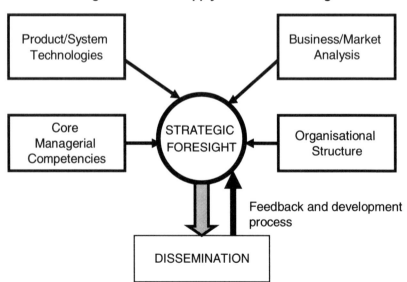

Strategic Dimension of SCM

Figure 4.6: Strategy-Based Organisational Development

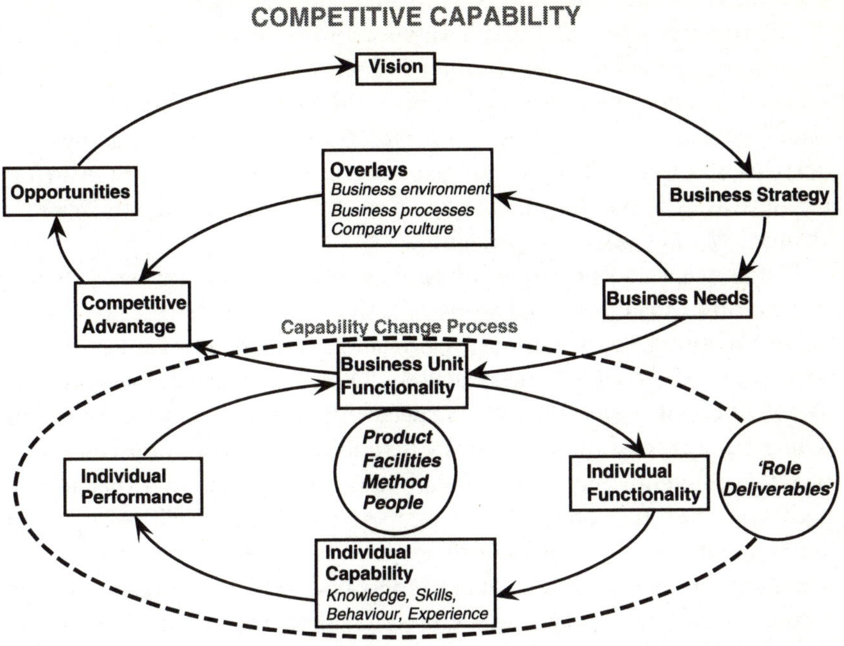

[Diagram: COMPETITIVE CAPABILITY — Vision connects to Opportunities and Business Strategy; Overlays (Business environment, Business processes, Company culture); Competitive Advantage ← Business Needs; Capability Change Process encompassing Business Unit Functionality, Individual Performance, Product/Facilities/Method/People, Individual Functionality, 'Role Deliverables', Individual Capability (Knowledge, Skills, Behaviour, Experience)]

Source: Reynolds, C. and Park, D. (2003), 'Senior Executive Development Plan', *Logistics Solutions*, 4, 12–13.

process as the programme and project structure changes over time. It is illustrated in Figure 4.6.

SCM, STRATEGY, ALIGNMENT AND AGILITY/RESILIENCE

As argued earlier, the basis of competition is moving from product/service to business model. For example, Dell succeeds in its industry, not because it offers highly differentiated products, but because of the significantly differentiated experience for the customer in dealing with Dell as a supplier. Dell configures and re-configures its supply chain on a sufficiently agile basis to enable it to achieve customisation of the product at the same time as maintaining consistency and commonality in the critical elements of the manufacturing process. In other words, Dell achieves *maximum* differentiation in the marketing dimension with *minimum* differentiation in the manufacturing dimension, and it achieves this with a high level of operational cost-effectiveness. Given that the process includes a high value of bought-in materials and components, it is the competence of Dell in SCM that gives it the competitive edge and, ultimately, the capacity to bring about or react to change in its business at the levels of (a) customer demand and (b) competitive activity.

The principles that Dell has developed for the personal computer business can be applied to other product and service markets – a strategy based on concentration, alignment and agility/resilience. As Hamel and Valikangas (2003) have put it, this is 'about continuously anticipating and adjusting to deep, secular trends that can permanently impair the earning power of a business. It is about having the capacity to change before the case for change becomes desperately obvious.'

The concept and principles of business strategy may not have changed significantly; the content and scope of activity certainly have. The ability of an organisation to derive differentiation and advantage from any part of the process of adding value is more acutely felt as the internationalisation and globalisation of businesses gathers speed. Efficiency in buying inputs and selling outputs remains operationally desirable, but it is not in itself enough. It is the differentiating *combination* of value-adding activities that increasingly wins customer preference. A strategic concept of 'built to last' is certainly moving into one of 'built to adapt and change'. The crucial strategic issues are the speed and cost-effectiveness with which an organisation can configure and re-configure resources to meet the requirements of an increasingly well-informed customer (whether a consumer or a business-to-business customer) in conditions of increasing proliferation of supplier and brand.

SCM is becoming central to this, and the importance of anticipating and taking advantage of change and value migration has been made more acute as economies and markets have become, and will continue to become, more open and globally accessible (Park 2006). Naturally, this increases opportunity and threat simultaneously. The role of the strategist is therefore to harness contemporary techniques such as SCM in serving the best available customers with high-preference top-quality products at prices that they are prepared to pay and, in so doing, make enough money to fund the continuous change that is necessary to secure the future of the enterprise.

For the most part, organisations have traditionally looked in detail at the impact and potential of SCM in operational management. However, against a background of increasingly rapid and, at times, discontinuous change we need to consider the broader value of SCM in creating a *differentiated business model* that determines competitive advantage in the judgement of customers. This constitutes the strategic dimension of SCM.

REFERENCES

Gattorna, J. (2003), 'Ireland: Backdoor or Gateway to the World – Aligning Ireland's Supply Chains with Customers to Create New Prosperity', Presentation to Logistics Ireland 2003, Supply Chain Management Forum, Dublin, 2 October.

Gattorna, J. (2006), *Living Supply Chains – How to Mobilize the Enterprise around Delivering What your Customers Want*, London: Prentice Hall.

Gregory, I.C. and Rawling, S.B. (1997), *Profit from Time*, London: Macmillan.

Hamel, G. and Valikangas, L. (2003), 'The Quest for Resilience', *Harvard Business Review*, September, 52–63.

Park, D. (2000), *What Is Business Strategy and Why Does It Matter?* First section of the manual for the module 'Introduction to Business Strategy' within the MSc Programme of NITL.

Park, D. (2006), 'Supply Chain Globalisation – Threat or Opportunity?' *Logistics Solutions*, 4, 15–19.

Porter, M.E. (1985), *Competitive Advantage: Creating and Sustaining Superior Performance*', New York: Free Press.

Porter, M.E. (1996), 'What is Strategy?' *Harvard Business Review*, November–December, 61–78.

Reynolds, C. and Park, D. (2003), 'Senior Executive Development Plan', *Logistics Solutions*, 4, 12–13.

Slywotzky, A.J. (1995), *Value Migration*, Boston: Harvard Business School Press.

5

The Financial Dimension of Supply Chain Management

DES LEE AND EDWARD SWEENEY

INTRODUCTION

The financial and economic aspect of supply chain management (SCM) can be considered from two perspectives. Firstly, supply chain costs represent a varying but significant proportion of total cost, and one of the overall objectives of SCM is to optimise total supply chain cost and investment.[1] Note that there are significant variations in this proportion between companies and in different industry sectors. The optimisation of total supply chain cost, therefore, contributes directly (and often very significantly) to overall profitability. Similarly, optimisation of supply chain investment contributes to the optimisation of return on the capital employed (ROCE) in a company. Secondly, SCM is concerned with the management of financial flows across a supply chain. As shown in Figure 5.1, financial funds flow from the final consumer, who is usually the only source of 'real' money in a supply chain, back through the other links in the chain (typically retailers, distributors, processors and suppliers). The integrated management of this flow is a key SCM activity,[2] and one which has a direct impact on the cash flow position of companies in the chain.

FINANCIAL MANAGEMENT

Financial management is fundamentally concerned with two things: securing financial resources from one or more of a number of sources (*the raising of funds*) and the effective deployment of these resources (*the use of funds*).

There are three main sources of funds for a company: share capital, loan capital (or debt capital) and reserves. Each comes with expectations and

---

[1] Optimisation of total supply chain investment and costs is part of *Fundamental One* of SCM (see Chapter 3).
[2] Integrated management of financial flows (along with material and information flows) is part of *Fundamental Three* of SCM (see Chapter 3).

Figure 5.1: Funds Flow (along with Material and Information Flows) in the Supply Chain

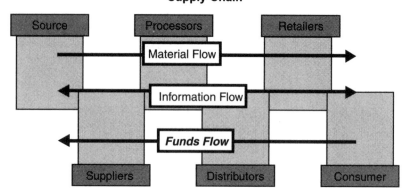

power on the part of the providers. Providers of *share capital* (i.e. shareholders) expect dividends and/or capital growth in share value. The ability of a company to pay dividends depends on profitability, while growth in share value is dependent on the re-investment of profits in the business. Striking the balance between dividend and re-investment levels is a critical strategic issue in most companies. The power of shareholders derives from their ownership of the company. Providers of *loan capital* (e.g. banks) expect repayment with interest.[3] Their power often derives from collateral (i.e. assets put up by the company as security against the loan). They may also have the right to demand immediate repayment under certain circumstances. *Reserves* are profits from previous trading retained within the business. While, in theory, these reserves belong to the business, in practice they represent past decisions on dividend payment versus retention within the business. There is no expectation that they will be disbursed to shareholders, at least not in the short term. There is, however, an opportunity cost associated with this form of capital (i.e. the opportunity of investing this capital to generate a 'safe' rate of return has effectively been foregone). Nonetheless, capital cost advantage can often be derived through the use of reserves as a source of finance.

Finance raised from the above sources is used in either of two ways. It may be invested in fixed assets, such as land, buildings, plant and equipment.

---

[3] As noted in Chapter 4, 'The managerial dimension of corporate finance is about identifying and harnessing a specific resource – capital – in the development of a business on the best available terms in the market.' This is central to the concept of the *Financial Supply Chain*.

From a supply chain perspective this is investment in *processes*. Alternatively, it may be invested in working capital (e.g. raw materials) – this is expenditure on *products*. The balance between fixed assets and working capital depends largely on the supply chain model adopted by a company. Traditionally, in manufacturing-based companies, the classical make-versus-buy decision was the major determinant of this balance. A company which carried out much of its manufacturing in-house had relatively high levels of fixed assets as a result of the need for significant investment in factories, plant and equipment. On the other hand, companies which had subcontracted much of their manufacturing to external suppliers tended to have lower levels of fixed assets, but proportionately higher working capital requirements. As companies concentrate on core supply chain activities and processes, 'non-core' activities and processes are outsourced. As noted in Chapter 2, this has resulted in a move away from vertically integrated architectures to more virtual configurations, with an associated shift in the fixed asset/working capital balance. At the extreme, a virtual organisation may have little or no fixed assets or working capital. Finally, the key strategic issue relating to the raising of finance is the need to ensure that the necessary funds are available for investment, whilst simultaneously ensuring that day-to-day financial commitments are met.

The Integrated Financial Model

Combining the two aspects of financial management – the raising and the use of funds – gives rise to the integrated financial model, as shown in Figure 5.2. The three main sources of funds are spent on either fixed assets or working capital. Fixed assets are used up over time, which is accounted for through depreciation. Working capital leads to sales and revenue. Calculation of profitability (before and after interest and tax) is carried out based on these revenues and the costs incurred in achieving them. These earnings are either paid out in dividends to shareholders or retained within the business (thus adding to reserves), thereby integrating the model. This model forms the basis of the standard systems of accounting practice, in particular the profit and loss account.

The overall SCM objective of optimising total supply chain cost and investment contributes directly to the overall profitability of a business. Figure 5.3 indicates how good SCM practice can impact on shareholder value, as measured by profit generated for every euro invested. Good SCM practice, first and foremost, aims to improve customer service. Improved customer service, for example in the form of greater product availability, results in greater sales revenue streams. Costs are reduced through improvements

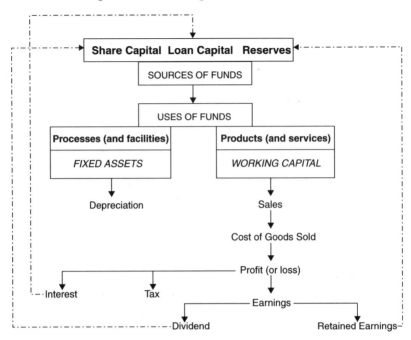

Figure 5.2: The Integrated Financial Model

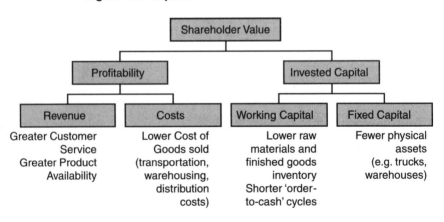

Figure 5.3: Impact of SCM on Shareholder Value

across the supply chain (e.g. improved transport, warehousing and distribution costs) due to the minimisation of non-value-adding activities (NVAs), which add cost to supply chain processes without necessarily adding value from a customer perspective. Good SCM practice has the potential to improve performance of both working capital and fixed assets. The major potential saving in working capital requirements results from lower inventory levels (raw materials, work in progress and finished goods stock). Furthermore, good SCM practice can improve order-to-cash cycle times. This releases working capital tied up in inventory and allows it to be used productively elsewhere in the business. Finally, SCM aims to make more efficient use of fixed assets such as trucks and warehouses. This reduces the amount of investment required in fixed assets.

The Working Capital Cycle

As noted in Chapter 3, of particular interest in SCM is the way working capital is used within a business.

The working capital cycle (see Figure 5.4) indicates that suppliers (i.e. creditors) supply raw materials (usually on credit) which are subsequently converted into work in progress and finished goods. These products are sold (also on credit) to customers (debtors) whose cash is used to pay suppliers. There are a number of SCM issues which relate directly to this cycle:

- *Value*: Value is added as raw materials are converted into finished products. Value-based accounting methods attempt to measure this in financial terms.
- *Speed*: A key objective is to increase the speed of the cycle or to maximise the 'working capital cycle circulation velocity'.
- *Creditor/debtor days*: Ensuring that customers pay in a timely manner, so that cash is available to pay suppliers on time, is an important element of liquidity.

Figure 5.4: The Working Capital Cycle

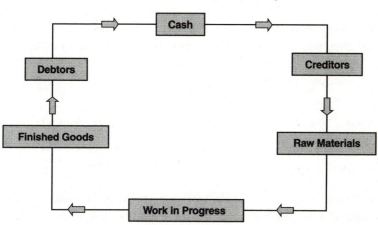

- **Liquidity**: The very existence of any business is dependent on its ability to meet short-term debts. The cycle provides some insights into this.

WORKING CAPITAL OPTIMISATION: INDIVIDUAL COMPANY

Every individual company in every supply chain is attempting to optimise its working capital position. This involves seeking to achieve the optimal value of each element of the working capital cycle. SCM, through its focus on transparency of information and velocity of movement, has contributed significantly to achieving the financial working capital optima.

Creditors

Companies buy goods and services (usually on credit) and at any one time there is an amount owing to suppliers or creditors in financial terms. These creditors are effectively lending money to the company which helps to fund its activities – they have provided goods and services which may be worked on or even sold but they have not yet been paid. Each company has a strong financial incentive to delay payment to suppliers for as long as possible without jeopardising supply or service. The common measurement of creditors is 'creditor days' which indicates how many days worth of purchases have currently not been paid for and, therefore, roughly how long it is taking the company to pay its suppliers.

Debtors

Most business-to-business (B2B) transactions are also on credit. The supplying company has a strong incentive to get paid as quickly as possible. Those customers who still owe (known as debtors) represent a cost that must be funded by the supplier. The common measurement of debtors is 'debtor days' which indicates how many days worth of sales have currently not been paid for and, therefore, roughly how long it is taking the company to extract payment from its customers.

Inventory

An ideal world would have no money tied up in inventory. While clearly unrealistic, minimal inventory for each category is desirable.

WIP: The minimum achievable work in process (WIP) inventory, consistent with efficient utilisation of capital and other resources, is defined by the lead time of the product. Any amount of WIP less than the lead time indicates unused resources; any amount over the lead time indicates queues. Financially, this is easily measured.

Finished goods: Finished goods inventory would be unnecessary if there were perfect information about future demand – that is if everyone in the supply chain had absolute certainty about the level of future demand for goods and services. Despite information sharing up and down the supply chain, many industry sectors suffer what is called 'lumpy' demands whereby customers demand product in unpredictable or large lumps. Unless there is a large amount of surplus capacity in the supply chain, the only way to satisfy this demand is through holding finished goods inventory. If capacity is available, additional production can quickly satisfy unexpected peaks in demand. If such spare capacity does not exist, the supply chain must hold inventory or risk stock outs in the event of an unexpected rise in demand. The risk of a stock out and its consequent effects on the downstream supply chain are very expensive, hence a certain level of finished goods stock will be held in most industries.[4] But finished goods inventory has the greatest risk of becoming obsolete. It cannot (easily) be converted into something else and must normally be sold as is. However, the optimum financial level for any one company is zero.

Raw materials: Raw material stocks are held to ensure supply and prevent disruption to value-add operations when supply is unpredictable or cannot respond fast enough to changes in demand. The cost of disruption varies in different industry sectors but can be as high as hundreds of thousands of euro per hour!

Therefore, every company has a need to hold some WIP and would like to hold little if any raw material and finished goods inventory. However, each company wants to have access to raw materials at very short notice and also wants to be sure that their customers have access to finished goods inventory.

Working capital represents the amount that must be funded to enable a company to operate. As companies grow, working capital requirements also grow. Efficient utilisation of working capital involves minimising the amount that must be funded and increasing the velocity at which working capital is turned over through the company.

---

[4]This provides the financial rationale for the SCM policy known as 'postponement', whereby final configuration of products is carried out as late as possible in the supply chain.

Companies such as Dell (through the 'Direct' model) and the large food retail multiples have the ability to generate cash from customers before (often quite a long time before) that cash needs to be paid to suppliers. Powerful customers or 'channel masters' have the power to demand better payment terms and/or demand that their suppliers and customers hold inventory, thus improving their own working capital position at the expense of others in the supply chain. The corollary of this is that many companies (often suppliers to these 'channel masters') struggle to meet their cash commitments as a direct result of delayed payment by customers. In the worst-case scenario, this has the potential to put even intrinsically profitable companies out of business.

WORKING CAPITAL OPTIMISATION: SUPPLY CHAIN

The fundamental objective of the supply chain is to add value for the customer. To do so, a certain amount of working capital is required – the minimum amount consistent with being able to meet the customers' needs. Local optimisation of working capital requirements inevitably involves higher levels of working capital being 'inflicted' on the weaker companies in the supply chain. This results in increased costs that must be reflected in the final value proposition for the customer.

The optimum working capital position for the entire supply chain is now outlined below.

Inventory

WIP: Each stage in the supply chain should hold its lead time worth of WIP.

Finished goods: Sufficient to ensure an adequate level of customer service/availability.

Raw materials: Sufficient to ensure an adequate level of customer service/ availability and no more. The key issue for supply chain optimisation is *where* inventory should be held. Each company in the supply chain would like their suppliers and customers to hold the inventory but only some have the power to enforce that position. Others have inventory holding costs imposed on them, leading to higher costs for the entire supply chain. The optimum for the supply chain as a whole should be similar to the optimum for a single, fully integrated supplier.

Debtors and Creditors

Debtors and creditors represent two sides of the one transaction – the buyer and seller – and any delay in payment results in increased costs for the supply chain as a whole and eventually for the customer. The optimum position for the entire supply chain is for both debtors and creditors to be as close to zero as possible, meaning that no supplier has to fund the materials for their customer downstream. This will minimise costs for the entire chain.

While great progress has been made in information and communications technology (ICT), manufacturing methods, inventory management and logistics, not as much progress has been made in financial payment systems. Many organisations practice leading edge supply management and inventory systems, while still using essentially the same invoicing and payment systems that existed 150 years ago. The typical cycle is for the customer to wait until they can match a purchase order, delivery docket and invoice before the payment cycle can even begin. And this cycle will be based on the standard payment terms (typically 30 days). Many companies do a 'cheque run' once a month, resulting in a minimum payment period of one month and a maximum of two months. But they will expect delivery in a much shorter period. The technology exists to enable payment cycles to closely match inventory, but it has not been deployed to any great extent. The result is a longer working capital cycle for many of the individual companies in the supply chain, reduced efficiency of the chain as a whole and consequent higher costs for the customer.

Good SCM practice has the potential to impact in a positive way on the working capital cycle through its focus on value and speed. As pointed out earlier, the effective integrated management of financial flows across the supply chain is an SCM fundamental. If this can be achieved, then working capital cycle performance can be enhanced.

SUPPLY CHAIN COSTS

While the quantity of inventory and its velocity through the supply chain are key elements in providing value for the end customer, and in contributing to minimum cost, inventory is not the only element of supply chain cost and working capital is not the only financial aspect of the supply chain. Every company in the supply chain must make investments in processes and facilities and must seek to gain an adequate return on those investments. Investing to facilitate an effective supply chain may mean additional investment in certain assets (e.g. additional logistics assets may be required to enable lower inventory levels and faster flows). The return on those assets is likely to be enhanced in an effective supply chain, making such investment more attractive.

Investment must also be made in processes and methods. The methods chosen will, of course, depend on the relative cost of the factors of production along with their relative returns. Thus, a company in India is likely to choose a process that uses more labour than a company in Western Europe, given the availability of much cheaper labour in India and the relatively small capital base.

Decisions about investment in fixed assets and about processes and methods of work within the supply chain must be made on the basis of financial information. The key issue is to identify the cheapest means of producing the stream of products and services required. This involves being able to ascertain the cost per unit of output, as well as the cost associated with choosing particular processes or locations. The challenge for generating useful costing information, even within a single company, is that products and services do not just consume those resources that are easily and directly attributable to them, but also require the presence of (and expenditure on) a wide range of supporting services and activities that make productive output possible. For example, the manufacture of a plastic moulding requires raw materials, a certain amount of time on a machine and the corresponding time of a machine operator, all of which can be fairly readily costed and attributed to an individual output (or batch of output). But there are many other costs incurred in this manufacture – materials handling, warehousing, waste disposal, transport, inventory management and production planning, production supervision and management, light, heat, insurance, etc. To obtain an accurate cost for a unit of output (or for a process) all of these indirect costs must be accounted for.

In reporting profitability of orders and customers, *traditional* cost systems (based on absorption costing) treat supply chain costs (and all other indirect costs) as overheads and allocate these costs to products/customers on the basis of volume drivers such as direct labour hours, units or turnover (Cooper 1988). However, this ignores the fact that different items of output can consume disproportionate resources (e.g. number and duration of machine set-ups; amount of time required to process). Allocating supply chain costs on the basis of volume may (and often does) lead to distortions in cost and profitability. The ever-increasing range of products and services offered, and the wide variety of channels and customers, make it difficult for supply chain costs to be modelled by volume drivers alone (Pohlen and La Londe 1994).

In the 1980s another system of costing was developed that directly links the costs of performing organisational activities to the products, customers or distribution channels. These links are usually unknown in advance and have to be identified at the level of the individual activities in the different overhead departments (Cooper and Kaplan 1998). Activity-based costing (ABC) is a costing method that first assigns overhead costs to activities and then to products, orders or customers, based on how much each of these cost objects uses the individual activities. ABC typically involves the following steps:

> Step 1: Identify the different overhead activities.
> Step 2: Assign the overhead costs to the different activities by a resource driver.
> Step 3: Identify the activity driver for each activity.
> Step 4: Determine the activity driver rate by dividing the total activity costs by the normal volume of the activity driver.
> Step 5: Multiply the activity driver rate by the activity driver consumption to trace costs-to-cost objects.

While ABC has been very successful in a wide range of industries and applications, a number of key difficulties have arisen:

1. *Measurement errors can lead to less accurate information.* ABC systems are set up to reduce specification errors. These errors arise when a volume-based allocation is used, while in reality costs are often driven by non-volume-related activities. ABC systems are also intended to reduce aggregation errors, since accuracy increases as more activity cost centres and cost drivers are used to assign costs to products (Datar and Gupta 1994). But information on the exact cost or the nature of resource usage is often difficult to obtain (Lin et al. 2001). Owing to these measurement problems, companies sometimes shift to a less detailed ABC system. Measurement of costs or units of activity drivers are further complicated when variables to be measured are not supported by well-defined measurement guidelines or measurement techniques. For example, consider the activity 'Order Processing'. Computing total costs incurred in order processing requires estimates of the percentage of time spent by various staff functions such as sales representatives, credit controllers and planners. The company typically estimates the time spent on the basis of *questionnaires and interviews* (Cooper et al. 1992) and these estimates are subject to measurement error (Datar and Gupta 1994).

2. *Enterprise-wide ABC models are becoming too complex.* Anderson et al. (2002) found more complex ABC models for companies facing a great deal of

competitive pressure. In a highly competitive environment, the need to focus on developing accurate product costs increases, because plant managers need more data on the cost of operations and opportunities for improvement. More accurate product costs are obtained in ABC as overhead support activities are broken down into finer components (Kaplan and Cooper 1998). Also Kaplan and Anderson (2004) argue that, when the activities become more advanced, ABC requires that activities have to be split into smaller activities leading to an *inflation of the number of activities*. For example, when the costs of order processing not only depend on the number of orders but also on the type of customer, accurate costing should use different order processing cost rates for every type of customer. A proliferation of activities and activity drivers is frequently found for staff functions (such as logistics and distribution), since these employees face less repetitive tasks than on the shop floor. Kaplan and Anderson (2004) argue that as the activity dictionary expands, either to reflect more accuracy and detail or to expand the scope of the model to the entire enterprise, the demands on the computer model used to store and process the data escalate dramatically. For example, a company using 150 activities in its enterprise ABC model, and applying the costs in these 150 activities to 600,000 cost objects (SKUs[5] and customers) and running the model monthly for two years requires data estimates, calculations and storage for more than 2 billion items (Kaplan and Anderson 2004). To reduce the difficulties of operating an enterprise-wide ABC model, companies often build separate ABC models for each of their sites or start with one product group, one time period and one type of distribution channel (Themido *et al.* 2000). In trying to coordinate cost estimates for products/customers, traversing multiple ABC models then becomes almost impossible.

3. *Time-consuming to build a complex ABC model.* Many ABC models languish when they are too complex, which in turn leads to long development times (Anderson *et al.* 2002). Survey research in different countries show that the amount of work involved is one of the biggest problems for the team designing the ABC system as well as for the accountants implementing it (Cobb *et al.* 1994; Pohlen and La Londe 1994). The analysis of activities involves many interviews, typically requiring about three people working full-time for between four and six months (Cooper 1990). Very often activities are crossing departmental boundaries and this means coordination of

---

[5]An *SKU* (stock-keeping unit) is an identification, usually alphanumeric, of a unique product that allows it to be tracked for inventory purposes.

information from many interviews to determine the major activities, again very time-consuming (Cobb *et al.* 1994).

4. *Difficult to update a complex ABC model.* Armstrong (2002) argues that since an ABC model is extensive in staff time to install, it will be even more expensive to update. Kaplan and Anderson (2004) observe that in dynamic environments, where activities, processes, products and customers frequently change, ABC might lead to a high cost of continually updating the model, out-of-date activity driver rates and inaccurate estimates of product, process and customer costs. Consider the following example in the activity 'ship order to customer', taken from Kaplan and Anderson (2004). Rather than assuming a constant cost per order shipped, a company might wish to recognise the cost differences when an order is shipped in a full truck, in a less than truckload shipment or using overnight express. In addition, the ship order might be entered either manually or electronically, and it might require either a standard or an expedited transaction. To allow for the significant variation in resources required by the different shipping arrangements, new activities must be added to the model, thereby expanding its complexity.

As a result of these difficulties, ABC has not been adopted as widely as it might have been, nor achieved the benefits of which it is capable. An adaptation of ABC has been developed that may overcome many of the difficulties noted above.

TIME-DRIVEN ABC

The concept of time-driven ABC was originally developed in 1997 by Anderson and practised through his company Acorn Systems, Inc. In 2001, Anderson teamed up with Kaplan of Harvard Business School to perfect the approach. This was consummated in several white papers that the two wrote starting later that year. This new approach requires only two parameters to estimate: the *unit cost* of the supplying resources and the *time* required to perform an activity by this resource group. The time-driven approach of ABC consists of the following steps (Kaplan and Anderson 2004):

1. Identify the various groups of resources that perform activities.
2. Estimate the cost of each group of resource.
3. Estimate the practical time capacity of each group of resource (i.e. available working hours).
4. Calculate the unit cost of each resource group by dividing the total cost of the resource group by the practical capacity.

5. Determine the required time for each event based on different time drivers.
6. Multiply the unit cost by the time required to trace costs to cost objects.

Earlier, Kaplan and Cooper (1998) suggested using the capacity of the resources supplied for assigning resource expenses to activities (see steps 3 and 4 above) in the traditional ABC system. New in time-driven ABC, the time required for performing the activity is now estimated for each event based on different characteristics, the so-called time-drivers. The breakthrough of time-driven ABC lies in the *time estimates* (see step 5 above). Again, consider the example of the sales order processing activity. Assume a total resource cost of €57,600 (payroll, depreciation, other supplies) per week related to a practical time capacity of 5,760 minutes (80 per cent of the theoretical capacity of 40 hours per week for three employees). So, the cost per minute for this group of resources is €10. The time required to process a standard order is estimated to be three minutes. Order processing for new customers requires a subtask of registration, taking an additional fifteen minutes. So the event of order processing for a new customer takes eighteen minutes, while the event of order processing for an existing customer takes three minutes. Hence, in the time-driven approach, the cost per order equals €30 for existing customers and €180 for new customers. By no longer using a transaction driver (number of orders) and instead using the time required to perform the order processing activity, the cost per order can be made *fully situation dependent*, without rebuilding the whole model. Based on the order processing characteristics, event 1 of order processing might take three minutes because it is an existing customer, event 2 might consume eighteen minutes because it is a new customer, while event 3 might require again three minutes, etc. Hence, the time-driven ABC uses *duration* drivers (such as set-up hours, material handling time, order processing time) instead of *transaction* drivers (such as the number of set-ups, the number of material moves, the number of orders). The reason is that, in complex environments, a particular activity does not always consume the same quantity of resources in every situation.

Rather than defining a separate activity for every possible combination of order processing characteristics, the time-driven approach estimates the resource demand by a *time equation* (Kaplan and Anderson 2004). The time equation for the simple example above is: *order processing time per order* = 3 + 15 *if new customer*.

Time-driven ABC allows the simplification of cost calculation and vastly increased flexibility in adapting the costing system to suit the circumstances.

CONCLUDING COMMENTS

From a financial perspective, companies aim to be both profitable and liquid. SCM contributes to profitability through the optimisation of total supply chain cost and investment. Financial management is concerned with the raising and the use of finance. This gives rise to the integrated financial model, which provides a financial framework for the analysis of the impact of SCM on overall profitability and shareholder value. SCM contributes to the liquidity and cash flow position of companies through its focus on the integrated management of financial flows across the supply chain. The working capital cycle provides a useful financial framework for the analysis of these flows. As emphasised in Chapter 3, understanding customer service sets the specification for supply chain design. In a similar way, as shown in Figure 5.5, improved financial performance measures the success of SCM.

In conclusion, every strategic and operational decision taken in a supply chain has financial implications. The approaches outlined in this chapter provide a framework for understanding these implications.

Figure 5.5: Improved Financial Performance Measures the Success of SCM

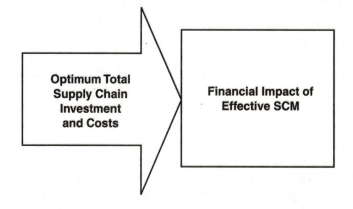

References

Anderson, S., Hesford, J. and Young, M. (2002), 'Factors Influencing the Performance of Activity-Based Costing Teams: A Field Study of ABC Model Development Time in the Automobile Industry', *Accounting, Organizations and Society*, 27(3), 195–211.

Armstrong, P. (2002), 'The Costs of Activity-Based Management', *Accounting, Organizations and Society*, 27(1–2), 99–120.

Cobb, I., Innes, J. and Mitchell, F. (1994), 'Activity-Based Costing Problems: The British Experience', *Advances in Management Accounting*, 2, 63–83.

Cooper, R. (1988), 'The Rise of Activity-Based Costing, Part Two: When Do I Need an Activity Based Cost System?' *Journal of Cost Management*, Fall, 41–48.

Cooper, R. (1990), 'Cost Classification in Unit-based and Activity Manufacturing Cost System', *Journal of Cost Management*, 4(3), pp. 4–14.

Cooper, R. and Kaplan, R.S. (1998), 'The Promise – and Peril – of Integrated Cost Systems', *Harvard Business Review*, Jul.–Aug., 109–119.

Cooper, R., Kaplan, R.S., Maisel, L.S., Morrissey, E. and Oehm, R.M. (1992), *Implementing Activity Based Cost Management: Moving from Analysis to Action*, Montvale NJ: Institute of Management Accountants.

Kaplan, R. and Anderson, S. (2004), 'Time-Driven Activity-Based Costing', *Harvard Business Review*, November, 131–138.

Kaplan, R. and Cooper, R. (1998), *Cost and Effect*, Boston, MA: Harvard Business School Press.

Datar, S. and Gupta, M. (1994), 'Aggregation, Specification and Measurement Errors in Product Costing', *The Accounting Review*, 69(4), 567–591.

Lin, B., Collins, J. and Su, R. (2001), 'Supply Chain Costing: An Activity-Based Perspective', *International Journal of Physical Distribution and Logistics Management*, 31(9–10), 702–713.

Pohlen, T.L. and La Londe, B.J. (1994), 'Implementing Activity-Based Costing (ABC) in Logistics', *Journal of Business Logistics*, 15(2), 1–24.

Themido, I., Arantes, A., Fernandes, C. and Guedes, A.P. (2000), 'Logistic Costs Case Study: An ABC Approach', *Journal of the Operational Research Society*, 51, 1148–1157.

Section 2
SCM: The Customer Perspective

6
Marketing and Supply Chain Integration: Substantiating Customer Service

NATALIE DESCHERES

INTRODUCTION

Traditionally, the marketing function of many organisations has operated in isolation from other, more operational, business processes. The former – including sales activity – were often seen as having primary responsibility for revenue generation, while the latter – including core supply chain management (SCM) activities such as production, warehousing and distribution – added cost in responding to the former's requirements (Laseter et al. 2002).

Indeed most companies' organisational structures and management incentives frequently discourage – and sometimes even obstruct – collaboration and communication between operations, sales and marketing functions, albeit being essential for cost-effective competitive advantage. According to Booz Allen (2004), cultural as well as structural differences make it tough for marketing and SCM to work together.

Often narrowly associated with sales or advertising, let us first define the marketing concept before analysing the rapid and progressive integration of SCM into marketing philosophies and practices.

MARKETING DEFINED

Kotler, in his book *Marketing Management: Analysis, Planning, Implementation and Control*, defined marketing as, 'the process of planning and executing the conception, pricing, promotion and distribution of goods, services and ideas to create exchanges with target groups that satisfy customer and organisational objectives' (Kotler 1996). In this context and based on her work in the field in recent years, the author has developed a model setting out the main constituent elements of marketing and the interactions between them. This is set out in Figure 6.1.

Figure 6.1: Model of Overall Marketing Elements and Interactions

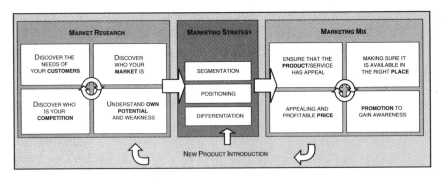

1. *Researching and understanding the market* and one's own capabilities in taking advantage of opportunities, which translates as:

   - Uncovering market needs or desires that are not fulfilled.
   - Matching customers to the above market gap.
   - Assessing who is directly or indirectly involved in this market.
   - Ascertaining organisational capabilities in fulfilling the uncovered needs/desires in an innovative way.

   In short, market research means understanding the market, customer, competition and one's own operations/capabilities.

2. Devising a *strategy* on how to fulfil the needs/desires best through:

   - Segmenting the market into manageable and self-contained parts and targeting the most suitable segments to limit risk and focus the organisation's relative strengths.
   - Positioning the organisation's own offering in a way that conveys positive feelings to the potential customer, highlighting and heightening the desire to buy and differentiating the offering from whatever competition may have on offer.

3. Designing an *overall tactical approach* that will ensure that the right product/service will be at the right place and at the right price with sufficient communication support to ensure a high level of awareness for customers. Branded by Kotler as the '4Ps', these are:

   - *Product*: What overall combination of product and service will fulfil the customer's needs/desires best (and better than the competitive offerings available)?
   - *Price*: What price will balance best what customers are ready to pay, what competition offers, and the necessary margin for the company?

- *Place*: Where and how can the final products/services be accessed, from channel management to aspects of merchandising?
- *Promotion*: What communication mix will advertise the products to the targeted customer segment as well as the identity attached to the product (branding)?

4. Ensuring future company survival through the development of new products or new markets. Marketing activities are sometimes limited to the marketing department, customer service or higher levels of management. Marketing is, however, above all a business philosophy that puts the customer first. As such, it should be omnipresent throughout the entire organisation. As markets are constantly evolving, marketing is an interactive and iterative capability, which fine-tunes a market position either through new product development and introduction (NPD and NPI) or the adoption of new approaches to existing markets.

The Origins of Marketing and SCM Integration

Historical Perspective

'Putting the customer first' or 'the customer is always right' mindsets have been present among forward-thinking entrepreneurs and companies throughout the ages. However, the formalisation of this business orientation has been a slow and maturing process, which can be broken down into four main phases (see Figure 6.2):

1. The Production Orientation.
2. The Sales Orientation.
3. The Marketing Orientation.
4. The Social Responsibility and Human Orientation.

The *Production Orientation* has been predominant ever since industrialisation, when the advance of machinery brought mass production into reality. As productivity became a key management focus, factories became larger, with an emphasis on long production runs and standardisation. Until World War II, except in the USA where a large cash-rich middle class constituted a ready market, European industries had to progressively expand geographically to be able to sell their wares. For example, the British Commonwealth and former colonies provided Britain with ready-made captive markets, which not only absorbed whatever was produced but also forced the development of increasingly complex distribution channels. The advent of the two world wars sped up the adoption of mass production techniques to cope

Figure 6.2: Historical Evolution of Marketing and Supply Chain Philosophies

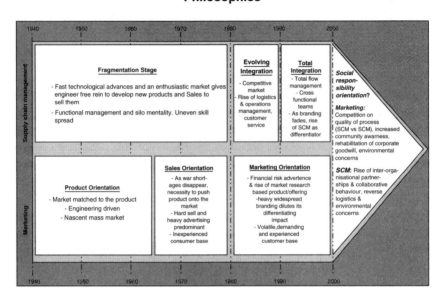

with the endless need for goods while, creating a strong middle class benefitting from the wealth redistribution characteristic of the post-war government policies. Until war shortages were over, the dynamic of matching a market to a given product was predominant.

However, from the 1970s, most markets started to get saturated, and this led to the *Sales Orientation* phase relying heavily on crude selling techniques. The logic was still that what could be produced could be sold, provided that inexperienced customers could be persuaded to buy. This gave a lasting bad aura to marketing, as well as sales, still persisting to a great extent to this day.

During the *Production and Sales Orientations* phases, organisations operated according to the principle that functions had to be clearly defined and compartmentalised in order to be managed. This vision of organisational design is still prevalent in the structure of businesses, often resulting in future supply chain inefficiencies (see Chapter 3).

The consequences were (a) strong functional management and (b) a 'silo' mentality, with the focus being distinctively on the sales force and the revenue generated. Any other functions were considered as pure cost contributors and typically had a less than glamorous image.

This meant that talented individuals would often be channelled unequally through the organisation and very little attempt was made to develop an overall picture of the entire process of conversion from raw material to end product. This resulted in a high level of *fragmentation* of the components of the process, and this was characterised by constant fire-fighting and massive inefficiencies in meeting the latest sales orders.

In the *Marketing Orientation* phase, markets saturated further and competition became more intense. Finding out what people needed/desired and producing matching products/services became a more constructive approach to managing the growing risks. In contrast with the previous production and sales orientations, the conscious decision by companies to ascertain and respond to market needs is the cornerstone of marketing.

While fulfilling needs locally can be done intuitively, on a larger scale a more systemic approach to analysing needs and market potential is necessary to reduce risks. As market research techniques became more widely understood and better applied, competitive advantage focused on how products were positioned or how organisations differentiated themselves. This led to an exceptional amount of effort and attention being paid to activities such as branding, of which advertising is part. As marketing became overwhelmingly focused on demand stimulation and generation, the more complex processes involved in satisfying demand received less strategic focus.

As branding became the dominant marketing approach, the scope for differentiation became narrower. This led to an escalation in the financial costs of branding and its heavy reliance on advertising. Indeed if differentiation cannot be substantiated then the 'message' has to be louder. The refocus towards effective and tangible processes instead of expensive advertising is partly due to the focus on creating shareholder value combined with the sheer confusion that brand proliferation eventually generated among customers.

Meanwhile, the progressive market saturation forced organisations to review the efficiency of their processes, and attempts at consolidating similar functions into a single cohesive system became more prevalent.

Market saturation was reflected in a broader diffusion of the tools and techniques used in product creation and of the knowledge base on which modern marketing is founded. Therefore it gradually became more difficult to achieve and sustain differentiation on the basis of product and/or service. Added to this, product life-cycles were beginning to shorten, and smaller increments to product and service specification were becoming more decisive in attracting consumer demand. Hence logistics and the broader field of SCM emerged *simultaneously* as the means of (a) achieving high quality at effective cost; (b) lowering inventory throughout the product creation and supply process; (c) accelerating the time-span of agreement-to-fulfilment and (d) shifting the basis of competitiveness away from increments to product and service (which were becoming increasingly easy to emulate rapidly) and into value-based business models. In other words, the basis of competitive performance moved from product-versus-product and service-versus-service to supply chain-versus-supply chain.

Thus, Dell in consumer and business-to-business marketing and Amazon.com in on-line retailing sought to differentiate themselves not by product specification but by the manner in which they could engage with customers. One model offered benefits of very close product specification allied to rapid delivery and high-quality post-sales service (Dell). The other model was based on offering the widest range of consumer choice at globally competitive prices, sourced and moved from anywhere using the fastest available logistics fulfilment services coupled with a low-inventory 'pipeline' of distribution (Amazon.com).

In this way, logistics, customer service and operations management issues became more prevalent *within* the concept of marketing. While still not focused on the flows that traverse the organisation or on the organisational design aspects of SCM, early attempts at examining organisations in a holistic and integrative way led to the *Evolving Integration* of the supply chain. It took nearly 20 years for the *Total Integration* to take place, with its emphasis not only on total flow management but also on the cross-functional performance indicators that support them and the required cross-functional teamwork (see Chapter 3). By this stage, branding strategy was striving to gain depth and substance. Not only was marketing ready to see SCM as a valid differentiator, SCM was finally mature enough to deliver its promises and offer a new basis for competitive differentiation.

It is always difficult to determine in which phase we live. However, several pointers such as the growth of environmental concerns, community awareness and the need to operate with business partners rather than individually might suggest that we are entering a *Social Responsibility Orientation* for both marketing and SCM. Marketing has now to deal with rehabilitating the damaged image that corporations have inflicted on themselves through the various scandals of the 1990s and is attempting to reposition itself, whilst relying on SCM to deliver the tangible goods. SCM is emerging from its long period of introspection to open itself to working collaboratively with its external partners. The focus on reverse logistics in many industries reinforces this new marketing approach and orientation.

Organisational Perspective

As discussed earlier, marketing has traditionally concerned itself largely with the issues of brand management, allowing other aspects of the marketing mix to move away from the marketing function (Hill *et al.* 1995). Branding is a very isolated aspect of marketing and requires little interaction with any other function. It is therefore easier to manage or coordinate, but does not offer the depth that true organisational alignment would provide in terms of cost, customer service or innovation. If brands can be copied with money alone, innovation – as an efficient market response strategy – requires vision and careful management. Also, with the rise of retailer power, many of the new and vibrant brands appear to belong to retailers rather than manufacturers, and have been created outside traditional product marketing altogether (Hill *et al.* 1995). Mainstream marketing is now facing a mid-life crisis and is increasingly being marginalised by other disciplines, most notably by SCM. Indeed, marketing has failed to recognise that demand stimulation alone is not, and cannot be, the only way to generate sales and satisfy customers in a sustainable manner, even in FMCG[1] markets (Tamilia 2000).

Three main environmental changes have deeply destabilised the foundations of marketing:

1. Standardisation of information collection and analysis.
2. High staff turnover.
3. Market fragmentation.

The very basis of marketing used to rely on 'secrecy': market intelligence and marketing strategies used to be seriously protected information. Today however, market research data collection and analysis use fairly standard approaches and technology. Also, changes in the psychological contract between employers and employees, where neither feel particularly bound to one another, has increased the level of staff migration within industry sectors, thus diluting proprietary knowledge. Finally, as markets become more and more fragmented, with smaller and smaller groups and more specific needs and buying behaviour, it is often uneconomical to address any one specific need and yet unrealistic to simply offer mass-produced solutions. Mass markets are fragmenting into niche markets, while – as noted in Chapter 3 – product standardisation is being replaced by the requirement for 'mass customisation' (Christopher 2003).

Based on these factors, new marketing approaches are emerging with the addition of *Process*, *Partnership* and *People* to the marketing mix. These refer directly to the role that SCM plays at the heart of the process of creating and sustaining differentiation for an organisation. Interestingly, the new focus does also emphasise the need to create new products based on latent, unmet needs,

---

[1]Fast Moving Consumer Goods.

that is an organisation must be able to develop a vision of the next generation of product even before the market becomes aware of it. This also puts SCM, coupled with market research techniques, at the heart of the process.

Marketing and Supply Chain Synergies

It would be wrong to believe that SCM only relates to the 'place' of the marketing mix. SCM and marketing are two faces of the same coin and are deeply complementary. Indeed, once a purchase has been made, the responsibility of logistics is to ensure that the customer will continue buying again and again with maximum ease and convenience. SCM, therefore, is not only concerned with supply management, but has a very important demand stimulation responsibility as well (Tamilia 2000).

Market Research

Market research is the process by which the needs or desires of the market are anticipated, probed and validated. To carry out such a process, tools such as questionnaires, interviews and focus groups are widely used, and analysis can be done at market, segment and niche levels.

Market research relies heavily on either direct input from individuals or economic data and statistics. This assumes, however, that individuals are fully aware and can articulate what their needs/desires are, and that the theoretical need can be turned into a real purchase, given the right circumstances. Unfortunately, both assumptions can be very misleading.

As most primary needs/desires are now fulfilled, needs are now very much driven by desires that will not affect our capacity to survive. Because *imagination* rather than *practicality* has become the drive for discovering new markets, most needs and desires are actually latent. This means that most individuals do *not* know what they need/want. In a market research context, potential targets end up validating whether a concept is a good idea. In the process of validating the idea, psychological aspects such as willingness to be seen in a positive light, double guessing the right answer or plain indifference might dramatically influence results and distort the findings on whether individuals would buy or not. This flaw is further exacerbated by the discrepancy existing in all of us between what is said and what is done (Argyris and Schoen 1974). The issue with market research is that it seeks to validate theoretical needs and behaviours instead of behaviour actually taking place.

While justified when completely new markets are being explored, true behavioural patterns can be defined from historical data, not extrapolation of theoretical ones. SCM captures real-life information since it covers all processes from order capture to invoicing, via transportation and delivery. It also does it in real time. This is particularly true since the rise of customer relationship management (CRM) approaches and systems.

CRM can be described as a business technique that involves focusing knowledge, business processes, and organisational structures around customers and prospects enterprise-wide to provide the ability to have a personalised dialogue/conversation with each individual customer seamlessly across channels/touchpoints and over time.

The strength of CRM relies on its ability to capture every single interaction with the customer on a *real-life* and *real-time* basis, whether by collecting sales reports, order and return history, feedback and enquiry information, patterns of ordering/buying, use of peripheral services, basic Internet roaming or channel usage. This information can be collected via the day-to-day management of the supply chain, and will provide information on what is truly happening rather than a theoretical model.

SCM activities also provide the widest exposure to human contacts since these will be established through sales and distribution channels, customer service and logistics. Not only will contacts be happening and often recurrent, it is usually a *nurturing* relationship where ensuring that the customer is satisfied is the key. In the context of traditional market research, the caring aspect is not so developed since the interaction is based on gathering information rather than nurturing relationships. Based on this dynamic, unlocking meaningful and true information and feedback can be very challenging.

CRM cannot replace traditional market research but it certainly can give it a credibility and a depth that is very beneficial. It is by balancing internal and external analyses that true understanding of the market can happen. CRM is discussed further in Chapter 7.

Marketing Strategy

Since marketing is the ability to interact with the environment, it is by definition an iterative process adjusting itself constantly on the basis of learning from customer reaction and feedback. The overall strategy, which focuses primarily on positioning (establishing a clear image in the customer's mind) and differentiation (being distinct from competition), should remain fairly stable as wide variation often results in confusion in the marketplace. In order to sharpen both of these concepts, market segmentation – the process of grouping similar customers into recognisable clusters – needs to happen.

Market segmentation traditionally tended to rely heavily on socio-economic parameters (e.g. the level of disposable income, postal code, number of cars, family patterns) to identify specific lifestyles. The theory goes that the more clearly identified the lifestyle, the easier it will be to design the right channel to either attract or communicate with the prospective customer. This type of segmentation was hence heavily geared towards supporting sales, advertising and branding, and would have had very little relevance for the supply chain. Mainstream marketing has become behaviourally and sociologically oriented with less focus on the economics of selling and with little concern for the cost of distribution in favour of a sharper focus on total cost of ownership and utilisation.

Such parameters may allow the achievement of highly targeted communication with the customer, but do not lead to substantiated customer service. Neither do they provide any guidance on how to, for example, prioritise a diverse order book. It is sales-focussed (i.e. geared at suiting the simple objective of raising short-term sales volumes) rather than customer-focused (i.e. geared at fulfilling customers' requirements either in terms of functionality, service or relationship).

When marketing came into prominence in the early 1970s, this approach was very successful as society was quite predictable and homogeneous. Today however, society has become more fragmented, diverse and multidimensional, and traditional segmentation has become more and more irrelevant. More importantly, prospective customers are no longer happy with a mass-produced solution; they want a solution that is customised and relevant to their needs. Such demands call for the alignment of the entire supply chain. Segmentation criteria must, therefore, reflect not only the diversity that characterises markets and segments, but it must also be meaningful to the supply chain that will respond to the demands. Table 6.1 details what such criteria might be.

Relevant and meaningful criteria could include time, speed and delivery pattern or requirement, reverse logistics parameters (packaging or obsolete items to be collected) or even payment flexibility. Based on how critical the customers are to the organisation and how efficiently demands can be fulfilled, customers can be tiered to allow the supply chain to prioritise demand fulfillment. As demand is then managed via different speed lanes (and consequently processes), the higher costs are recovered through greater efficiency. Indeed, as speed increases and cycle time decreases, the financial cash flow is accelerated, while working capital decreases (see Chapter 5). Additionally, as better prioritisation allows for better planning, performance on the ground often improves dramatically, which in turn reinforces the overall strategic goal of strong customer service differentiation and positioning.

Differentiation strategy can be achieved through strong branding. Branding is the creation of a set of expectations in the mind of the customers about

Table 6.1: Logistics Segmentation Factors

Example factors	Specifics
Buying relationship • Demand forecasting • Price determination	*Buying relationship* • Limited, extensive, joint forecasts/schedules • Basic volume, agreed return on investment
Ordering and billing • Order entry mechanism • Billing mechanism • Order confirmation • Order tracking	*Ordering and billing* • Phone, fax, EDI • Invoice, COD, EFT, EDI • Immediate 2 days • Visibility, bar coding
Delivery and support services • Use of time slots • Driver unloading role • Order receiving • Delivery requirements	*Delivery and support services* • None, strict • None, expected • ASN, automated receiving support • Special pallets, special barcodes
Ordering complexity • Variability of demand • Regularity of orders • Order Predictability (size and product mix) • Order frequency • Average order sizes	*Ordering complexity* • Low, medium, high • High, medium, low • High, medium, low • Weekly, monthly • Boxes, pallets, truck loads
Delivery complexity • Drop-off points • Site accessibility • Emergency deliveries • Requirement for reverse logistics	*Delivery complexity* • Central, single, multiple • Low, medium, High • None, expected • None, expected

Source: Torres, L. and Miller, J. (1988), 'Aligned Logistics Operations: Tailoring Logistics to the Needs of the Customers', Chapter 3, in J. Gattorna, and T. Jones (eds.), *Strategic Supply Chain Alignment: Best Practice in Supply Chain Management,* Aldershot: Gower, 42–59.

purpose, performance, quality and price. But, as discussed earlier, it is not only often overused, but it also relies on large amounts of money being spent on the promotional aspect of the marketing mix.

The obvious weakness is that even strong branding does not guarantee the satisfaction of the end user; it is also open to competition spending even more cash to establish its own brand. When SCM is being used as the main differentiator, the capability for planning, organising and coordinating is much more difficult to copy and reproduce and is, therefore, more likely to preserve competitive advantage.

The Marketing Mix

Out of the '4Ps' (i.e. price, product, place, promotion), promotion is the element that is probably the most isolated from the rest of the organisation. It is also the one that got the most interest through branding despite the fact that measuring its impact is near-impossible. The sustained focus on promotion, communication and branding is partly the reason for the disconnection between the marketing philosophy – which should be all-encompassing in terms of culture and process – and the reality of marketing, which seems disconnected from the other areas of the organisation. There is, however, an argument that promotion and SCM are very complementary since it is in the supply chain that real contact with real customers takes place.

During the pre-marketing era, *products* were produced in the hope that a market would absorb them due to a diligent and convincing sales force that was usually paid on commission. The marketing philosophy identifies the needs of the market, designs a product accordingly and then produces it. As such, marketing has a massive input when it comes to NPD. Successful NPD comes from the synergy between all parts of the organisation in making it happen. New products cannot emerge successfully if marketing comes up with an idea, and research and development (R&D) with a solution, with manufacturing left to produce it. Successful NPD requires the simultaneous involvement of all to come up with a product that will satisfy the needs of the market and the organisation optimally.[2]

Balancing external knowledge with internal capabilities is essential. Too often new products are the result of too much emphasis on one or the other. The result is total costs that are unnecessarily high, jeopardising the profit that must be generated and threatening the long-term survival of the organisation. As product life-cycles are now compressing and much shorter in time-span, optimising costs and development time have become the key competencies that organisations must master.

Profit is the difference between revenue and cost. The revenue is directly affected by *price*. Setting the right price is a combination of what the customer is willing to pay, what the competition is charging and the total cost generated by the supplier in supplying the product and the user in using it. By letting total cost be higher than necessary, profit will either be diminished

---

[2]This is the concept of *simultaneous* or *concurrent* engineering.

or non-existent. Profitability is enhanced through optimisation of the NPD process as well as through flexible interaction with the business environment.

Place, particularly when the Internet is used as a channel to market, can be merged with the *promotional* aspect of the mix. When independent intermediaries are used, such synergies can be more difficult to achieve since the growing power of retailers has, in many cases, shifted loyalty and brand recognition to the benefit of the latter rather than the manufacturer. Flexibility comes from merging internal and external market data to minimise risks as well as being discriminatory on the financial costs associated with different customer service levels. In other words, flexibility is achieved by merging marketing and the management of the supply chain.

THE 7PS OF SUPPLY CHAIN-BASED COMPETITION

To regain market credibility, the 4Ps not only need to be reconciled with their operational roots, but they also need to be extended to include the *process*, *people* and *partnership* elements that add depth to any customer orientation claims.

Process

In the context of a fast-moving environment, demand satisfaction requires efficient processes that can cope with a wide variety of end products with shortening product life-cycles. The focus requires flexibility and speed with an added focus on quality of product/service and quality of the experience for the end customer. In other words, processes need to be agile to cope with market unpredictability (Christopher 2005). The shift needed is illustrated in the Table 6.2.

Whether internal or inter-organisational, all processes must be aligned into a coherent stream of flows focused not on complexity reduction and cost efficiency, but on revenue and margin enhancement via high levels of customer service, to the extent of providing for occasional 'profitable inefficiencies' (Torres and Miller 1998). Supporting processes will consequently need to be reviewed collectively (in terms of product, information and financial flows) and individually (e.g. receiving, storage, packing, scheduling).

People

However, processes are not run by machines; *people* are at the heart of processes and new market demands cannot be met if the 'people' dimension

Table 6.2: The Key Business Transformations and the Implications for Management Skills

Business transformation	Leading to	Skills required
From supplier centric to customer centric	The design of customer driven supply chains	Market understanding: customer insight
From push to pull	Higher level of flexibility and agility	Management of complexity and change
From inventory to information	Capturing & sharing information on real demand	IS and ICT expertise
From transactions to relationships	Focus on service and responsiveness as the basis for customer retention	Ability to define, measure and manage service requirements by market segment
From, 'trucks and sheds', to end-to-end pipeline management	A wider definition of supply chain costs	Understanding of the cost to serve and time based performance indicators
From functions to processes	Creation of cross functional teams focused on value creation	Specific functional excellence with cross functional understanding; team working capabilities
From standalone competition to network rivalry	More collaborative working with supply chain partners	Relationship management and win-win orientation

Source: Christopher, M. (2005), *Logistics and Supply Chain Management: Creating Value-Adding Networks*, London: FT Prentice Hall.

is not also reviewed. If one was to describe the organisational structure of the marketing era, 'silo' is probably the first thought that would spring to mind. In the era of SCM, cross-functional (or cross-organisational) teams are the norms and the focus has shifted from functions to the holistic management of the related flows. This is in line with *Fundamental Three* and *Fundamental Four* of SCM (see Chapter 3).

The traditional hierarchical, command and control organisations have evolved into more federalist, de-centralised and networked organisations with clear conflict resolution and decision-making processes focused on knowledge transfer and organisational learning. Former organisational cultures which relied heavily on analysis, uniformity and control must learn to discriminately use cooperative and competitive skills in line with environmental requirements (Giles and Hancy 1998). This assumes a workforce that is empowered to change behaviour in real time. In networked organisations, 'getting the job done' means working with people over whom one has no direct authority, who are typically located elsewhere and often work in different time zones. The 'trust-based' way of working – in contrast with traditional 'control-based' approaches – lies at the heart of making this successful (Walt and Gattorna 1998).

Partnership

This leads to the final element necessary for ensuring responsiveness to market needs, for which the concept of trust through partnership is absolutely essential. Partnership is quite different from outsourcing as the latter is often focused on reducing cost from the contracting organisation (see Chapter 9), while the former is based on 'mutual benefit by two or more parties having compatible or complementary business interests or goals' (Segil 1996). Cost reduction is not the primary goal; it is usually a consequence. Satisfying the end customer in terms of the nature, process and timing of their choice is usually what drives partnership, shifting the focus from internal organisational issues to the end customer. This aim, in fact, comes closest to the fundamental philosophy of marketing that was introduced earlier.

More than ever, many of the skills and resources essential to a company's future prosperity lie outside the firm's boundaries and outside management's direct control. Partnership – when executed properly – provides a valid business arrangement supporting the concept of agility (Doz and Hamel 1998). In many respects, one could argue that agility is the result of complete integration of marketing and SCM, combined with the ability to deal collaboratively with selected business partners. Indeed, agility

Figure 6.3: Marketing and Supply Chain Integration

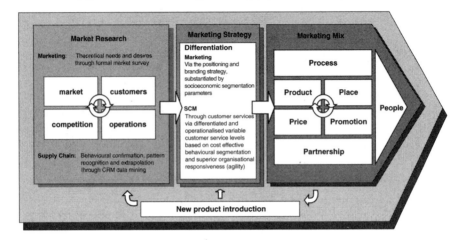

requires a level of creativity that partnership can provide by focusing on satisfying the end customer. Alliances not only serve the purpose of bringing together complementary strengths, but also combine insight and understanding to reduce uncertainties and accelerate learning (Doz and Hamel 1998).

Figure 6.3 illustrates how the marketing model introduced earlier (see Figure 6.2) can be reconsidered in the light of the foregoing issues relating to marketing/SCM integration. It should also be noted that the 3Ps of *process*, *people* and *partnership* rely much more on integrative management than the more clear-cut, analytical approach of traditional marketing. However it is also from these 3Ps that the traditional marketing mix and strategy gain meaningful and tangible differentiation that is difficult to replicate. The clothes chain Zara has been around for the past twenty years with an operating model that is in many ways still unmatched.

Marketing and SCM: The Role of Mass Customisation and Postponement Strategies

In line with the 7Ps, two related SCM concepts are worthy of particular consideration.

As noted in Chapter 3, the mass customisation (MC) concept was first introduced in the 1980s and it promotes the ability to provide individually designed products and services to every customer. This contrasts starkly with the Henry Ford Model T paradigm of the mass production era. In many respects the MC concept is a logical consequence of the evolution of marketing, as discussed earlier. Furthermore, it illustrates very clearly the trend towards the integration of marketing and SCM thinking. The underpinning logic of MC is that, as markets become more competitive and customers more discerning, there is a need to move towards the MC ideal and supply chain agility is the route to making this happen. One approach which facilitates the implementation of MC is known as postponement.[3]

Postponement is about delaying (or *postponing*) final product configuration until as late as possible in the supply chain. This allows inventory to be kept in as generic a format for as long as possible, thereby increasing the number of final product configurations for which that inventory can be deployed. This allows the twin objectives of SCM (in terms of cost and service as outlined in *Fundamental One*, see Chapter 3) to be addressed simultaneously. Cost is reduced by lowering supply chain inventory requirements; service is improved by allowing products to be tailored to customer requirements with shorter lead times than would otherwise be possible, thus making the MC ideal more achievable. Postponement can only be possible by designing and developing products with due consideration of all supply chain implications. Sectors such as consumer electronics and automotive have pioneered postponement strategies, based on late final product configuration.

New Market Entry

It is in the sphere of new market entry that SCM can make perhaps its greatest impact in modern marketing.

Traditional approaches to new market entry can be costly, time-consuming and risky. The classic model is to move via stages in which different organisational forms are adopted, from working via an agent in the country through to setting up a wholly owned marketing/sales office through to establishing production and distribution facilities and finally into integrated full-function multinational/global operations.

In fact the move towards multinational/global operations involves the establishment of internal supply chains and the introduction of the concept of internal suppliers and customers. The rationale for this is to achieve internal economies of scale and scope. However the advances that we have

---

[3]The financial rationale of postponement strategies was introduced in Chapter 4.

seen in SCM involving external partners now give rise to alternative routes to new market entry that can overcome the challenges of cost containment, time compression and risk reduction. Principally this involves partnership and collaboration, sharing facilities, knowledge and human resources: in short, utilising and leveraging any resource irrespective of ownership for joint advantage.

An excellent example of SCM in new market entry is that of the Spanish ceramics company Roca into the People's Republic of China. In establishing facilities in China to meet national as well as export demand, Roca collaborated financially and operationally with a division of BSC Group, a leading Hong Kong importer/distributor of ceramic products under an agreement in which BSC acts as the 'marketing division' of the collaborative venture, applying its specialist knowledge of China market conditions and approaches to distribution and retailing. This achieved three main benefits: (i) it ensured that Roca gained access to specific marketing expertise quickly, cost-effectively, and at low risk; (ii) it enabled the two companies to capitalise on their core competencies and create an agile, differentiated organisation in the market and (iii) it ensured that transmission of information concerning movements in consumer preferences and competitive marketing activity can be factored quickly into the Chinese and European manufacturing and primary logistics operations. Above all, it overcomes one very significant barrier to entering into the Chinese market – the time (and hence cost) involved in the creation of all-important personal business relationships.

In line with *Fundamental Four* of SCM, collaboration and partnerships are discussed in other contexts elsewhere in this book. The point here is that they can make as powerful a contribution to marketing as to other elements of the supply chain. This marketing model will generally be applied more frequently in the future, especially in relation to new market entry.

CONCLUSION

Markets are becoming more complex and sophisticated, and customers more discerning. Marketing is now being recognised as an evolving, intelligent and unique entity with concrete demands regarding the product, the fulfilment of the need and the political context associated with the supplier. SCM, through its contact with customers, suppliers and third parties, plays a vital role at all levels. The value perception of the customer is no longer split between traditional, internally focused 'marketing' and 'operations' orientations; these must be considered in an integrated manner with a view to delivering consistently to secure loyalty. This transition is facilitated by adding *people*, *process* and *partnership* to the traditional '4Ps'.

In this way, marketing and SCM can be viewed as a single integrated process, with both concepts contributing equally to a company's strategic development.

REFERENCES

Argyris, C. and Schoen, D. (1974), *Theory in Practice: Increasing Professional Effectiveness*, San Francisco CA: Jossey Bass.

Christopher, M. (2003), 'Creating Agile Supply Chains', in J. Gattorna (ed.), *Handbook of Supply Chain Management*, 5th edition, Aldershot: Gower, 283–95.

Christopher, M. (2005), *Logistics and Supply Chain Management: Creating Value-Adding Networks*, London: FT Prentice Hall.

Doz, Y. and Hamel, G. (1998), *Alliance Advantage*, Boston MA: Harvard Business School Press.

Giles, P. and Hancy, A. (1998), 'Alternative Organisation Options: Moving from Lines of Hierarchy to Network of Alliances', in J. Gattorna (ed.), *Strategic Supply Chain Alignment: Best Practice in Supply Chain Management*, Aldershot: Gower, 410–424.

Hill, S., Newkirk, D. and Handerson, W. (1995), 'Restoring Relevance to the Marketing Department: Dismantling the Brandocracy', *Strategy and Business*, Fall, 2–16.

Kotler, P. (1996), *Marketing Management: Analysis, Planning, Implementation and Control*, Englewood Cliffs, NJ: Prentice Hall.

Laseter, T., Kandybin, A. and Houston, P. (2002), 'Marketing and Operations: Can this Marriage be Saved?' *Strategy and Business*, First Quarter, 26, 22–27.

Segil, L. (1996), *Intelligent Business Alliances: How to Profit Using Today's Most Important Strategic Tool*, New York: Random House.

Strategy and Business/Knowledge@Wharton (2004), 'The Challenge of Customization: Bringing Operations and Marketing together', available at: <http://www.strategy-business.com/sbkwarticle/sbkw040616?pg=all>, accessed April 2007.

Tamilia, R. (2000), 'What is the Importance of Logistics to Marketing Management', *Rencontres Internationales de la Recherche en Logistique (RIRL)*, available at: <http://www.uqtr.uquebec.ca>, accessed April 2007.

Torres, L. and Miller, J. (1998), 'Aligned Logistics Operations: Tailoring Logistics to the Needs of the Customers', in J. Gattorna (ed.), *Strategic Supply Chain Alignment: Best Practice in Supply Chain Management*, Aldershot: Gower, 42–59.

Walt, C, and Gattorna, J, (1998), 'Aligned Logistics Operations: Tailoring Logistics to the Needs of the Customers', Chapter 29, in J. Gattorna (ed.), *Strategic Supply Chain Alignment: Best Practice in Supply Chain Management*, Aldershot: Gower, 472–401.

7

Understanding Customer Service

LIZ CARROLL

CUSTOMER SERVICE IN THE SUPPLY CHAIN: INTRODUCTION AND BACKGROUND

In today's competitive environment, as product quality is expected and differentiation is becoming more and more difficult, the concept of customer service is progressively becoming more and more important. As noted earlier, customers now expect a quality product or service at a competitive price which is delivered where and when the customer wants. This means that many companies now compete largely through customer service – it is supply chain management (SCM) that delivers the required levels of customer service.

Before any strategy can be put in place to enhance service to customers, it is necessary for companies to clearly identify who their customers are and will be by segmenting and analysing them for requirements (order qualifiers and order winners, i.e. what do they consider value for money) and profitability. It is then necessary to determine the performance standards that will consistently meet and exceed the expectations of the target customers. This changing role of customer service requires companies to become market focused by measuring, monitoring and managing customer relationships with the objective of developing suitable supply chains to consistently deliver value for money to their customers.

The key to effective customer service is *understanding* – understanding what customers you should target, understanding how profitable they are and what they contribute to your business, understanding what they perceive as value for money, how you create value (and reduce waste) for the effectiveness and efficiency of the supply chain and how you monitor this to understand the dynamics within the supply chain to enable your company to continuously improve on the delivery of value for money. This comes from understanding your customers' businesses, probably better than they do, and developing relationships of trust and transparency which lead to clarity and consequently the required level of understanding.

Customer Service Defined

Customer service in business is *not* about:

- 'Yes' men (women).
- Making promises that cannot be delivered.
- High levels of entertainment.
- Transactions (e.g. putting up sales orders).
- Being overly aggressive to your support functions.

It *is* about every encounter between a customer and a business that results in a negative or positive perception by a customer. According to Christopher (1998), 'Customer service is concerned with making the product available to the customer ... there is no value in the product or service until it is in the hands of the customer.' The level of customer service delivered is determined by the interaction of all the elements of the supply chain which enables the availability of products and services to the final customer.

La Londe and Zinszer (1976) put forward three headings under which customer service can be examined: pre-transaction, transaction and post-transaction.

1. Pre-transaction elements include:
    - written customer service policy;
    - accessibility;
    - organisation structure.
2. Transaction elements include:
    - order cycle time;
    - inventory availability;
    - order fill rate;
    - order status information.
3. Post-transaction elements include:
    - availability of spares;
    - call-out time;
    - product tracing/warranty;
    - customer complaints, claims, etc.

However, each market attaches different importance to different service elements and it is the responsibility of each company to work this out for each of their customers. Some of these issues will be discussed in more detail later in this chapter.

The 10 Commandments of Customer Service

In his book *Ten Deadly Marketing Sins: Signs and Solutions*, renowned marketing expert Philip Kotler identifies the 'ten most common and most damaging mistakes marketers make, and how to avoid them' (Kotler 2004). The following *Ten Commandments* are adapted from this work[1] and can act as a guide to achieving excellent customer service:

1. The company will segment the market and target appropriately.
2. The company will map its customer needs, preferences and behaviours, and motivate stakeholders to deliver.
3. The company will know its current and potential major competitors and complete regular SWOT analyses on all.
4. The company will build partnerships with stakeholders and reward them.
5. The company will develop sales and service processes to capture and measure opportunities.
6. The company will identify and rank opportunities.
7. The company will develop product and service policies to meet targeted market demand.
8. The company will develop brands by using cost-effective communication tools.
9. The company will invest in appropriate skillsets and communication with employees.
10. The company will use technology that gives it a competitive advantage in the marketplace.

Customer Segmentation

As customers become more discerning in their selection of products and services, and more demanding of their suppliers, it is no longer possible to be 'all things to all men' and, as noted in Chapter 6, it becomes necessary to segment the market. A market segment is a part of the market which is distinguished from other parts of the market by one or more characteristics. Market segmentation is the process of dividing the market into a number of

---

[1] Specifically, it is based on 'The Ten Commandments of Marketing Effectiveness' in the epilogue of Kotler (2004).

segments, each having one or more unique characteristics. Some examples of the characteristics used for segmentation are:

- Size, growth, demography, geography.
- Seasonality.
- Consumer/buyer attitudes.
- Price bands.

The following are the issues which a company typically considers in targeting a particular market segment:

- Past growth record and future growth potential of the segment.
- There needs to be an attractive volume in relation to current and affordable capacity.
- Price levels relative to investment and operating costs need to be adequate.
- How resistant to substitution is the product/service?
- Logistics (e.g. do accessible distribution channels exist?).

In general, however, the reason why a company targets certain customers is to make a profit. Hence, it is really about identifying customers who are profitable for a company. It should also be noted that a profitable customer for one company is not necessarily a profitable customer for another.

CUSTOMER PROFITABILITY

Common wisdom is that *customers create sales and the most successful companies are those that win the most customers and keep them*. However surely 'success' would be defined by most CEOs and shareholders as relative profitability. Therefore it is more likely that *the most successful companies are those that win the most profitable customers and keep them*. Below is a simple formula proposed by Christopher (1998) for calculating a customer's profitability for a company:

$$\text{Lifetime Profitablility} = \text{Average Transaction Profit} \\ \times \text{Yearly Frequency of Purchase} \\ \times \text{Customer 'Life Expectancy'}$$

In reality, there are significant differences in the profitability of customers. There are different quantities bought, products bought and different costs to service. This means it is necessary to know the profitability of each product and the cost of delivering every element of service. What is required is an appropriate level and mix of service depending on customer type. According to Thomas *et al.* (2004), 'Stable, healthy growth is built on the profitability of customers, not on their raw number or their loyalty.'

Figure 7.1: The Cost/Benefit of Service

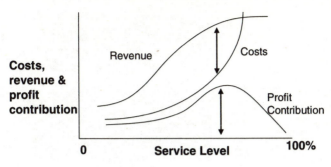

Figure 7.2: Customer Type Matrix

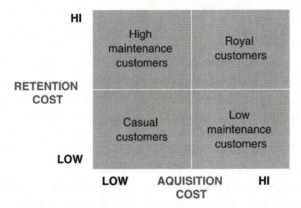

Source: Thomas, J.S. *et al.* (2004), 'Getting the Most out of your Customers', *Harvard Business Review*, Jul.–Aug.

It is necessary to carry out a cost/benefit analysis of servicing customers. At a certain point there will be no increase in revenue, no matter the increase in service level. It is therefore essential to understand the nuances of the level of service perceived as value by the different customers and the relative price they are prepared to pay. This is illustrated diagrammatically in Figure 7.1.

Thomas *et al.* (2004) have carried out more detailed analysis on the profitability of customers based on the cost to acquire them and then the cost to retain them. When looking at the results for a catalogue retailer over three years, tracking the same cohort of customers who began their relationship with the company in the same quarter, it was the high acquisition cost but low retention cost customers who provided the most profit. This can be seen diagrammatically in Figures 7.2 and 7.3.

Figure 7.3: Customer Classification and Profitability

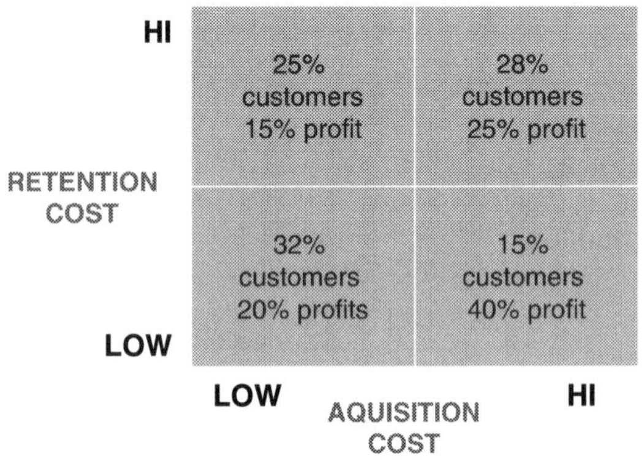

	LOW AQUISITION COST	HI AQUISITION COST
HI RETENTION COST	25% customers / 15% profit	28% customers / 25% profit
LOW RETENTION COST	32% customers / 20% profits	15% customers / 40% profit

Source: Thomas, J.S. et al. (2004), 'Getting the Most out of your Customers', *Harvard Business Review*, Jul.–Aug.

Thomas *et al.* (2004) point out that profitability is driven by:

- Acquisition likelihood: Factors which affect the likelihood of becoming a customer (e.g. acquisition expenses, number of face-to-face contacts and number of telephone contacts the sales representatives make, number of customer-initiated contacts to company enquiring about its products or services, demographics, customer base of customer).
- Relationship duration: Factors which affect the relationship duration (e.g. retention expenses, number of face-to-face contacts and number of telephone contacts the sales representatives make, number of customer-initiated contacts to company enquiring about its products or services, usage by customer of type of product/service delivered by company).
- Factors affecting profitability: The costs of acquisition and retention and factors affecting brand and possible substitution (e.g. acquisition and retention expenses, number of face-to-face contacts and number of telephone contacts the sales representatives make, number of customer-initiated contacts to company enquiring about its products or services, usage by customer of type of product/service delivered by company, estimated relationship duration).

Each customer's profitability can be measured using the following steps:

STEP 1: Measure product and service profitability taking into account all costs, including capital costs, rent, power, and other overheads as well as direct costs.

STEP 2: Once the true profitability of your products/services is identified, check which customers buy which ones. Assess the preliminary profitability of your customers.

Understanding Customer Service

STEP 3: Subtract all direct or customer-specific costs from the preliminary estimate (e.g. time costs with sales representatives, returns costs, late paying, special deliveries).
STEP 4: All costs not already assigned (e.g. CEO costs, HQ building) should be divided between all customers.

These steps can be replaced by the use of activity-based costing (ABC) which is a more effective way of monitoring the supply chain than traditional costing systems. ABC is discussed in some detail in Chapter 5.

Figure 7.4: Customer Categorisation

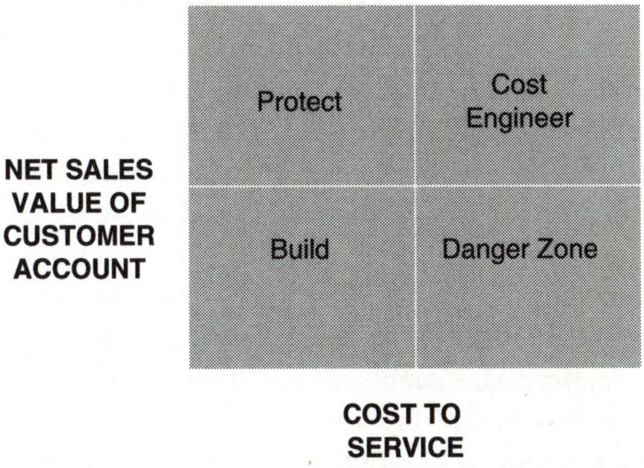

NET SALES VALUE OF CUSTOMER ACCOUNT	Protect	Cost Engineer
	Build	Danger Zone
	COST TO SERVICE	

Source: Christopher M. (1998), *Logistics and Supply Chain Management: Strategies for Reducing Cost and Improving Service,* 2nd ed., Upper Saddler River, NJ: Prentice Hall.

Figure 7.4 classifies customers by their net sales value and their cost to service. Those that you want to protect and keep from competitors are those that have a high net sales value but a low cost to service. In the opposite corner are those that are low in sales value but high in cost to service. These are the customers that you need to move into one of the neighbouring quadrants and hopefully move them eventually into the opposite quadrant. However, if this is not working, they are either customers that you want to lose or customers that you want to create a new supply chain for. For those in the 'build' category you want to grow their net sales value, while those in the 'cost engineer' category are the ones for whom you want to reduce the cost to service without impacting their sales value.

CUSTOMER REQUIREMENTS: ORDER QUALIFIERS AND ORDER WINNERS

If service offerings can be differentiated to customers, then it follows that customers will also view the performance of certain service criteria as being more important than others. Order winners allow orders to be won in favour of the competition – they change over the course of the product life-cycle, whereas order qualifiers have to be *in situ* just to compete. Higher performance than that required will not necessarily gain additional business.

It is most useful to identify and distinguish qualifying and winning characteristics at the start of customer service strategy formulation. Their determination should be used as a framework for system design decisions to be evaluated, such as policy decisions regarding inventory management, warehousing objectives, order processing considerations and formulating transport requirements. But these are not isolated activities! Aligning and integrating component activities into the supply chain involves evaluating trade-offs between sequentially aligned upstream and downstream activities.

Evaluation of design and improvement processes without recognition of this influencing and shaping consideration will lead to, at best, an effective and optimal sub-function but an ineffective and sub-optimal supply chain. In such instances, any competitive advantage provided by a sub-optimal supply chain can only be provided by that supply chain working 'harder' than its nearest competitor. As pointed out in Chapter 3, supply chains compete and inappropriate supply chain designs can be inflexible, costly and disruptive to change (see Figure 7.5).

It is therefore prudent to identify customer requirements through identifying the customer service elements which are key to them. These need to be objectively assessed as to whether they are order winning or order qualifying factors. This can be undertaken by applying a quantitative rating that scores the company's performance both in terms of their importance

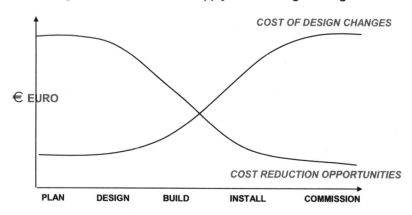

Figure 7.5: The Cost of Supply Chain Design Changes

to the customer and when compared to competitors. The following is a well-known step-by-step approach which can be used in the process of identifying what elements need to be developed to create value for specific customers.

Stage 1 – Identify performance factors, based on:
- benchmarking reports;
- customer interviews;
- competitor analysis;
- market research;
- performance established through completion of a questionnaire.

Stage 2 – Rate the factor in terms of its importance to the customer:
- Does the factor provide a crucial advantage with customers?
- Does the factor provide an important advantage factor with customers?
- Does the factor provide a useful advantage with customers?
- Does the factor need to be of a good standard?
- Does the factor need to be mid-point standard?
- Can the factor afford to be of lower standard?

A scoring system may be used based on: '1 – crucial' (order winning) to '9 – lower standard' (order qualifying).

Stage 3 – Rate performance factors relative to the competitors:
- Do we perform consistently considerably better?
- Do we perform consistently largely better?
- Do we perform consistently marginally better?
- Do we perform often considerably better?
- Do we perform often largely better?
- Do we perform often marginally better?
- Do we perform usually about the same?
- Do we usually perform worse?

Again a scoring system may be used based on: '1 – consistently considerably better than' to '9 – worse than'.

Stage 4 – Plot the results and determine action.

Take the average score for each service factor surveyed in relation to its importance to the customer, and its performance relative to the competition. Design a graph with the X-axis running from '9' at the origin through to '1' for customer importance – from unimportant to order winning. Design the Y-axis to run from '9' at the origin through to '1' for competitor performance – from worse than to better than. Plot these paired average

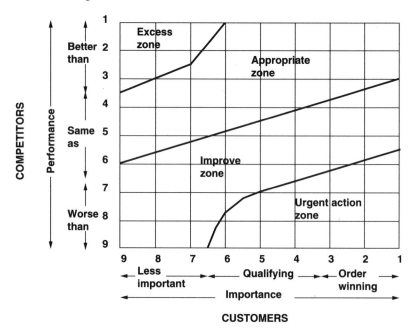

Figure 7.6: Customer Service Performance Grid

scores for each customer service factor for both customer importance and competitor performance onto the graph, as shown in Figure 7.6.

It is necessary to use judgement to determine the 'excess zone' for the performance of activities relative to competitors and to determine the 'urgent action zone' for the importance of performance to customers. Inappropriate zoning will either create unnecessary decisions and actions – which will lead to a false promotion of order qualifiers to order winning status – or it will fail to identify appropriate decisions and actions necessary to improve performance based on 'true' order winning criteria. Additional 'value-add' has to be assessed from raising the split point for the 'improve' and 'appropriate' zones. Sensible splitting can only be achieved by thorough knowledge of the business.

Historically, SCM has often been regarded as a rearward-facing function as its activities were directed at meeting the demands of customers – considerably so in the days when SCM was evolving from physical distribution, through to logistics (see Chapter 3). On the other hand, customer relationship management (CRM) has often been regarded as a forward-facing function, evolved from marketing (see Chapter 6), with its activities

Figure 7.7: Trade-offs Required to Meet Customer Expectations

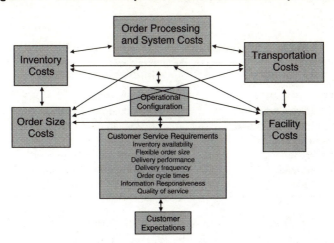

directed at understanding customer needs, satisfying them, and continually adding value. However, true competitive advantage will only be achieved by integrating both component parts, which can only occur through understanding the practice of trade-offs that occur, as the performance and characteristics of elements within each component part are sought to be optimised (as shown graphically in Figure 7.7). The end objective is a holistically managed entity that synchronises information, material and financial flows to provide superior value to the end consumer, while delivering cost-effective competitive advantage to the company.

IMPLICATIONS FOR SUPPLY CHAIN DESIGN

Once customer requirements are identified it is then necessary to design a customer focused supply chain strategy that meets these needs. Some of the issues which it is necessary to think about are:

- Matching supply with demand.
- Nature of products and services.
- Types of supply chain (e.g. lean or agile?).
- Industry environment and organisational capabilities/alignment.

Initially it is useful to identify if the products or services required are *functional* or *innovative* and what the nature of demand is for them. In defining these it is necessary to consider the product life-cycle, demand predictability, product variety and market standards for lead time. According to Fisher (1997) the following is how a company's products and services can be classified (see Table 7.1).

Table 7.1: Functional versus Innovative Products

Functional Products	Innovative Products
• Staples	• High variety
• Satisfy basic needs	• Additional reason to buy product
• Demand does not change much over time	• Volatile demand
• Long life-cycles	• Short life-cycles
• Highly competitive	• Competition from imitators
• Low profit margins	• High profit margins

Fisher (1997) goes on to relate aspects of demand to the two classifications of products/services as can be seen in Table 7.2.

Of course all products and services do not fit nicely into this dichotomy and it is in reality more of a spectrum. However, looking at them from this perspective helps identify what in actual fact supply chains are attempting to achieve. In this context, every supply chain could be regarded as having two main functions: the physical function and market mediation function. Physically, it is looking to convert raw materials into parts, work in progress (WIP) and finished goods or services, and moving them along the supply chain to the final customer. In addition, it is trying to ensure that the variety

Table 7.2: Aspects of Demand for Functional and Innovative Products

ASPECTS OF DEMAND	FUNCTIONAL	INNOVATIVE
PRODUCT LIFE CYCLE	2 years +	3 months–1 year
CONTRIBUTION MARGIN	5%–20%	20%–60%
PRODUCT VARIETY	Low (10 to 20 per category)	High (often millions)
AVERAGE MARGIN OF ERROR IN FORECAST AT TIME PRODUCTION IS COMMITTED	10%	40%–100%
AVERAGE STOCK OUT RATE	1%–2%	10%–40%
AVERAGE FORCED MARKDOWN AS % OF FULL PRICE – END OF SEASON	0%	10%–20%
LEAD TIME REQUIRED FOR MADE TO ORDER PRODUCTS	6 months–1 year	1 day to 2 weeks

Table 7.3: Physically Efficient versus Market Responsive Products and Services

	PHYSICALLY EFFICIENT	MARKET-RESPONSIVE
PRIMARY PURPOSE	Supply predictable demand efficiently at the lowest possible cost	Respond quickly to unpredictable demand in order to minimize stock outs, forced markdowns and obsolete inventory
MANUFACTURING FOCUS	Maintain high average utilisation rate	Deploy excess buffer capacity
INVENTORY STRATEGY	Generate high turns and minimise inventory throughout the chain	Deploy significant buffer stocks of parts or finished goods
LEAD-TIME FOCUS	Shorten lead times as long as it does not increase cost	Invest aggressively in ways to reduce lead-time
APPROACH TO CHOOSING SUPPLIERS	Select primarily for cost and quality	Select primarily for speed, flexibility and quality
PRODUCT-DESIGN STRATEGY	Maximise performance and minimise cost	Modular design to postpone differentiation

Source: Tables 7.1, 7.2 and 7.3 from Fisher, M. (1997). 'What is the Right Supply Chain for your products?' *Harvard Business Review*, Mar.–Apr.

of products in the marketplace is what the customer wants to buy. For example, Fisher (1997) divides the products/services as shown in Table 7.3.

Different types of products and services require different supply chains. On the one hand, functional products focus on minimising physical costs. The key to this is to meet predictable demand at the lowest cost. On the other hand, as far as innovative products are concerned, market mediation costs are the primary focus and the key is to read market signals and react quickly (see Figure 7.8).

Monitoring and Managing Customer Service: Customer Performance Measures and SLAs

Having designed and developed the appropriate supply chain to deliver the required customer service levels it is then essential to monitor and manage these levels. Performance measurements can create transformational change,

Figure 7.8: Matching Supply Chains to Products/Services

	FUNCTIONAL PRODUCTS/ SERVICES	INNOVATIVE PRODUCTS/ SERVICES
EFFICIENT SUPPLY CHAIN	MATCH	MISMATCH
RESPONSIVE SUPPLY CHAIN	MISMATCH	MATCH

build commitment, motivate teams and generate forward momentum. Measurements calibrate the effectiveness of activities (see Chapter 14). *Performance measurement* is the process of assessing progress towards pre-determined goals, while *performance management* is the use of performance measurement information to either confirm or change current policy and programme direction to meet the pre-determined goals. As noted in Chapter 3, to effectively manage performance it is important to set 'SMART' objectives:

- **Specific**: One clear goal with sufficient detail so that there is no question as to what is being measured and how the measurement is to be calculated.
- **Measurable**: Ensure that there is a system that accurately records performance.
- **Aligned**: The target should fit in with overall strategic objectives.
- **Realistic**: The targets should be challenging and stretching, but not unrealistic.
- **Time-based**: Identify when the target will be attained.

However, it is also important that the measurements selected need to provide an indication of the value delivery that is being provided by the supply chain to customers, employees and shareholders. This implies that corporate measurements need to transcend all functions in line with SCM thinking.

As regards customer service, the key objective is to achieve service excellence in a cost-effective way. The concept of the *perfect order* is useful when contemplating the meaning of service excellence. The perfect order is achieved when the customer's requirements are completely met. One common way to measure the perfect order is to measure *on-time, in-full* and *error-free*. The service level achieved for a customer can then be calculated by multiplying together the percentages achieved in each element. For

Understanding Customer Service

example if, during the period being measured, a company has achieved on-time deliveries 98 per cent of the time, in-full deliveries 95 per cent of the time, and error-free deliveries 90 per cent of the time, then the perfect order or service level achievement measure is 98 per cent × 95 per cent × 90 per cent, with the result that the likelihood of a perfect order being achieved is 83.79 per cent. It is important to note that even though the levels in each category are up in the 90+ per cent arena, the overall service level is actually significantly below 90 per cent.

However, as different customers may have different requirements and it is also important to keep the service cost elements under control, there are numerous possible ways of measuring customer service. The metrics for customer service can be broken down into four main areas as follows:[2]

1. Service metrics;
2. Speed metrics;
3. Asset metrics;
4. E-Commerce metrics.

See Part 5 of the Appendix to this chapter for examples of each of these metrics.

SERVICE LEVEL AGREEMENTS

As noted by Coyle *et al.* (2003) and others, companies leverage each other on an operational basis so that they perform better than they did separately. When two or more companies elect to work (partner) together, synergy is a common outcome – which, if extended forward, suggests that competencies can be created when collaborative activity takes place (e.g. perform more efficiently for the same cost *or* perform at the same level for a lower cost). But to achieve either of these, management of these relationships for the services and products the partners provide is key and can be supported through the use of service level agreements (SLAs).

The SLA is *not* a catchall term for attempting to meet minimum acceptable levels of service. Its main aim is to attract and maintain customers and, as such, it should be designed to provide customers with the service they require to build sustainable competitive advantage. Properly created SLAs, based on a company's analysis of customer requirements, an objective assessment of their competencies and prudent management of resources by the contractor, can

---

[2]With due acknowledgement to Rose McCarthy.

develop customer loyalty and create a competitive differentiation. SLAs develop a relationship between cost and service – that is, ill-defined specification of requirements can lead to 'wanting a Rolls Royce but only willing to pay for a Mini'. The division of service into 'Basic', 'Enhanced' and 'Premium', for example, may enable resources and cost trade-offs to be viewed for differing levels of service and a valuable by-product is the development of trust – if comprehensive SLAs can be developed and the terms met, then it allows your customers to extend the same service to their customers.

An SLA defines the obligations of both parties which set out the negotiated terms. There are three kinds of obligations:

1. 'Expressed terms' contained in clauses in the SLA;
2. 'Incorporated terms' contained in additional documents specifically referred to in the contract document;
3. 'Implied terms' contained in relevant prevailing law.

Key ingredients for successful long-term SLAs are:

- Constant evaluation of the strengths and weaknesses of each partner – that is, competency analysis;
- Company values that are clearly understood by each side of the arrangement;
- Measurable objectives – early identification and declaration of deviances together with proposed corrective action;
- Committed staff;
- Fair and negotiated recompense;
- Significant levels of contact to monitor and control the arrangement;
- Trust in each partner to the agreement.

The Appendix to this chapter outlines the key elements of a typical SLA.[3]

Customer Relationship Management

As noted by Nemmers (2005), 'getting close to the customers is not so much a problem that the IT or marketing department needs to solve as a journey that the whole organisation needs to make.' The importance of market and detailed customer information in devising a customer focused supply chain, and how to achieve this operationally through performance measurement and SLAs, has been outlined. However, there is a more subtle and culturally

---

[3] With due acknowledgement to John Mee.

ingrained system that also needs to be in place to achieve true customer focus. There are three keys to this:

1. There is a need to learn everything there is to learn about a company's customers at the most granular level, creating a comprehensive picture of each customer's needs – past, present and future.
2. Employees must be able to share what they learn about customers.
3. This insight guides not only product and service decisions but also the company's basic strategy and organisational and supply chain structure.

According to Gulati and Oldroyd (2005), the stages necessary to achieve a highly developed customer focus are as follows.

1. *Communal Coordination*

The first stage involves creating a central repository of customer information, which records each interaction a customer has with the company. First of all, companies bring together information drawn from customer touch points throughout the organisation into one format and location. This information is organised by the customer, that is the customer is the fundamental unit of analysis. To gather, standardise and organise customer information from throughout the organisation, it is necessary to establish a coordination infrastructure. Each group contributes its information to a central pool and taps into it as necessary.

2. *Serial Coordination*

At this stage the company moves from assembling customer information to drawing inferences from it. The centralised coordination role expands to manage a sequence of tasks performed by different functional units so that the information can be analysed and the resulting insights shared throughout the company. This is done by collated information being passed to business analysts; analysis results are then passed on to business users and users apply it to marketing efforts, building on local knowledge. This may not occur smoothly or spontaneously, and may need a unit to take a leadership role to ensure that all steps are accomplished and properly coordinated.

3. *Symbiotic Coordination*

At this stage the focus moves from an analysis of past customer interactions to anticipating and even shaping the future. This necessitates companies moving to a dynamic 'give-and-take' information flow (or two-way communication) throughout the organisation. It is an experimental stage with four discrete sets of activities:

1. Creating models to predict customer behaviour;
2. Experimenting with interventions designed to alter customer behaviour;
3. Measuring the results of these interventions;
4. Using feedback from the front line to improve the models.

4. *Integral Coordination*

There is now a sophisticated understanding of the customers which is apparent in the day-to-day operations of the company. Customer focus has become part of the culture and is incorporated into the informal values and daily behaviour of all employees. In fact, the outside world perceives the company as customer-focused.

If an organisation reaches this stage, it has come along a learning journey. There are four elements to this journey, each with its own challenges and each necessitating more sophisticated ways of coordination and cooperation between its staff.

Conclusion

In essence, customer service is delivered by the supply chain. To do this in the most effective and efficient manner, it is necessary to have a clear understanding of what delivers value to each customer and what information is needed to facilitate the monitoring and management of the delivery of this value through continually developing and improving the organisation's customer service strategy and related supply chains. It is necessary to understand the dynamics within the supply chain to enable a company to continuously improve on its delivery of value for money. This comes from understanding customers' businesses – probably better than they do – and developing relationships based on trust and transparency, which lead to clarity and consequently the required level of understanding to enable the development of an appropriate supply chain.

REFERENCES

Christopher, M. (1998), *Logistics and Supply Chain Management: Strategies for Reducing Cost and Improving Service*, 2nd ed., Upper Saddler River, NJ: Prentice Hall.

Coyle, J.J., Bardi, E.J. and Langley Jr, C.J. (2003), *The Management of Business Logistics, a Supply Chain Perspective*, Mason, OH: South-Western, a division of Thompson Learning.

Fisher, M. (1997), 'What is the Right Supply Chain for your Products?', *Harvard Business Review*, Mar.–Apr., 105–116.

Gulati, R. and Oldroyd J.B. (2005), 'The Quest for Customer Focus', *Harvard Business Review*, April, 92–101.

Kotler, P. (2004), *Ten Deadly Marketing Sins: Signs and Solutions*, New York: John Wiley & Sons.

La Londe, B.J. and Zinszer, P.H. (1976), *Customer Service: Meaning and Measurement*, National Council of Physical Distribution Management, Chicago.

Nemmers, M. quoted in Gulati, R. and Oldroyd, J.B. (2005), 'The Quest for Customer Focus', *Harvard Business Review,* April, 92–101.

Thomas, J.S., Reinartz, W. and Kumar, V. (2004), 'Getting the Most Out of Your Customers', *Harvard Business Review*, Jul.–Aug., 116–123.

APPENDIX: KEY ELEMENTS IN A SERVICE LEVEL AGREEMENT (SLA)

1. Specification of requirement
2. Contract term
3. Buyer's obligations (Company's)
4. Provider's obligations (Contractor's)
5. Payment methods
6. Performance measures
7. Insurance and indemnity provisions
8. Dispute resolution
9. Prevailing legal conditions
10. Signatures

1. Specification of Requirement

- The detail that will allow a contractor to provide the offering as required.
- The clarity should be such that if the process involved tendering, all interested parties could tender without consulting the company.
- All supporting materials have to be included in drawing up the requirement specification.
- Failure to understand the requirement could lead to fulfilment of a contract that does not deliver expectations.
- Failure to be exacting in detail could lead to the impression that the contractor is failing to perform.
- Specification of requirements is the cornerstone of the SLA process – 'a chain is only as strong as its weakest link.'
- If your supply chain is 'weaker' than that of your competitors, then your supply chain will have to work 'harder' to yield the same level of competitive advantage.

2. Contract Term

- The term should be of such a length that the contractor can offer a competitive pricing/service.
- Contractors will require longer length contracts if costly/extensive capital assets are involved.
- Users tend to require shorter length contracts, allowing the ability to switch/take recognition of market dynamics.
- Terms may roll forward. Often a lack of contest from the customer implies acceptance of continuation.

- Break clauses sever the term, often against inadequate performance/non-compliance – but these have to be specified at the commencement and agreed.
- Depending on the assets involved, there may still be a break cost to the customer.
- *Force majeure* provisions render the contract impossible to conclude. They are outside of the control of either party.

3. *Buyer's Obligations (Company's)*

The company is obligated to include specifics that allow the contractor to undertake the tasks required. These might include:

- Forecasts of workload;
- Appropriate assets;
- Declarations with regard to product quality and fitness for purpose;
- Failure to provide all specifics that are required to enable the contractor to deliver on the contract may render the agreement 'in dispute' at some future point.

4. *Provider's Obligations (Contractor's)*

The contractor should ensure that the main body of the SLA includes:

- A general description of the services to be provided against agreed service levels;
- Obligations of the contractor including an understanding of punitive penalties where appropriate;
- Key legislation to be adhered to;
- If the contract involves premises not owned by the company, in other words an obligation to allow access to the company.

5. *Payment Methods*

- Methods are dependent on the services/products that are supplied.
- Performance data may have to be supplied by the contractor to sanction payment.
- Incentives might be available if the contract involves the provision of a service – the optimum contract to cement collaborative activities involves 'gain-sharing'.
- There are, however, contract types that might not (need to) encourage improvements to minimum acceptable standards.

Compensation Methods

- Unit Rate

Advantages	Disadvantages
Easy to use.	No incentive to share productivity gains with customer.
Costs vary with volume.	Possibly inflated to include risk element.
Easily coupled with incentive programmes.	Difficult to use if unit rate is difficult to define.
Can be adjusted in line with volumes achieved.	

- Cost Plus

Advantages	Disadvantages
Contractor profit is known and capped.	Needs mechanism to establish what are reasonable costs – benchmarking.
Effective in start-ups when costs are uncertain.	No built-in incentive to provide productivity improvements.
Productivity benefits accrue to the customer.	
Contractor does not suffer if volume estimates are inaccurate.	

- Management Fee

Advantages	Disadvantages
Useful when units are difficult to define and volumes are uncertain.	Difficult to determine the appropriate level of fee.
The levels of profit and overhead are fixed and known.	No built-in device to pass on benefits of productivity improvements.
Provides incentive to improve productivity.	No incentive to expand management team if necessary.

6. Performance Measures

Service Metrics

- On-Time Order Delivery Performance Percentage (Total number of orders delivered on time during the period/Total number of orders originally requested during the period).
  - Ideal to analyse by individual drop point, customer group, route.
  - Often combined with 'order fill' to create one measure of 'in full and on time'.
- On-Time Line Delivery Performance Percentage (Total number of lines delivered on time during the period/Total number of lines originally requested during the period):
  - Ideal to analyse by individual drop point, customer group, route.
- On-Time Case Delivery Performance Percentage (Total number of cases delivered on time as originally requested during the period/Total number of cases originally requested during the period):
  - Ideal to analyse by individual drop point, customer group, route.
- Order Fill (Total number of complete orders supplied/Total number of orders supplied):
  - 750 orders supplied in full/760 orders supplied.
  - 98.68 per cent order fill.
- Line Count Fill (Total number of complete lines shipped/Total number of lines shipped).
- Case Count Fill (Total number of cases shipped in full/Total number of cases shipped).
- Value Fill Rate (Value of order shipped/Value of initial order).
- Shipment Visibility/Traceability Percentage (Total number of shipments via carrier with order tracking/Total number of shipments sent in period):
  - Indicator of sophistication of carrier base.
  - A measure of the non-price value of the carrier base.
- Availability (Total number of SKUs in stock/Total number of SKUs offered). 90 SKUs in stock/100 offered = 90 per cent availability.
- Demand Failure:
  - 1 − (Total cases supplied/Total cases demanded).
  - 1 − (80 cases supplied/100 demanded) = 20 per cent demand failure.
- Backorder Analysis
  - Backorders created against an item when there is insufficient stock to satisfy the demand.
  - (Percentage of total SKUs in queue/Total SKUs in portfolio).
  - (Percentage of total cases in queue/Total cases dispatched this period).

- (Value of queue/Value of posted invoice values this period).
- Aged analysis where the total number of days outstanding for each backordered instance for all SKU, is aggregated.
- POD Accuracy (Error-free PODs/Total number of PODs in period).
- Perfect Order Measurement:
  - A combined multiplicative measure from each stage of the order cycle.
  Example:
  Order entry accuracy: 99.95 per cent.
  Available to allocate: 98 per cent.
  Warehouse pick accuracy: 97.4 per cent.
  Delivered on time: 100 per cent.
  Shipped without damage: 99.2 per cent.
  Invoiced correctly: 99.9 per cent.
  Perfect order measurement: 99.95 per cent × 98 per cent × 97.4 per cent × 100 per cent × 99.2 per cent × 99.9 per cent = 94.5 per cent.
- Warehouse Error Rate as a Percentage of Dispatches:
  - It is important to have a check on the damages, shortages and picking errors that a warehouse operation are responsible for – even more so in contracted-out situations.
  - Errors are all warehousing instances that stop the invoice being raised for 100 per cent of stock allocated – picking errors/shortages.
  - In an established manual operation it would not be uncommon for this figure to be in the region of 0.25 per cent.
  - (Total number of cases with errors/Total number of cases dispatched).
- On-Time Pick-Ups (Number of pick-ups made on time/Total number of pick-ups made in the period).
  - Indicates freight carrier performance on customer service.

Speed Metrics

- Cycle Time to Process Product Returns for Resale:
  - The finite number of days/hours required, from the day of returned receipt, to process the returned goods into fit goods available for re-selection.
- Supply Chain Cycle Time:
  - The total time it would take to satisfy a customer order, if all inventory levels were at zero.
  - A measure of both depth of partnerships and flexibility of operations it is calculated by adding up the longest lead times in each stage of the cycle.
- Upside Flexibility:
  - The ability to respond to an increase in demand over and above original order.

- Measured as percentage over original order or measured in finite days.
- Can be measured by labour, material and capacity.
- Transit Times:
  - Measured by the time it takes in hours/days/weeks/for a delivery to arrive at the receiving location.
- Truck Turnaround Times:
  - The average time between a truck's arrival at the facility and its departure.
  - Measures dock/loading bay efficiencies.
- Inventory Turnover:
  - The velocity at which the inventory passes through the organisation.
  - (Cost of goods sold/Average inventory):
    e.g. €70,000/€50,000, 1.4 turns per annum.

Asset Metrics

- Total Supply Chain Costs:
  - The total costs as a percentage of net sales to manage the entire function.
  - Includes the costs of all supply chain activities.
- Cash to Cash Cycle Times:
  - The number of days between paying for raw materials and getting paid for product.
  - (Inventory days of supply + Days of sales outstanding − Average payment period for material).
- Total Warehousing Costs to Net Sales Value:
  - Expressed as a percentage figure this KPI will provide a measure of the absolute cost sustained by the warehousing operation, in support of the actual level of sales. (Total warehousing costs/Total net sales value).
  - The measure becomes more pertinent in outsourced operations at the annual budgetary process, when expected sales growth in value can be compared to expected cost increase from third-party contractors.
- Stock Adjustments per Period (day/week/month/quarter) in Terms of Value, or Number of SKUs:
  - Once the contractor assumes responsibility for inventory integrity, then they will probably introduce an ongoing process for re-balancing inventory levels, such as cycle counting monthly stocktakes.
  - The stock value written off per day/month will drop straight into the stock/loss provision account and be debited from profit.
  - The total accumulating value over a period of time would be a measure of how accurate all preceding control operations have been executed by the contractor.

E-Commerce Metrics

- Conversion Rate to Purchase:
  - A measure of the proportion of total visits that lead to purchases.
    (Number of site visits producing a purchase/Total number of site visits) × 100 per cent.
- Digital Sales Conversion Rate:
  - A measure of all sales that originate and complete via the web, as distinct from completing via an 0800 number, or in store.
    (Number of sales originated and completed on the web/Total number of sales originated and completed).
- Bricks and Mortar to Web Sales Ratio:
  (The total number of sales originated and completed via traditional channels/The total number of sales originated and completed via the web) × 100 per cent.

7. Insurance and Indemnity Provisions

- The company should define all its liabilities to the contractor and its customers and ensure they are covered by third-party insurance.
- The contractor needs to understand all of its liabilities to the company and ensure these are managed by a third party.
- The company should insist that the contractor provides evidence of insurance cover.
- Neither company can accept risks or liabilities for situations that they have no control over – these should be defined in a broad fashion as exclusions or limitations.

8. Dispute Resolution

- Breach of contract usually involves the award of damages – to place the company back in the position it would have been in had the contract been fulfilled properly.
- Conciliation, arbitration and negotiation.
- Conciliation and arbitration involve a third party whose involvement is agreed to by both company and contractor.
- Conciliation involves a settlement being promoted.
- Arbitration involves an award of compensation or remedial course of action.
- Negotiation procedures for escalating dispute resolution whilst contract is in force should be detailed.

- If differences cannot be resolved, then there may only be two courses of action:
  - 'Leak' that you are seeking alternative suppliers and are prepared to 'buy out' the contract.
  - Terminate the contract on expiry date or earlier.

9. *Prevailing Legal Conditions*

- Regulatory compliance – that the products and services provided by both sides will be in accordance with prevailing local/market laws.
- In the case of product supply, the customer will have to inform the contractor of any regulations that relate specifically to their products.

10. *Signatures*

- Appropriate levels of responsibility to agree the terms and conditions that will bind the companies.
- Dated and witnessed.
- 'For and on behalf'.

8

Customer Service and Supply Chain Design

RANDAL FAULKNER

INTRODUCTION

This book explains how the traditional view of management as a series of independent buy, make, move and sell functions, each managed in isolation and often at cross-purposes, is necessarily replaced in today's complex, global and competitive environment, by a supply chain management (SCM) approach, where the different functions are managed in a holistic fashion.

When explained to a business management team, the SCM philosophy usually makes sense. However the question most commonly asked by managers sold on the concept is, 'How do we start to implement SCM?'. And the place to start is with customer service. This chapter explains how, through customer service, SCM is a key part of any company's marketing mix and, as a result, how customer service 'sets the spec for the design of the supply chain'.

CUSTOMER SERVICE AND THE MARKETING MIX

The marketing mix involves blending a number of variables, often with different mixes for different market/customer/product categories (see Chapter 6). Six of the common variables are listed below, but additional variables may be important to some businesses:

Product Quality: The quality of the product is a key variable, often regarded as a 'given' in today's competitive environment and with little or no flexibility.

Branding/Image: 'Brand' is the value attached to an entity such as a product or a business resulting from an accumulation of factors developed over years (e.g. the brands Guinness or iPod have an inherent value).

Customer Service: Customer service as the deliverable of SCM is the subject of this chapter and the elements that comprise customer service and their role in the design of the supply chain will be explained below.

Technical Support/Knowledge: Successful business is not just about supplying product; it is also about supporting that product whether with technical knowledge or warranty or the like.

Price: Price is often considered, particularly by sales personnel, as the most important variable in the marketing mix. Setting the right price, including 'price pointing' – that is, setting the price relative to competitors or competing products – is important, but is often not considered the most important by customers.

Terms of Business: Credit terms, vendor managed inventory (VMI), returns policy, minimum order size, discount structure, etc. are all elements of the terms of business which can be offered to a customer and these form an important part of the marketing proposition to customers.

To assess the relative importance of each of these, customer service in particular, as part of the marketing mix, a company can conduct a survey of its customers using for example Table 8.1, where 1 indicates the most important and 6 indicates the least important.

Based on experience of a number of such surveys in a variety of business sectors, companies are often surprised to find customer service coming second only to product quality in the eyes of the customer, and often being more important than price. Marketing management are also often surprised to see that money spent on brand development (e.g. advertising and promotional spend) is often not as important as money spent on improving service levels. Customer service is a very important factor in a customer's decision to do business with a company.

Table 8.1: Assessing Marketing Mix Variables

Function	Ranking 1–6
Product Quality	
Branding/Image	
Customer Service	
Technical Support/Knowledge	
Price	
Terms of Business	

Customer Service and Competitive Advantage

Competitive advantage is achieved by delivering a market-driven customer service strategy at optimum supply chain cost. The words 'market-driven' are important. Understanding the level of service that is required to be competitive is critical. It is not necessary to provide a level of service that customers do not need. A food company promised its customers any order received by 4.00 p.m. would be delivered the next day and failed miserably to meet this level of service. A survey of their customers revealed that this level of service was not required, and so the company was able to relax the service constraint, meet it consistently, have happier customers and, save money because the new service level incurred lower costs.

Successful businesses today focus first on their customers and their needs. Increasingly, the customer comes first in business decision-making in all parts of the operation. As will be discussed below, customer service is the deliverable of SCM. The whole chain from suppliers via production through the distribution channels (such as retailers, wholesalers or direct) to the end customer must work efficiently and effectively all the time to ensure that customers receive the right products reliably and consistently on time. As noted in Chapter 3, understanding customer requirements in the marketplace and current supply chain cost elements and drivers then becomes the starting point for the supply chain improvement/re-engineering process. The development of a market-driven customer service strategy sets the specification for SCM. Improved financial performance measures the effectiveness of SCM. Figure 8.1 shows how achievement of the two objectives combines to create competitive advantage through integrated SCM.

Figure 8.1: Achieving Competitive Advantage through Integrated SCM

Universal Success Factors → *Impact*

- Market-driven Customer Service Strategy
- Optimum Total Supply Chain Investment And Costs

→ Competitive Advantage Through Integrated SCM

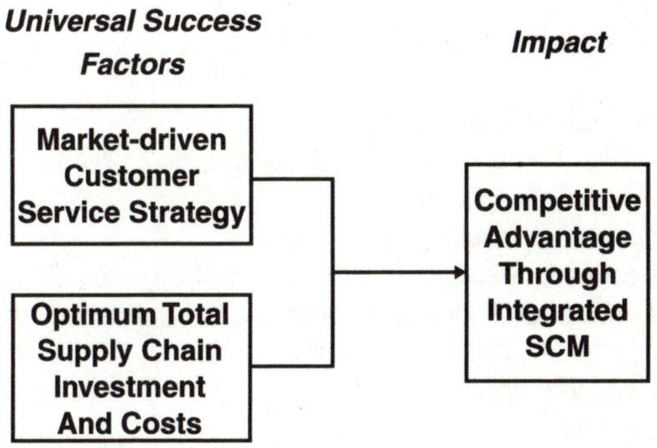

Source: Modified from Faulkner, R. (2002), 'You Need to Think Supply Chain Management', presentation at European Union Asia ICT Workshop, October, Bangkok.

Elements of Customer Service

The first thing to ask is: *What do we mean by customer service?* As pointed out in Chapter 3, NITL (2001) noted that, 'To some organisations it means dealing with customer complaints; to others it is about after-sales service, and to yet others it is the 'have a nice day' attitude to customers.' In SCM, customer service means something quite specific. Customer service includes all the service factors involved in supporting and getting product to customers (see Table 8.2), and these are reviewed below.

The list of customer service elements below is not intended to be exhaustive and some companies may have additional elements which they consider important.

Product Availability: This customer service element is also sometimes referred to as 'fill rate'. It is how much of a customer order can be supplied when required. It is often measured as a percentage (e.g. 99 per cent fill rate), and can be measured as 'order fill' (e.g. what proportion of the orders can be supplied complete) and sometimes as 'line fill' (e.g. what proportion of each line in orders can be supplied). Different fill rates can apply to different products. Critical products might be 100 per cent and non-critical can be less.

Length of Order Cycle Time: This is the length of time between placing and delivering an order. In some sectors (e.g. in pharmaceutical distribution)

Table 8.2: Elements of Customer Service

Customer Service Elements
- Product Availability (Can orders be filled?)
- Length of Order Cycle Time (Time it takes from order to delivery, usually counted in days)
- Consistency of Order Cycle Time (Always the same length of time from order to delivery)
- Invoice/Billing Procedures/Accuracy
- Irformation Request Responsiveness (How fast does company respond?)
- Flexibility in Resolving Problems
- Distance to Supplier's Warehouse
- Special Customer Requests
- Frequency of Damaged Goods (Do products get damaged on the way to the customer?)
- Quality of Order Department
- Emergency Coverage
- On-time Delivery

Source: National Institute for Transport and Logistics (2001), 'Customer Services', *Technical Fact Sheet*, Dublin: NITL.

the order cycle time is a few hours; in food it might be 24 or 48 hours; in motor distribution it can be several months for new cars, but 24 hours for spare parts.

Consistency of Order Cycle Time: Often more important than the length of the order cycle time is the consistency of that order cycle time. If a customer knows that the supplier consistently delivers orders 48 hours after order placement, then they can plan for such an order cycle time. If sometimes it is 24 hours and other times it may be a week, then it is difficult to plan. Consistency is often more important than speed.

Order Accuracy: Delivering exactly what was ordered is a basic and critical element of customer service. Checking the 'pick accuracy' is a fundamental of good order processing.

Invoice/Billing Procedures/Accuracy: A most annoying feature of many suppliers is the inaccuracy of the paperwork. A wrong invoice can incur a lot of unnecessary cost in terms of administrative time and even cash flow.

Information Request Responsiveness: Responding to customer requests for information, for example about order status, is another key element of customer service. In fact, companies can turn poor service into excellent service by keeping the customer informed.

Flexibility in Resolving Problems: Good management is about flexibility. The one reality of business life is that things do not always go to plan. Being able to resolve problems when they arise is considered good service.

Special Customer Requests: Dealing with special requests by customers (e.g. early delivery, less than minimum order, etc.) is appreciated by customers and can represent positive marketing, provided customers understand it is 'special' and therefore cannot be allowed on a regular basis.

Frequency of Damaged Goods: Damage to goods in transit is a business reality. For the customer, damaged product may be the same as no product, and should be minimised.

Packaging: The way a product is packaged can be important to customers. Product which comes ready for merchandising can save time and labour.

Quality of Order Department: The order department, like the delivery driver, is often the most visible face of a company from the customer's perspective. The quality of the order department and how easy it is for a customer to place an order are important elements of the service offering.

Emergency Coverage: Emergency situations always arise and the ability of a company to cater for such emergencies determines its image in the eyes of the customers.

On-Time Delivery: Last, but by no means least, is the ability to deliver on time. Indeed, for many customers '100 per cent on time', meaning receiving 100 per cent of what they ordered on time, is the basic requirement.

As noted in Chapter 7, different sectors/products/markets/customers will have different requirements for each of these elements. Understanding the relative importance of each is fundamental to developing a market-driven customer service strategy. Additionally, understanding how competitors are rated in each of the important service elements is fundamental to developing a competitive customer service strategy. It has long been recognised that both of these can be discovered by surveys or audits of customers (see, for example, Sterling and Lambert 1989).

CUSTOMER SERVICE SURVEYS

First of all, customers can be asked to rank the service elements in order of importance. Thirteen or fourteen elements might be too many for customers to sensibly rank, in which case they can be asked to rank the top five or six. Then they can be asked to rate the company's performance, and also the performance of the leading competitor or competitors, in relation to these customer service elements (or the top five or six) on a scale of one to five.

The company can then start to develop strategies for actions which deliver the level of service that customers actually want and are willing to pay for, and exploit the company's strengths and the competitors' weaknesses. In this way, the customer service strategy becomes part of the marketing mix. Logistics and SCM help to sell products. The company is in effect developing a market-driven customer service strategy.

Table 8.3 sets out an appropriate set of questions that customers might be asked. It may be introduced as follows: 'Please tell us how we perform

Table 8.3: Ranking Customer Service Performance

Ranking:	Self	Competitor
Product Availability (Order Fill)	1 2 3 4 5	1 2 3 4 5
Length of Order Cycle Time	1 2 3 4 5	1 2 3 4 5
Consistency of Order Cycle Time	1 2 3 4 5	1 2 3 4 5
Order Accuracy	1 2 3 4 5	1 2 3 4 5
Invoice/Billing Procedures/Accuracy	1 2 3 4 5	1 2 3 4 5
Information Request Responsiveness	1 2 3 4 5	1 2 3 4 5
Flexibility in Resolving Problems	1 2 3 4 5	1 2 3 4 5
Special Customer Requests	1 2 3 4 5	1 2 3 4 5
Frequency of Damaged Goods	1 2 3 4 5	1 2 3 4 5
Packaging	1 2 3 4 5	1 2 3 4 5
Quality of Order Department	1 2 3 4 5	1 2 3 4 5
Emergency Coverage	1 2 3 4 5	1 2 3 4 5
On-Time Delivery	1 2 3 4 5	1 2 3 4 5

for you on the elements shown in Table 8.3. 1 indicates poor performance and 5 indicates strong performance. Please rank us against our competitors.'

USING CUSTOMER SERVICE INFORMATION IN SUPPLY CHAIN DESIGN

Combined with the knowledge about what customers think is most important to them, a company can begin to design the supply chain configuration to deliver the right level of service. Customer service expectations set the agenda for supply chain design. Once a company knows what is important to its customers, it can develop the right set-up in terms of suppliers, production and distribution channels to give the customers what they want. Not all customers are the same, and what customers want changes over time. It is therefore important to repeatedly ask customers for their opinions and be flexible enough to adapt to changing customer requirements speedily. It might sometimes be necessary to divide customers into different types depending on their needs, and serve each customer segment with a different logistics set-up. This is called customer segmentation by logistics characteristics, and can be very effective. For example:

- If a customer values consistency, but is not worried about length of time from order to delivery, more cost-efficient distribution channels can be used.
- If order fill rates are important to the customers, then inventory policies can be planned to meet this requirement.

- If a fast response time to orders is critical, then inventory levels, warehouse locations, modes of transport, etc. can be planned to deliver the required level of service.

In a situation where additional marketing expenditure will generate an uncertain return, and production costs are honed to the bone, and further cuts would jeopardise quality, customer service and related logistics management represent a real opportunity to generate competitive advantage.

Conclusion

In today's competitive and global marketplace, where product quality is becoming a given, and price is dictated by the marketplace and is out of the control of management, then customer service becomes the key differentiator between competing companies.

With customer service determining the design of the supply chain and then being dependent on how well companies manage their supply chains, this makes SCM a critical value-adding activity in successful businesses, alongside other key business activities such as product innovation and brand development.

The importance to business and supply chain success of understanding and managing customer service cannot be underestimated.

REFERENCES

Faulkner, R. (2002), 'You Need to think Supply Chain Management', Presentation at *European Union Asia ICT Workshop*, Bangkok, Thailand, October.

National Institute for Transport and Logistics (2001), 'Customer Service', *Technical Fact Sheet*, Dublin: NITL.

Sterling, J. and Lambert, D. (1989), 'Customer Service Research: Past, Present and Future', *International Journal of Physical Distribution and Materials Management*, 19(2), 1–23.

SECTION 3
SCM: THE SUPPLIER PERSPECTIVE

9

Outsourcing and its Role in the Supply Chain

Aoife O'Riordan and Edward Sweeney

Introduction

As noted earlier (see in particular Chapters 2 to 4), companies are increasingly focusing on what they regard as their core activities or competencies. Oates (1998) defines core competencies as 'the central things that organisations do well.' The corollary of this is that activities regarded as 'non-core' are being outsourced. Greaver (1999) states that 'non-core competencies take up time, energy and workspace and help management lose sight of what is important in an organisation'. Furthermore, the trend towards economic and business globalisation (see Chapter 2) has facilitated the outsourcing of various activities to overseas locations (offshoring). Key supply chain activities are increasingly being outsourced to third-party organisations. Furthermore, in the increasingly knowledge-based economies of developed countries, shared knowledge – which one can acquire by outsourcing – is a potentially important element of competitive capability. What was once known as ***power is knowledge*** is now known as ***shared power is knowledge*** (Connolly *et al.* 2004). This chapter provides an overview of outsourcing in the context of wider developments in the supply chain.

Background and Development

Traditionally, outsourcing is an abbreviation for 'outside resource using' (Arnold 2000). Currently, in the simplest of forms, outsourcing takes place when an organisation transfers the ownership of a service or function that used to be done in-house to a supplier. The degree of transfer of control is the defining characteristic of outsourcing. It concerns 'the transfer of routine and repetitive tasks to an outside source'; 'having an outside vendor provide a service that you usually perform in-house'; and 'paying other firms to perform all or parts of the work' (Zineldin and Bredenlow 2003).

Outsourcing, or offshoring as it is now known in many circles,[1] has been around for many decades. In the beginning, outsourcing was a relatively peripheral activity and related mainly to the blue collar or lower-skilled operations of organisations. However, with rising labour costs and the increasing use of robots for automation purposes, those jobs would have been lost anyway. Now, the fear of many skilled workers or managers is that their jobs are going to be outsourced as the global economy has opened up and the cost of communication is cheap. Organisations can now outsource virtually anything they wish within the organisation.

Historically, outsourcing was used when an organisation could not perform to world-class standards in all aspects of its work due to many factors, including: incompetence of staff and/or management; lack of capacity within the organisation; financial pressures and/or technological pressures. In its most basic of forms it started from the outsourcing of a single service such as canteen management, buildings management, or computing. In addition, outsourcing was applied in overhead functions or activities with no potential for competitive advantage and business processes where an end user could create a competitive advantage through partnerships with vendors specialising in a particular area (Dole 1998). Now, outsourcing is used to build on core competencies and organisations recognise that serving the customer is critical: 'Anything that distracts us from this focus will be considered for outsourcing' (Greaver 1999).

Outsourcing is not simple or easy to create, develop and support, and it can have both positive and negative effects on key areas of the supply chain (Mason *et al.* 2002). There are many implementation problems and the failure rate is often quoted to be as high as 70 per cent (Zineldin and Bredenlow 2003). In addition, it can adversely affect employees and many transitions have been unsuccessful. Even with these problems recent studies have indicated that 85 per cent of all companies outsource at least one function or service (Logan 2000).

So, why outsource? According to Dole (1998):

> To compete in today's information age companies must re-evaluate the way they do business in the light of rapid, unrelenting change in the marketplace. The need to improve productivity, quality and flexibility has led companies to examine their organisational structures and to realise that

---

[1] The terms 'offshoring', as the name suggests, is usually used in the context of the outsourcing of activity to an overseas-based provider.

creating the greatest value does not require them to own, manage, and directly control all of their assets and resources. Rather, strategic alliances and partnerships with those who provide expertise in a particular area may be the most effective way to gain results.

It permits organisations to enhance effectiveness by focusing on their core competencies while using specialist suppliers for non-core activities, and as a result they should have better overall performance.

Furthermore, it can be applied to most functions and services (see Figure 9.1) within an organisation. Today, what an individual company outsources depends on the core competencies,[2] core activities[3] and critical functions (see Figure 9.2) within the organisation.

Core competencies are one of the keys to customer satisfaction and superior performance. They combine three features: (1) They differentiate between the company and its competitors; (2) Resources and know-how for the product must be unique over time, (there must be something to prevent

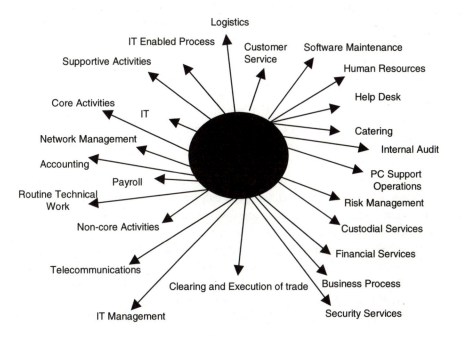

Figure 9.1: Examples of What is Outsourced

---

[2]'The central things organisations do well' (Oates 1998).
[3]'Things that are central to what organisations do' (Oates 1998).

Figure 9.2: Examples of Core and Non-core Parts of a Business

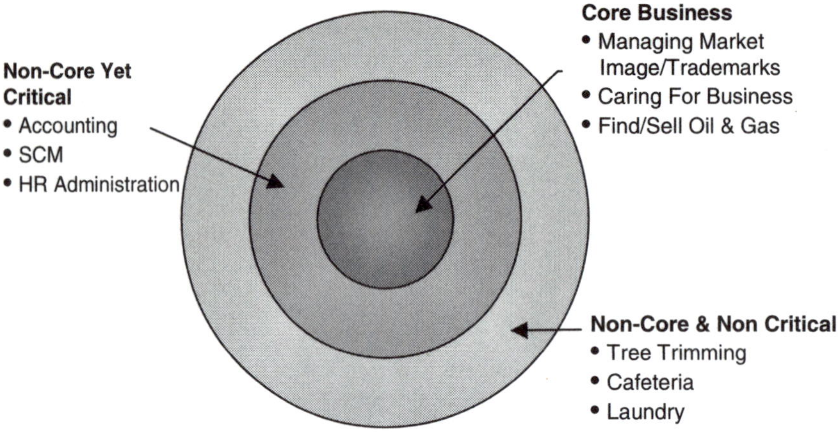

Non-Core Yet Critical
- Accounting
- SCM
- HR Administration

Core Business
- Managing Market Image/Trademarks
- Caring For Business
- Find/Sell Oil & Gas

Non-Core & Non Critical
- Tree Trimming
- Cafeteria
- Laundry

Source: Adapted from Dole, R. (1998), *Business Process Outsourcing: A Case Study*, KPMG Peat Marwick LLP.

it against an influx of imitators); and (3) The core competencies should never be outsourced (Arnold 2000). To hand over core functions to a third-party supplier is to hand over the things that make a company what it is and what differentiates it from others, in essence what makes the company profits.

Non-core competencies take up time, energy and workspace, and help management to lose sight of what is most important in the organisation (Greaver 1999). Non-core activities can be farmed out to specialists if they conduct them better, more cheaply or both.

Nowadays there are two main types of outsourcing: total outsourcing and selective outsourcing. *Total outsourcing* happens when companies outsource all the activities within the selected function or service of the company. *Selective outsourcing* on the other hand can be done in four separate and distinct ways. The first is outsourcing on the individual level. It involves moving specific positions out of the organisation, for example the management of a poorly performing function or service. The second type is outsourcing on the functional level. The next type of selective outsourcing is the process level. The final level is outsourcing on the component level, which involves outsourcing the manufacture of component parts or sub-assemblies.

Other types of outsourcing that are used, though not as widely as total outsourcing and selective outsourcing, include *co-sourcing*, whereby the client company keeps responsibility for the management and strategic aspects of the outsourced activity while the outsourced supplier provides a consultancy service and often experienced personnel to help to keep the business streamlined.

Another is *insourcing*. Insourcing is the outsourcing of some work to other countries but, instead of transferring all the responsibility, the company sets up, staffs and runs the business except with much lower costs (King 2003; Arnold 2000). This can help to overcome the problems of skill shortage, particularly in the areas of project management and technical work. A major advantage of the insourcing option is that, because the suppliers are inside the organisation, they are living with their clients and because they are, for example, attending in-house meetings they understand the business, thus allowing the company to retain critical business knowledge and intellectual capital. KPMG (2004) claim that 41 per cent of information technology outsourcing (ITO) users intend to insource some components of their IT systems because they fear a loss of control.

Examples of Outsourced Services/Functions

Logistics Outsourcing

Logistics is the process for the efficient and timely flow of goods, services, and information from the point of origin to the point of consumption. (Candler 1994)

Logistics outsourcing has become really important in the supply chain in the past twenty years as it was traditionally handled by firms internally as a support function. At that time logistics activities such as warehousing, distribution, transportation, and inventory management had been given low priority compared with the other business functions within the organisation. However, since the customer has become more demanding, the logistics function has now become a source of competitive advantage (see Table 9.1),

Table 9.1: Types of Logistics Services that can be Outsourced

Warehousing	Outbound Transportation	Freight Bill Auditing/Payment	Inbound Transportation
Freight Consolidation/ Distribution	Cross-Docking	Product Marking/Labeling/ Packaging	Selected Manufacturing Activities
Product Returns and Repair	Inventory Management	Traffic Management/ Fleet Operation	IT
Product Assembly/ Installation	Order Fulfilment	Order Entry/Order Processing	Customer Service

Source: Cap Gemini Ernst & Young (2001), *Third Party Logistics Study – Results and Findings of the 2001 Sixth Annual Study*, <http://www.tli.gatech.edu/downloads/3PLStudy_2001.pdf>.

and there has been a growing emphasis on providing good customer service (Razzaque and Sheng 1998).

According to Wilding and Juriado (2004), about 40 per cent of global logistics is outsourced. According to Razzaque and Sheng (1998), the management of the logistics function in modern organisations involves decision-making for the complete distribution of goods and services with a view to maximising value and minimising cost. What has become apparent is that competitive advantage now comes as much from the delivery process as from the product being delivered (Razzaque and Sheng 1998), which has transformed logistics from a traditional back-room function to a front-office function. Consistent service at appropriate levels is necessary for a well-run and well-designed logistics system.

However, for an organisation to handle its logistics activities effectively and efficiently, it must consider the following:

1. Can it provide the service in-house?
2. Can it outsource the function?
3. Can it set up a subsidiary by buying a logistics firm which will provide its logistics function?

IT Outsourcing

In the late 1980s and early 1990s senior executives sought ways to use outsourcing as a way to control and shape IT costs in conjunction with changing business requirements (Currie 2000). The 1990s witnessed the growth and maturing of the IT outsourcing market.

Electronics Outsourcing

Electronic manufacturing comprises the process of 'design, development, fabrication, assembly, and testing of electronics parts, tools, technology, components, and systems' (Mason *et al.* 2002). The evolution of electronics manufacturing started with the development of new and better technologies to produce smaller and more reliable electronic components at a much lower cost than previously. But, at the same time, the manufacturing process has become more complex and costly than ever before. As a result, there is now a very high cost of entry into the market, which has caused many start-up electronics manufacturers to outsource.

The effective management of this supply chain is important due to the existence of short product life-cycles and the resulting cyclical demand. The outsourcing of electronics typically results in significant reductions in costs and production time. Some of the major players in electronics contract manufacturing today include Celestica and Flextronics (Mason *et al.* 2002).

Business Process Outsourcing (BPO)

> [BPO is] the delegation of one or more IT intensive business processes to an external provider that owns, administers, and manages the selected processes based on defined and measurable performance metrics. (Dole 1998)

A unique characteristic of BPO is that it operates in conjunction with other activities and, as global economic transformations force both public and private sectors to identify, protect, and grow their core competencies, BPO is emerging as a viable and even critical part of these organisations.

Dole (1998) suggests that BPO is growing for seven main reasons:

1. An awareness of outsourcing solutions.
2. Technological and organisational imperatives.
3. Acceleration of change.
4. Global competition.
5. Mounting price/cost pressures across organisations.
6. Focus on the customer.
7. Increasing customer expectations.

Transportation Outsourcing

Transportation outsourcing is a function of logistics outsourcing, but is important in its own right, and that is why it is being explained separately. According to Logan (2000), transportation is one of outsourcing's biggest players, and one of the major challenges faced by transportation outsourcing providers is the establishment of trust and confidence.

The switch to outsourcing of transportation was fuelled by two environmental elements:

1. *Deregulation of the trucking industry*: This allowed competition to drive costs down and transportation specialisation upwards. This market forced companies to be more efficient and effective.
2. *The use of technology* (changing technology): This, including the use of global positioning systems (GPS) and optimised logistics programmes, allowed logistics providers to offer highly technical services that would be too costly for a single company to offer in-house (Logan 2000).

Perspectives on Supply Chain Management and Logistics

Reasons for Outsourcing

Across the academic literature five recurring categories can be identified for companies deciding to outsource (see Figure 9.3). But it should be noted that none of the categories are mutually exclusive.

It appears that the main reason that companies outsource is financial. According to Clinton (2004), 90 per cent of organisations say that cost saving is the primary reason to outsource. Stakeholders are increasingly demanding cost-effective business practices to improve productivity and profitability. Tyson (2004) claims that service costs can fall by a dramatic 50–60 per cent; Farrell (2004), the head of research in the McKinsey Global Institute, claims that by reorganising production intelligently, multinational organisations can hope to lower their costs by as much as 50–70 per cent. In short, outsourcing is 'an easy way to achieve more functionality for less money, with less aggression' (Perkins 2003).

In addition, companies outsource to reduce the cost pressures caused by shrinking budgets within their organisations and to improve the cost control structure (Dole 1998). Companies can also outsource to reduce their investments in expensive technology, warehousing, trucks and other equipment, leaving them with a better-looking profit-and-loss account that does not have to take into account depreciation or the cost of maintenance of the equipment. An example of this would be outsourcing the logistics function within the organisation. If the company does not have to invest heavily in equipment, labour and software, then they save on logistics costs provided the

Figure 9.3: Reasons to Outsource

initiative is constructed correctly. Cost reduction can also come as a result of superior supplier performance and the provider's lower cost structure – the provider can do this by doing things faster and more efficiently.

Secondly, the service category gives the company even more reasons to outsource. The simplest reasons are: (1) staff may not be able to provide adequate service; (2) the service/function cannot be provided in-house; or (3) a lack of specific knowledge required for the service or function that is being outsourced (Razzaque and Sheng 1998). Also, the more specialised the business, the more likely it is that the expertise required can be found only outside the organisation rather than inside it. Another reason which has been widely mentioned in the literature is that it can help companies to improve process discipline and service, but to make it successful one must benchmark beforehand (e.g. Wilding and Juriado 2004).

Outsourcing to improve agility within the organisation is the third category. In today's fast-changing environment, there is a premium on knowledge and the competition is getting greater. Components and services can now be more efficiently and economically sourced outside the organisation. Outsourcing can also allow companies to add capacity and to better utilise their employees, gain world-class expertise in all the areas that deliver value, reliability, speed and innovation, which can support an organisation's international expansion if required. It can improve the business focus of meeting customers' needs by concentrating on the broader business issues while having operational issues assumed by outside experts. Outsourcing can also allow companies to become more flexible (Wilding and Juriado 2004), more dynamic and better able to meet changing opportunities and to redirect resources to meet more strategic activities that provide a greater return by serving the customer, and using these to allow companies to respond faster to competitive pressures. Furthermore, outsourcing allows companies to become more agile and to deal with situations more easily as they occur.

Many of the organisational reasons in the fourth category have already been mentioned within the previous three categories. Outsourcing can be used to improve and strengthen relationships and to gain technologies and economies of scale that may not be attainable within the organisation. Improving relationships allows organisations the opportunity to give more responsibility and trust to the outsource supplier, thus creating more time in the organisation and improving performance. Furthermore, the reasons for outsourcing could be based on factory capacity or constraints during high seasonal demand, unforeseen changes in demand and/or the proprietary nature of the products to be manufactured (Mason et al. 2002).

The fifth category – technology – is summed up by Brown and Browning (2003) in their claim that outsourcing is to 'ensure that critical technology service delivery is achieved and can grow over time without directly investing in costly skills, hardware and software'. Moreover, it can help organisations to access higher levels of functional technology and business process expertise, and can help companies when they decide to upgrade their IT systems. What is more, according to (Dole 1998) they can help to step up internal demand for 'more robust technologies and solutions to better enable customer services'.

Drivers of Outsourcing

Drivers for outsourcing are in some ways similar but are in most ways quite different from the reasons companies decide to outsource. Drivers are the factors within the organisation (internal) or factors outside the organisation (external) that dictate if a company should outsource or not.

Chohan (2004) claims that the organisational drivers for outsourcing are to benefit from: (1) greater financial resources; (2) greater technological resources; and (3) increased economies of scale. Cohen (2003) suggests that the key drivers are the economic downturn and the climate of uncertainty that surrounds us, and claims that these are forcing organisations to move towards outsourcing to reduce costs and improve efficiencies.

The trends in outsourcing depend on the type of organisation one is in. It has been influenced by management techniques such as business process re-engineering (BPR) and the theory of core competence which claims that organisations are only able to perform a certain number of 'core' activities. In medium- to large-sized organisations the trend is to outsource entire processes, and according to Greaver (1999), in large diversified organisations, the trend is to outsource global functions and processes to large providers with a stronger global presence and expertise. This is in comparison to small- and medium-sized organisations (SMEs) which tend to outsource individual activities.

The digital revolution which included the introduction of the Internet and Broadband, accompanied by the falling costs of transport and telecommunication, all played a part in opening up the global economy and in the growth of outsourcing.

At the beginning of the 1990s, the market for outsourcing was developing at a very fast pace but it was still immature. This was the time when many organisations were considering or entering into a significant degree of outsourcing for the first time. Incognito (1995) claims that the growth of outsourcing in the early 1990s equalled that of the previous fifteen years. The outsourcing market has grown rapidly since the early 1990s; however, 'experts' cannot agree on what the actual overall growth of outsourcing has been (see Table 9.2):

Table 9.2: Outsourcing Spending (in billions of dollars)

(a)	$	(b)	$
1994	49.5 bn	1996	41 bn
1999	70 bn	2001	107 bn
2000	121 bn		

Source: (a) Sanders, J. (1999), *Outsourcing in Action*, The Institute of Chartered Accountants in England and Wales, London: Chartech Books, and (b) Oates, D. (1998), *Outsourcing and Virtual Organisation – The Incredible Shrinking Company*, London: Century Business.

Greaver (1999) argues that the outsourcing market is expected to grow at double digits until 2009. This was backed up by a Fortune 500 chief executive officer (CEO) survey carried out in 1996 where 94 per cent of the companies surveyed said they would outsource and 86 per cent of them expected to outsource additional processes up until 2004. Sanders (1999) also estimated that outsourcing would grow by more than 15 per cent per annum until the end of 2009.

Who is involved in outsourcing? According to Clinton (2004), nine out of ten of the largest firms in New York are predicted to perform IT or business process work offshore. In addition, according to Barthelemy (2003), 34 per cent of firms outsourced all or part of their IT in 1997. This proportion of firms is expected to reach 58 per cent by 2010. Similar increases are expected for activities such as telecommunications, accounting and human resources. How does this amount of outsourcing affect the numbers of employees displaced by it? According to Garten (2004), this is one to two million workers in the USA (a tiny percentage of the 140 million workforce). However, it is predicted that another three to five million more jobs will be transferred within the next five to ten years (Garten 2004).

RISKS WITH OUTSOURCING

According to Greaver (1999), risks can be categorised into three main categories (see Figure 9.4): risks inherent in any project; general risks inherent in any outsourcing project; and specific risks.

Category 1: *Risks Inherent in Any Project*

These include lack of management commitment, employees reacting negatively to the initiative, employees resistant to change, intellectual property

Figure 9.4: Categories of Risk

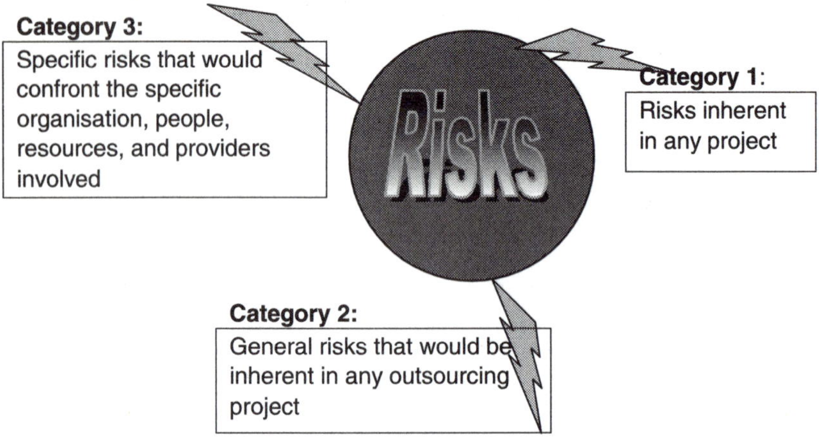

Category 3:
Specific risks that would confront the specific organisation, people, resources, and providers involved

Category 1:
Risks inherent in any project

Category 2:
General risks that would be inherent in any outsourcing project

Source: Greaver II, M.F. (1999), *Strategic Outsourcing – A Structured Approach to Outsourcing Decisions and Initiatives*, New York: Amacom.

rights (IPR), breach of confidentiality, and security problems (see, for example, Greaver 1999; Croom *et al.* 2000).

Category 2: General Risks that Would be Present in Most Outsourcing Projects

These concern the management team and the scope of the project. It is vitally important that the project managers and members are chosen appropriately so that the project team has the necessary skills and expertise required to fulfil its roles.

Category 3: Specific Risks that Would Confront the Specific Organisation, People, Resources and Providers Involved

The main problem is that outsourcing affects the whole company and the main risk is that, if the initiative is not part of the overall company strategy, and resources required are not available, this would lead to insufficient support when problems arise. It can lead to a weak project which may ultimately fail.

Some of the main risks that vendors and outsourcers worry about can be seen in Figure 9.5.

However, Logan (2000) proposes that a company can mitigate much of the risk by encouraging performance to be measured by behaviour-based measures and by developing controls for each risk.

Figure 9.5: Perceived Risks by Participants

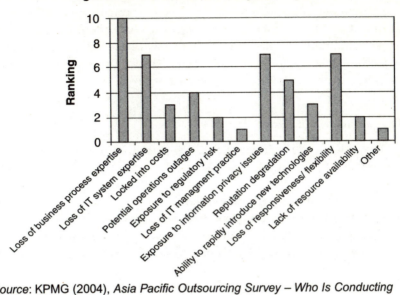

Source: KPMG (2004), *Asia Pacific Outsourcing Survey – Who Is Conducting the Orchestra?* <http://www.kpmg.fi/Binary.aspx?Section=174&Item=1552>, November.

Concluding Comments

What's the Bad News?

It is unfortunate that outsourcing has come to be regarded as a kind of panacea or 'magic solution' in some organisations. Several examples of failure with which the authors are familiar have resulted directly from this approach. The move towards outsourcing of labour-intensive manufacturing activities, with a view to gaining access to relatively low labour cost production, is a particular case in point. Such moves have frequently failed to achieve anything close to the expected (or, indeed, potential) benefits. In some extreme cases it has directly contributed to corporate collapse. As Greaver (1999) very aptly put it: 'Like marriage, outsourcing is much easier to consummate (improperly) than it is to terminate, and recover from, if done poorly.'

So What's the Good News?

The good news is that many companies have derived significant benefits from the outsourcing of various supply chain activities. This is true in traditional industries such as clothing and textiles, as well as in hi-tech sectors such as electronics. In some cases, companies can attribute their very survival to successful outsourcing. As pointed out earlier, outsourcing and the development of effective collaborative arrangements have the potential to contribute significantly to value-adding potential. In the oft-quoted words of Dr. Joachim Milberg, former Chairman of BMW: 'Those who work alone can only accumulate, but those who collaborate intelligently can multiply.'

What are the Key Lessons?

The key lessons are that the potential benefits of outsourcing can only be achieved if:

1. It is not regarded as a 'magic solution'.
2. It is implemented as an integral part of supply chain design.
3. All analysis, planning and implementation is carried out logically and systematically, with proper attention to detail.

An overview of a methodological approach to tackling outsourcing projects is contained in the Appendix to this chapter. In short, outsourcing cannot be carried out in a vacuum — rather, it needs to be a part of an overall integrated approach to SCM.

REFERENCES

Arnold, U. (2000), 'New Dimensions of Outsourcing: A Combination of Transaction Cost Economies and the Core Competencies Concept', *European Journal of Purchasing and Supply Management*, 6(1), 23–29.

Barthelemy, J. (2003), 'The Seven Deadly Sins of Outsourcing', *Academy of Management Executive*, 17(2), 87–100.

Brown, R.H. and Browning, J.A. (2003), *SMBs: The Biggest Little Outsourcing Market in the World*, Stamford CT: Gartner Research Group.

Candler, J. (1994), 'You Make it, they Distribute it', *Nation's Business*, 82(3), 46–48.

Cap Gemini Ernst and Young (2001), *Third Party Logistics Study – Results and Findings of the 2001 Sixth Annual Study*, available at: <http://www.tli.gatech.edu/downloads/3PLStudy_2001.pdf>, accessed April 2007.

Clinton, H. R. (2004), ' "Bestshoring" Beats Outsourcing', 1 August, available at: <http://www.opinionjournal.com/extra/?id=110005429>, accessed April 2007.

Chohan, S. (2004), 'GECIS Spinoff could Redraw the Global Outsourcing Map', Stamford, CT: Gartner Research Group.

Cohen, L.R. (2003), 'How to Get and Sustain an Outsourcing Deal', Stamford CT: Gartner Research Group.

Connolly, K., Sullivan, E., Brennan, L. and Murray, J. (2004), 'International Supply Chain Management: A Walk Around the Elephant', *Irish Journal of Management*, 26(1), 149–162.

Croom, S., Romano P. and Giannakis, M. (2000), 'Supply Chain Management: An Analytical Framework for Critical Literature Review', *European Journal of Purchasing and Supply Management*, 6(2), 125–141.

Currie, W. (2000), 'The Supply Side of IT Outsourcing: The Trend towards Mergers, Acquisitions and Joint Ventures', *International Journal of Physical Distribution and Logistics Management*, 30(3–4), 238–254.

Dole, R., Switzer, J and KPMG Peat Marwick LLP (1998), *A Case Study Guide to Business Process Outsourcing*.

Economist, The (2004), 'The Luck of the Irish', 14 October, available at: <http://www.economist.com/surveys/displaystory.cfm?story_id=E1_PNGTDST>, accessed April 2007.

Farrell, D. (2004), 'Can Germany Win from Offshoring?', *The McKinsey Quarterly*, No. 4, McKinsey Global Institute, available at: <http://www.mckinseyquarterly>, accessed April 2007.

Garten, J. E. (2004), 'Offshoring: You Ain't Seen Nothin' Yet', *Business Week*, 21 June.

Greaver II, M.F. (1999), *Strategic Outsourcing – A Structured Approach to Outsourcing Decisions and Initiatives*, New York: Amacom.

Incognito, J.F. (1995), 'The 10 Most Powerful Words in Outsourcing', Sunnyvale CA: WHL Architects Planners Inc., available at: <http://www.whlarchitects.com/articles/feature7.html>, accessed April 2007.

King, J. (2003), 'The Best of Both Shores: Slashing labor costs while retaining control over IT staff and project quality is at the heart of offshore insourcing', *ComputerWorld*, 21 April.

KPMG (2004), *Asia Pacific Outsourcing Survey – Who is Conducting the Orchestra?'* available at: <http://www.kpmg.fi/Binary.aspx?Section=174&Item=1552>, accessed April 2007.

Logan, M.S. (2000), 'Using Agency Theory to Design Successful Outsourcing Relationships', *International Journal of Logistics Management*, 11(2), 21–32.

Mason, S.J. et al. (2002), 'Improving Electronics Manufacturing Supply Chain Agility through Outsourcing', *International Journal of Physical Distribution and Logistics Management*, 32(7), 610–620.

Oates, D. (1998), *Outsourcing and Virtual Organisation – The Incredible Shrinking Company*, London: Century Business Books.

Perkins, B. (2003), 'Look Before you Leap to Outsource', *ComputerWorld*, 10 March.

Razzaque, M.A. and Sheng, C.C. (1998), 'Outsourcing of Logistics Functions: A Literature Survey', *Journal of Physical Distribution and Logistics Management*, 28(2), 89–107.

Sanders, J. (1999), *Outsourcing in Action*, The Institute of Chartered Accountants in England and Wales (ICAEW), London: Chartech Books.

Tyson, L.D. (2004), 'Offshoring: The pros and cons for Europe', *Business Week*, 6 December.

Wilding, R. and Juriado, R. (2004), 'Customer Perceptions on Logistics Outsourcing in the European Consumer Goods Industry', *International Journal of Physical Distribution and Logistics Management*, 34(8), 628–644.

Zineldin, M. and Bredenlow, T. (2003), 'Strategic Alliance: Synergies and Challenges – A Case of Strategic Outsourcing Relationship "Sour"', *International Journal of Physical Distribution and Logistics Management*, 33(5), 449–464.

APPENDIX: A METHODOLOGICAL APPROACH TO OUTSOURCING

Introduction

Outsourcing of various elements of supply chain functionality has sharpened the focus or the need for methodological approaches to the planning and implementation of effective outsourcing. This appendix provides an overview of such an approach, developed by the authors.

Overview and Rationale

This approach is based on answering three key questions:

- To outsource or not to outsource (that is *the* question!)?
- Outsource to whom?
- How are relationships managed and performance improved?

Answering each of these questions invariably involves consideration of a range of quite often interdependent variables and is, therefore, quite a complex process. The following sections provide some guidance in terms of the main issues that need to be addressed and the steps that should usually be followed.

To Outsource or Not to Outsource?

The approach adopted will depend on whether one is dealing with the decision-making at a strategic level or at a more tactical or operational level. What follows is based largely on the former, which usually involves a quite fundamental assessment of the nature of the business:

- Identification of core competencies.
- Identification of 'non-core' activities.
- Assessment of potential benefits of outsourcing.
- Assessment of risks associated with outsourcing.
- Identification of potential activities for outsourcing.
- Prioritisation of these activities.

Outsource to Whom?

- Detailed definition of requirements.
- Development of Request for Quotation (RfQ) or equivalent.
- Identification of possible suppliers/partners.
- Selection of preferred supplier(s)/partner(s).

The latter stage in turn typically involves the following steps:

- Establishment of short-listing criteria.
- Short-listing of potential suppliers/partners.
- Establishment of more detailed assessment criteria.
- Detailed assessment of short-list.
- Selection of supplier(s)/partner(s).

The latter stage in turn typically involves the following steps:

- Assessment of *current performance* levels.
- *Financial assessment*.
- *Strategic assessment*.
- *Supply chain audit*.

Assessment of *current performance* involves analysing, wherever possible, current levels of quality (mainly in terms of product/service performance and functionality), cost (total landed cost rather than simply unit price) and customer service. However, it is not sufficient in itself that a candidate company currently performs well in these areas. It is also important that it can at least sustain, and preferably improve, its level of performance. The *financial assessment* ensures that a company is robust financially and, for example, will not become overly dependent on our business. The *strategic assessment*, which involves an objective critique of the company's strategic objectives and plans, is designed to ensure that a company has a viable future. Finally, the *supply chain audit* examines all aspects of the company's supply chain.[4]

How are Relationships Managed and Performance Improved?

As pointed out in this chapter, this is a complex and multi-dimensional activity. Ensuring that information flows are managed as effectively as possible is one important element. IT connectivity (part of the 'hard wiring') plays a potentially key role in terms of day-to-day operational management of the relationship. A properly formulated service level agreement (SLA) is also an important tool (see Chapter 7). Part of an SLA is the agreed performance standards and metrics. These are important as they provide the basis for continuous improvement. Finally, collaborative approaches to planning

---

[4]NITL has developed a separate checklist of the types of information which typically need to be collected as part of such an audit.

(e.g. collaborative planning, forecasting and replenishment or CPFR) and problem resolution can often provide a useful platform for improvement.

Conclusions

The approach outlined in this appendix provides the basis of a logical and systematic approach to the analysis, planning and execution of outsourcing opportunities. Furthermore, it helps to ensure that outsourcing is considered as part of an overall approach to integrated SCM. Finally, it should be remembered that every project is unique and that methodologies exist only to provide guidance. The detailed approach adopted in individual projects must be properly thought through. Never forget that 'the devil is in the detail.'

10

Procurement and Purchasing in the Supply Chain

MICHEAL O'FEARGHAIL

INTRODUCTION

The purchasing activity in firms is a critical one. Effective purchasing can contribute to profitability and competitiveness. All industries, and most firms, have seen a transition from reactive buying of materials and services to a more planned approach, and there is a bigger distinction now, between operational replenishment, strategic planning of procurement and the management of special purchases, than previously. Good purchasing decisions are founded on good information, and the primary questions remain: *What to buy*, *how much to buy*, *when* and *from whom*? The management of demand information and the building of good supplier relationships are, therefore, the cornerstones of well-managed purchasing functions.

It is in the management of supplier relationships that purchasing moves outside the boundary of the firm. These relationships are the 'weld' that holds the links in the supply chain together. In this context, then, we see a supply chain role for the purchasing function.

This chapter examines the nature and role of purchasing in the firm, and its role in relation to the management of the firm's place in the supply chain. It looks at how supply decisions need to be reviewed over the life of the product. It goes on to outline how the fundamental make/do or buy decision evolves into outsourcing, and how this concept and the emergence of world-class, turn-key, outsourced service providers have impacted on global supply chains.

DEFINING THE ROLE OF THE PURCHASING FUNCTION IN THE FIRM

The purchasing activity has existed as long as trade has existed. Purchasing has a role to play in all organisations, from service industries to manufacturing. Baily *et al.* (2005) still hold to their long-standing explanation of the role of the purchasing function as 'to acquire the right quality of material, at the right time, in the right quantity, from the right source at the right price'. They go on to acknowledge that this simple definition belies the complexity of the activity in the modern business environment and talk also of the importance of the continuity of supply, managing the flow of materials and the importance of relationships. These relate directly to *Fundamental One, Fundamental Three* and *Fundamental Four* of supply chain management (SCM), respectively, as discussed in Chapter 3.

Lysons and Farrington (2006) explain that a distinction can be made between the purchasing function and the purchasing department. The former is the activity related to the acquisition of materials and supplies, while the latter is an organisational unit. They also talk of purchasing as a process, a discipline and a profession, and refer to supply chain links and relationships. These writers and others explain how the role of purchasing in the manufacturing firm, particularly, has changed and evolved over the years, as industries have progressed from craft production, through mass production and onto lean production and world-class manufacturing. Womak *et al.* (1990) clearly show how Japanese firms, notably Toyota, have introduced new developments in supply management. Burt *et al.* (2003) acknowledge this and also list the emergence of electronic purchasing systems and a 'growing recognition of senior management of the critical role that must be played by purchasing', as factors that have greatly influenced the role that the purchasing function plays in the modern firm.

Purchasing's role had traditionally been a supportive one, the importance of which was determined by the objectives and strategies of the firm. Purchasing's role in manufacturing firms was seen as one of procuring materials as cheaply as possible to enable production to continue uninterrupted and to gain the benefit of economies of scale in the manufacturing process. Purchasing's role was to support manufacturing. The purchase of non-manufacturing and supply items is again seen as a support to the various functions of the firm. In service organisations purchasing may not be a core activity, but provides support for the other functions of the firm. When purchasing is viewed in this way – as a supporting role – it is evidence of insular thinking by the firm. Until recently, firms did tend to behave as separate island kingdoms, closing their borders and carefully guarding their information. Global competition has changed all that.

The new reality is that firms are no longer able to compete in the marketplace, one for one. Cooperation and collaboration with other firms is an absolute necessity. The supply chain concept is founded on this new-found belief. Each firm must align itself into a network of business partners that will each adopt the supply chain role for which they are best equipped, the one which provides the best match with their own core competencies (see Chapter 4). This new reality has had a number of profound consequences.

One such consequence is that the focus on core competencies has fragmented the manufacturing process: firms will now focus on the manufacture of specific components, on sub-assembly, or on final assembly. Some will concentrate on product development and outsource the manufacturing activities to specialist firms and manage the process from a distance. Very few firms will continue to keep the entire process in-house. Saunders (1997) observes that 'the bought-in content of products made by firms has been increasing, thus reducing the significance of internal operations.' In the new scheme of things, purchasing's traditional support role to manufacturing has changed.

Another consequence is that the new alliances and dependent linkages between firms need to be managed. Supplier relationships are sometimes difficult but they are now seen as an important element of the supply chain – as noted earlier, the 'weld' that holds the links in place. Purchasing professionals find themselves positioned at the boundary of the firm and acting as the custodians of these relationships as shown in Figure 10.1.

Lysons and Farrington (2006) contend that 'purchasing is increasingly ceasing to be a discrete function and becoming a group of activities within an integrated supply chain.'

Figure 10.1: Purchasing's Role in Supply Chain Relationship Management

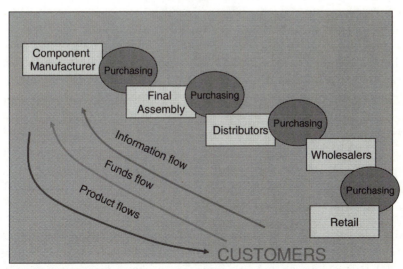

Purchasing, Procurement and Supply Management

Purchasing and procurement are terms that are used interchangeably by many. A distinction can be made in that there are more ways of procuring an item than purchasing it. Purchasing an item involves taking ownership of it. Lysons and Farrington (2006) define procurement as 'the process of obtaining goods or services in any way, including borrowing, leasing and even force'. (We should, however, confine the definition, in relation to commercial activities, to procurement by legal means!) Procurement can also cover joint venture approaches to manufacturing and customer service, and outsourcing. There is now a marked reluctance in firms to 'own' anything. In particular, there is a move to delay taking ownership of materials until the latest possible time. Just-in-time (JIT) manufacturers arrange daily deliveries from their suppliers, and only take ownership when the component arrives on the production line or even, in many cases, delay taking ownership until the finished product containing the component is shipped. The title is passed immediately to the customer, the manufacturer only owning the component momentarily.

Against this background, *purchasing* hardly seems the appropriate word to use. *Procurement* may be used and *supply management* is becoming more popular as it better describes the activity. As far back as 1993, Lamming suggested that *external resource managers* was a term that purchasing managers might adopt.

The external resource is to be found at the supplier's plant or in the service they provide. Managing the external resource *de facto* means managing the supplier. Lysons and Farrington (2006) define this activity as 'that aspect of purchasing or procurement concerned with rationalising the supply base and selecting, coordinating and appraising the performance of and developing the potential of suppliers and, where appropriate, building long-term collaborative relationships'. It can be seen then that, today, finding and developing the 'right source' emerges as the primary objective and incorporates the other 'rights' of price and quality. Timing and quantity decisions are nowadays mostly automated and receive little management attention.

Once appropriate suppliers have been sourced the focus is on sharing information so that the production and distribution activities of both (i.e. the supplying and buying firms) can be synchronised. In the supply chain context, this backward flow of information starts at the retail outlet, where sales data is collected electronically at the point of sale, and transmitted electronically to the immediate upstream supplier, often in real-time. As noted in Chapter 3, this is a key element of the efficient consumer response (ECR) strategy in the grocery business, and the quick response (QR) approach in the clothing industry. Suppliers then schedule production and arrange delivery accordingly, and share their schedules with their own suppliers. In such cases, the buying firm's inventory status and production schedules are made visible to the supplier, who then takes on the responsibility for initiating the flow of materials.

STRATEGIC PROCUREMENT MANAGEMENT

According to Dobler and Burt (1996), 'strategic procurement planning is concerned with the development of a firm's plans for its long-term material requirements, as contrasted with its plans for foreseeable, near-term requirements.' They further explain that strategic planning focuses management's attention on long-term competitiveness and profitability, rather than on short-term bottom-line considerations.

Cox (1996) explains that the process is one which requires that external sourcing and supply is linked at all times with the internal strategic goals of the organisation, and it cannot operate independently of the other functions of the organisation. He outlines a four-step approach to its implementation – value chain positioning, business reorganisation, supply management evaluation and feedback – of which value chain (or supply chain) positioning is the first, and arguably the most important. This refers to the firm deciding on its role and its position within the supply chain, as well as its resulting strategies aimed at extracting the best value from its adoption. The concept of core competencies is closely linked.

Saunders (1997) looks at all aspects of supply chain from a strategic point of view and again stresses the management of external resources as an important aspect of the discipline. He also notes the need to separate activities from functions and the importance of relationships and strategic issues relating to quality, material flow and human resources in the supply chain.

In 1991, Heinritz *et al.* suggested that the emphasis on strategic planning for materials appeared to be driven primarily by pragmatic considerations tied to the stability of the markets for a given basic material. They contended that when markets are unstable, major buying organisations assess the environment more carefully and develop longer range plans that assure the availability and affordability of the materials in question. This is undoubtedly true but their view that, as markets become more stable, the need for such planning becomes less imperative, meaning less strategic planning is carried out, needs closer scrutiny. They believed that as firms moved into the 1990s most major markets would be relatively stable, and that less strategic planning for materials would be done by major manufacturing organisations. This is now shown not to be the case. Markets have not become more stable and are not likely to. The need for strategic procurement planning is more imperative than ever. However firms will continue to attempt to bring stability to their own supply chains by building better relationships with their supply chain partners, improving information flows and structuring as much of the decision-making as is possible.

A number of issues in the past decade (for example the millennium bug fear, international terrorist activities, rising oil prices and certain disruptive natural disasters) have diverted the supply chain community's attention from efficiency to the vulnerability of the new, leaner supply chains. Currently the debate (amongst academics, notably Christopher *et al.* (2002) and Juttner *et al.* (2003)) seems to have shifted away from the matter of inventory and cycle time reduction – areas in which huge strides have already been made – to the issue of supply chain vulnerability. Consequently, strategic purchasing now includes contingency and recovery planning, and risk management.

INTEGRATING SUPPLY MANAGEMENT AND PRODUCT LIFE-CYCLE MANAGEMENT

The Role of Purchasing in New Product Introduction

If the supply chain's *raison d'etre* is to provide consumer satisfaction through the concerted effort of constituent firms, perhaps the most important activity is the conception, development and introduction of new products. The new product development (NPD) process can be considered to be the start of all supply chain activities. It is during this stage that the supply chain is designed, in tandem with the design of the product, and alliances are forged. Dobler and Burt (1996) have advised that 80 per cent of the product's cost is committed at the design stage (i.e. when the specification is fixed the cost is 80 per cent fixed) and that, subsequent to this, the best efforts of the purchasing function can do little to impact the product's cost. There is a clear recognition that the purchasing function's work must start at this stage.

As noted in the Preface to this book, in the past product development was conducted serially, each relevant function doing their bit and passing the project over the fence to the next function. All too often, it came back again for modification. The NPD process is now seen as a multi-disciplinary process in which the necessary activities progress concurrently. This has the advantage of shortening the time-to-market cycle. Though occurring simultaneously, the process can be seen to follow a number of stages and purchasing can contribute in many practical ways. Purchasing – and key suppliers – will typically only become involved when there is a clearly defined product concept, although sometimes earlier than this.

Purchasing's role in relation to NPD has increased in importance due to the increased levels of outsourcing and a greater need to control and influence external manufacturing operations and the imperative that new products get into markets faster. Also, the more recent focus on SCM points to a greater need to integrate the different links in the chain to ensure faster information flows and shorter lead times.

The purchasing function's contribution can be of a very practical nature as follows:

1. Purchasing can provide a window to new components which suppliers have developed and which might cause marketing/engineering to identify new product possibilities.
2. Purchasing can provide information and contact with potential 'partners' and introduce suppliers to the NPD process.
3. Purchasing can provide information on cost, performance, availability, quality and reliability of components that may be used.
4. Purchasing can assist in the make or buy decision.
5. Purchasing can have suppliers and systems in place prior to production.
6. Above all, purchasing can promote such cost-saving ideas as standardisation, fitness-for-purpose and value addition.

According to Saunders (1997) 'there is a growing recognition of the increasing importance of the value-added to products by suppliers as companies continue to pursue policies of concentrating on core manufacturing processes.' The importance of getting existing and potential suppliers involved in the process is critical.

Following on from NPD is NPI (new product introduction). However, these two might often occur at different locations. For example, in the case of the many multinational corporations manufacturing in Ireland, it is often the case that the product development activity is performed elsewhere and yet the new product needs to be introduced to the manufacturing operation based in Ireland, and perhaps ultimately introduced to the market from there. The involvement of supply management is critical to this activity. This may mean establishing or developing local sources of supply, booking capacity with suppliers and arranging delivery schedules. In JIT manufacturing it will extend to working closely with production engineers on materials handling systems, factory layout and supplier communication systems. It will invariably mean integrating a firm's scheduling systems with those of the supplier.

The Role of Purchasing throughout the Product Life-Cycle

Once the product is launched and in the marketplace, managing the supply side of that product and its components is essential (see Figure 10.2). This is not a time for complacency. Demand for products and consequently volumes changes over time. In line with the classical product life-cycle, the following pattern typically exists: *introduction, growth, maturity* and *decline* stages. Many decisions made at the early stages of a product's life concerning suppliers, manufacturing methods, logistics and so on, need to be reviewed as volumes change.

In the early stages if volumes are low, products may be manufactured in batches. Certainly, in relation to bought-in components, this is likely to be the case at the supplier's plant. As volumes increase, JIT might be favoured, and also the likelihood is that mass production of components might be a more viable option. For example, components that were machined in the early part of the product's life-cycle might be die-cast when volumes increase. If different production methods are to be considered, then different suppliers might also be required. Expansion into different geographical locations might necessitate local sourcing in those markets.

Existing supply strategies need to be reviewed over time, for example whether a component is single-sourced or whether competition between suppliers is to be encouraged. Supplier performance may vary and new suppliers brought in. Quality may need to be improved; changes to the

Figure 10.2: Purchasing's Role Throughout the Product Life-Cycle

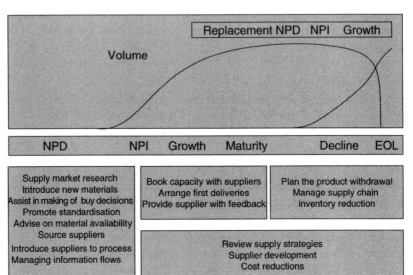

product design (e.g. additional features) will ensure that the purchasing function's relationship with the product will continue throughout the product's life.

Purchasing's Role at the End of the Product Life-Cycle

Careful management of supply at the end of a product's life is critically important, not only to the firm but also to the entire supply chain. The purchasing function typically takes a lead role in this.

When the product is in the mature phase, with demand steady, supply lines established and most decision-making structured and routine, a sort of complacency may set in. The early stages of decline may not be seen as such, and ignored. As the decline speeds up, the unwary firm may suddenly find itself with more stock than it needs. The situation is usually much worse for the supplier (or the supplier's supplier) who will have even less visibility of the impending end of a product lifecycle. The result of this complacency will often be obsolete stocks throughout the supply chain.

Progressive firms now manage the end of the product's life as carefully as they do its introduction, and will typically adopt the same team-based, concurrent approach, involving the same players, including the purchasing function and key suppliers.

PURCHASING AND LOGISTICS

The firm's inbound supply chain involves, for each item purchased, the supplier, the carrier and the user within the firm. The task of coordinating the information and product flows through this supply chain typically falls on the supply management function.

Grant *et al.* (2006) define logistics as 'that part of SCM that plans, implements and controls the efficient, effective forward and reverse flow and storage of goods, services and related information between the point of origin and the point of consumption, in order to meet customers, requirements'. In this context, transport and distribution, and warehousing are all elements of logistics.[1]

In the past, transport inwards (collections from suppliers) and transport outwards (to customers) were typically managed as distinct and separate activities and firms tended to own their own transport fleet, often in addition to hiring carriers. Responsibility for inbound transport often rested with the purchasing function, and outbound with the sales function. In the day-to-day

---

[1] For a more detailed discussion of the role of logistics in SCM, see Part C of Chapter 3.

routine of dealing with the detail – and because of the disjointed nature of the activity – the 'big picture' was often lost and there was little time spent on the strategic planning aspect. The integration of inbound and outbound transportation, under one logistics manager, has had many benefits (for example the hiring of carriers is done centrally, allowing better rates to be negotiated). The requirements of purchasing, manufacturing and sales are dealt with centrally also, avoiding inefficiencies. Greater focus can be placed on cycle times and the flow of materials into, through and out of the firm (i.e. on the 'big picture') in line with *Fundamental Two* of SCM (see Chapter 3).

Following the move from 'Transport Management' to 'Logistics Management' in the firm, the total cost of logistics becomes more apparent. With increased global competition, it has become a critical issue. These forces and deregulation of the transport industry combined to create greater competition between inter-modal and intra-modal carriers. The cost of hired transport has come down and, when compared with the cost of owning and managing their own fleet, most companies now choose to engage the services of an outside carrier. With the greater volume of business, and a higher level of competition between carriers, the transport industry response has been the emergence of the one-stop logistics company – the third-party logistics (3PL) service provider.

Consequently, the logistics function in very many firms is now outsourced. The important result, for purchasing professionals, is that an appropriate logistics provider needs to be sourced and integrated into the firm, and the ongoing relationship managed. The Appendix to this chapter provides some guidelines on the selection and management of 3PLs. It will be clear by now that, as more and more activities are outsourced, the supply chain role of the purchasing function expands.

Purchasing and the Management of the Financial Supply Chain

Traditionally, the flow of supply chain finance has been disjointed and not assisted by the involvement of a number of different functions in the firm. Contracts, including terms of trade and price, are agreed by the purchasing function, but payment is only made when the matching process is complete. This process may involve confirmation of receipt of the goods by the stores function (possibly under the control of production), inspection by quality control personnel, and completion of the paperwork by the finance department. Payment may be further delayed by cash flow considerations. This scenario is not conducive to good supplier relations and efficient SCM.

As more and more firms get in tune with the requirements of world-class manufacturing, and with the move towards the adoption of JIT and lean production principles, the flow of finance is (slowly) receiving attention (see Chapter 5). The speed of that flow could be described as the 'grease' that keeps the supply chain in good working order.

As noted in Chapter 3, SCM involves the management of the forward flow of material and the backward flow of demand information and funds. The forward flow of material is speeded up by automatic replenishment systems (such as QR, ECR) and continuous replenishment (CR) programmes at retail level and by JIT in manufacturing. The flow of information is aided by Internet technology and real-time communications (see Chapter 12). The circle is completed by the automatic transfer of funds, triggered by receipt of the material (or increasingly on dispatch of the products containing the material) from the manufacturing firm.

The responsibility for any of the critical flows (materials, information and funds) cannot be divided between different functions without creating the potential for disruptions. In practice, this responsibility increasingly rests with the supply management function.

Outsourcing, De-capitalisation and the Virtual Corporation

The concept of core competencies and the reluctance of firms to take ownership of materials and resources has already been noted. The focus has switched to managing the forward flow of product through supply chains, with title only changing to facilitate the backward flow of funds. The close management of the flow of product, information and funds is made possible by the recent advances in information and communications technology (ICT), often in the guise of e-business (see Chapter 14), with its myriad of applications and possibilities.

Lysons and Farrington (2005) define outsourcing[2] as 'a management strategy by which major non-core functions are transferred to specialist, efficient external providers'. Outsourcing arises when a firm takes a decision that a certain activity can be handled more efficiently and more effectively by a third party. Outsourcing differs from sub-contracting in that, in the latter situation, the firm retains control over the management of the activity, often supplying detailed specifications and materials to the sub-contractor and monitoring quality closely. When an activity is outsourced, the firm stands back from it completely, in recognition of the reality that the outsourced provider is, in fact, more expert than themselves at the task.

---

[2]Chapter 9 discusses outsourcing in more detail.

Figure 10.3: Traditional Asset-Based Model versus New De-capitalised Model

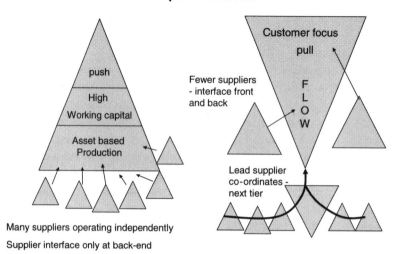

Source: Means, G. and Schneider, D. (2000), *Meta-Capitalism*. © 2000 John Wiley & Sons, Inc. Reprinted with permission of John Wiley & Sons, Inc.

Many commentators will suggest that there are functions that should not be outsourced. Even so, recent trends and the emergence of, for example, the so-called fourth-party logistics (4PL) providers who take on the management and integration of the outsourced functions, point to the new reality that innovative corporations are outsourcing almost all functions and are concentrating on such issues as brand management and customer service.

To better leverage their capital, and to focus on core competencies, the major brand-owning companies now feel compelled to transform from conventional asset-based business models to a new de-capitalised model, as described by Means and Schneider (2000) (see Figure 10.3). These firms adopt the strategy of outsourcing non-core physical capital activities across the supply chain, as well as outsourcing support functions.

The implication for those involved in the purchasing function is that their role is no longer confined to the 'back-end' but is now active in managing external resources at all levels. Where once they managed short-term contracts with large numbers of separate suppliers, they now manage longer-term relationships with selected business partners and outsourced providers.

SUMMARY AND CONCLUSION

Many reasons are given to explain how the concept of SCM came about (see Chapter 3). The shift in thinking that created the environment where new ideas could take hold occurred in parallel with a maturing of the role of the purchasing function in organisations. A review of the purchasing-related literature over the incubation period shows clearly that purchasing professionals were often the first to grasp and promote the new idea. In the author's experience, operations functions rowed in quickly with the marketing function somewhat later, while finance functions are still trying in many cases to come to grips with it.

The various definitions of SCM that are discussed in this book – in particular *Fundamental Two* of SCM (see Chapter 3) – demonstrate the need for higher levels of integration in the activities of upstream and downstream business partners that are, legally and *de facto*, independent entities. This integration is enabled by the sharing of demand and other information and by building open, honest and long-standing relationships. The purchasing function's traditional role at the supply side boundary of the firm, and its early adoption of the SCM concept, has dictated that it is often well placed to be the custodian of the supply chain linkages.

A summary definition of the key activities of the purchasing function that might capture the foregoing is: *purchasing initiates and controls the flow of materials into the firm, strategically plans the supply side of the operation over the life of the firm's products, and manages the relationships with the firm's upstream business partners.*

REFERENCES

Baily, P., Farmer, D., Jessop, D. and Jones, D. (2005), *Purchasing Principles and Management*, Essex; Pearson Education Ltd.

Burt, D., Dobler, D. and Starling, S. (2003), *World Class Supply Management*, New York: McGraw Hill.

Christopher, M., Peck, H., Chaoman, P. and Juttner, U. (2002), *Supply Chain Vulnerability*, Bedfordshire: Cranfield School of Management.

Cox, A. (ed.) (1996), *Innovations in Procurement Management*, Lincolnshire: Earlsgate Press.

Dobler, D. and Burt, D. (1996), *Purchasing and Supply Management*, New York: McGraw Hill.

Grant, D., Lambert, D., Stock, J. and Ellram, L. (2006), *Fundamentals of Logistics Management*, Berkshire: McGraw Hill.

Heinritz, S., Farrell, P., Giunipero, L. and Kolchin, M. (1991), *Purchasing Principles and Applications*, New Jersey: Prentice Hall.

Juttner, U., Peck, H. and Christopher, M. (2003), 'Supply Chain Risk Management: Outlining and Agenda for Future Research', *International Journal of Logistics: Research and Applications*, 6(2), 197–210.

Lamming, R. (1993), *Beyond Partnership*, Hertfordshire: Prentice Hall International (UK) Ltd.

Lysons, K. and Farrington, B. (2006), *Purchasing and Supply Management*, Essex: Pearson Education Ltd.

Means, G. and Schneider, D. (2000), *Meta-Capitalism*, New York: John Wiley & Sons, Inc.

Saunders, M. (1997), *Strategic Purchasing and Supply Chain Management*, London: Pitman Publishing.

Womak, J, Roos, D. and Jones, D. (1990), *The Machine that Changed the World*, New York: Rawson Associates.

Appendix: Purchasing Logistics Services – Guidelines on Selecting and Managing the Right 3PL[3]

Background

The focus of Chapters 9 to 11 is on the 'buy' link (i.e. the outsourcing, purchasing and procurement dimension) of the supply chain. Outsourcing of logistics services has long been a feature of SCM and this type of outsourcing continues to grow rapidly. It is crucial that prospective customers of 3PL services be extremely thorough in their purchasing of logistics services through the use of a robust evaluation, selection and bidding process. This appendix provides guidance on selecting and managing the right 3PL provider, adopting appropriate elements of purchasing best practice throughout.

Key Elements of a Process for Selecting and Managing a 3PL

1. *Set and define internal and external goals and objectives*

    The company's main objectives and expectations for outsourcing need to be clearly defined. What is the company trying to accomplish in its relationship with a third-party provider? A clear understanding of the goals serves as a guideline as well as a way to measure the project's success. A clear set of SMART (Specific, Measurable, Aligned, Realistic and Time-based) objectives helps potential 3PLs to identify clearly what they are bidding on. The main objectives need to relate to the overall supply chain objectives of optimising total supply chain cost and meeting defined customer service requirements.

2. *Develop 3PL selection criteria*

    The evaluation of a 3PL starts with the establishment of selection criteria based on the agreed objectives. The basic criteria should include service quality, cost, capacity and delivery capability – these are traditionally used to evaluate providers' core capabilities. As detail is added to the selection process, other criteria such as financial strength, information systems infrastructure, operating and pricing flexibility and management expertise play a vital role in the process. The 'cultural fit' with potential providers is another important criterion. The agreed criteria form the basis of a company's RFP (request for proposal).

---

[3]This appendix is based on a 'Technical Focus' which originally appeared in *Logistics Solutions* in 2003 (Sweeney, E. (2003), 'Purchasing Logistics Services: Guidelines on Selecting and Managing the Right 3PL', *Logistics Solutions*, 6(5), 34, October).

3. *Identify potential providers*

   Once the selection criteria have been identified, a list of potential 3PL candidates is developed. Potential candidates should have experience in the industry and geographical coverage which satisfies location requirements. Other important issues in developing this list are the providers' ability to develop long-term customer partnerships and their record of producing continuous improvement. This needs to be combined with the assessments of existing customers of the various potential providers regarding their key competencies.

4. *Develop the RFP*

   The RFP should have all the project requirements for warehousing, transportation or any other services that are being outsourced. Specific information about the candidate's pricing model, organisation, capabilities and current customers also needs to be requested. This format should be such as to enable convenience in the evaluation process. It is a comprehensive document and potential providers should be allowed a reasonable period of time to respond to this request.

5. *Review the proposals*

   All candidates' bids are thoroughly reviewed and assessed in areas such as financial stability, strategic fit, management philosophy and culture. It is important that the chosen 3PL has the financial and strategic capability to grow and invest in new technologies and solutions. A well-developed information infrastructure and high levels of ICT connectivity are also desirable. Good proposals should be creative in nature – you should look for providers who are developing solutions that will meet your current and future needs. Site visits are used to allow providers' management, facilities, procedures and employees to be assessed. Successful outsourcing logistics is about trust. Without trust any relationship is doomed to failure. Site visits attempt to assess these trust issues as objectively as possible.

6. *Review proposed SLA/contract*

   Once the final candidate is selected, a service level agreement (SLA) and contract is drafted. The review should include transport and warehousing contracts, schedules, tariffs and rates. Service guarantees and the monitoring of performance reliability of the provider are critical elements of any 3PL agreement. Conflict resolution mechanisms also need to be agreed. Once the contract is agreed, the parties begin implementation. Implementation often involves a learning curve and being prepared to be as flexible as possible as operations are being established is imperative.

Concluding Comments

As the logistics capabilities of 3PLs improve, so do higher expectations of the services being provided. Higher expectations in areas such as speed, accuracy and flexibility will increase. The ideal 3PL will not only meet these expectations, but exceed them. In order for 3PL providers to continue to grow and be competitive, they must demonstrate a clear market or cost advantage. Users are looking for logistics expertise, improved service, and lower cost, not outsourcing for the sake of outsourcing. Success requires that the process of selecting a preferred provider is carried out in a logical and systematic manner based on the guidelines outlined above. It also requires that the ongoing relationship is well managed, and based on the key partnership principles of trust and transparency. In this way sustainable relationships based on a 'win–win' philosophy can be developed.

11

Purchasing Management: Elements of Good Operational Practice

GRAHAM HEASLIP

INTRODUCTION

The boundaries between functions or departments inside organisations and those between firms competing in both supply and customer markets have become somewhat blurred. Acceptance of this view means that it is harder to define clearly the roles and responsibilities of specialists and 'professionals' as they become involved in cross-functional organisational units and cross-organisational groups as well as in project or multi-functional teams. Paradoxically, there is a view that the more important purchasing and supply issues are seen to be, the less they can be managed solely within a tightly demarcated department. Purchasing and supply matters become a wider corporate concern, and it is argued that others need to be involved in managing them.

The level of planning and control of the purchasing activity in firms depends on a number of variables, but it can be seen that its perceived importance has traditionally been greater in manufacturing than in services, and that the nature and role of purchasing in the retail sector has changed considerably in the recent past. It is in manufacturing industry that the most evolved systems and procedures can be found, but best practice quickly migrates between industries and into retailing and services.

This chapter looks at how firms manage the purchasing activity in relation to a number of key areas of operational practice.

PURCHASING AS A FUNCTION

As noted in Chapter 10, a distinction can be made between the purchasing function and purchasing department. Lysons *et al.* (2006) argue that the purchasing function in a business context involves acquiring raw materials, components, goods and services for conversion, consumption or resale.

Figure 11.1: The Purchasing Process Chain

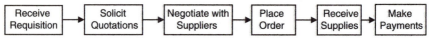

Source: Lysons, K. and Farrington, B. (2006), *Purchasing and Supply Chain Management*, 7th edition, Harlow, England: Pearson Education Limited.

They also highlight that the purchasing department is the organisational unit responsible for carrying out this function.

As shown in Figure 11.1, purchasing according to Lysons *et al.* (2006) can be viewed as a sequential chain of events leading to the acquisition of supplies.

The key link in the purchasing process chain is information. Thus, each sub-process in the chain is responsible for capturing or otherwise processing information that enables some questions to be answered, specifically: 'What are we required to purchase?' and 'Where and how can the required suppliers be obtained?' A process chain relationship can therefore be considered a message chain relationship. Previously messages, both internal (such as requisitions) and external (such as orders and payments), were transmitted on paper documents via the mail. Electronic transmission, as shown later, has revolutionised the cost and speed of purchasing.

Baily *et al.* (2005) argue that the main stages in the purchasing process are as follows:

- Recognition of need.
- Specification.
- Make or buy decision.
- Source identification.
- Source selection.
- Contracting.
- Contract management.
- Receipt, possibly inspection.
- Payment.
- Fulfilment of need.

The idea of the purchasing cycle is often employed to indicate the main activities in which purchasing might be involved. The activities included in the cycle do not indicate all of those that purchasing staff might be involved with; there are many activities (such as negotiation, vendor rating and source development) that are not specifically included. It should be observed that the early and late stages in the cycle may not necessarily involve specialist purchasing staff, the core purchasing contribution to the cycle being the items included in the central part of the list.

PROACTIVE PURCHASING

As the level of attention paid to purchasing and supply increases, the work tends to become more strategic in emphasis, concentrating more upon such activities as negotiating longer-term relationships, supplier development and total cost reduction, rather than ordering and replenishment routines (Baily *et al.* 2005).

On examination of buyers in large organisations with a well-developed function – such as IBM, Nissan, Ford and Hewlett Packard – we find that a relatively small proportion of their time is devoted to administrative and clerical activities. Most of their activity concentrates on the establishment and development of appropriate relationships with suppliers. The emphasis in such organisations has evolved beyond simply reacting to the needs of users as and when they arise, to a forward-looking proactive approach that more fully reflects the contribution that the management of inputs can make. Table 11.1 compares and contrasts reactive and proactive purchasing.

Table 11.1: Changing Purchasing Roles–Reactive and Proactive Buying

Reactive Buying	Proactive Buying
• Purchasing is a cost centre.	• Purchasing can add value.
• Purchasing receives specifications.	• Purchasing (and suppliers) contribute to specification.
• Purchasing rejects defective material.	• Purchasing avoids defective supplies.
• Purchasing reports to finance or production.	• Purchasing is a management function.
• Buyers respond to market conditions.	• Purchasing contributes to making markets.
• Problems are supplier's responsibility.	• Problems are shared responsibility.
• Price is the key variable.	• Total cost and value are the key variables.
• Emphasis on today.	• Emphasis strategic.
• Systems independent of suppliers.	• Systems may be integrated with suppliers systems.
• Users or designers specify.	• Buyers and suppliers contribute to specification.
• Negotiations win–lose.	• Negotiations win–win (or better).
• Plenty of suppliers = security.	• Plenty of suppliers = lost opportunities.
• Plenty of stock = security.	• Plenty of stock = waste.
• Information is power.	• Information is valuable if shared.

Source: Baily, P., Farmer, D., Jessop, D. and Jones, D. (2005), *Purchasing Principles and Management*, 9th edition, Harlow, England: Pearson Education Limited.

A simplistic view of purchasing activity is that it merely involves buying: that in essence it consists of finding a supplier who is willing to exchange the goods or services for an agreed sum of money. This perception of purchasing has become known as the 'transactional' view, and is based on the idea that purchasing is concerned with simple exchanges, with buyers and sellers interacting with each other on an arms-length basis. The underlying interest of the buyer in this rather simple scenario is to acquire as much resource as possible for as little money as it is necessary to pay.

It is true to say that this transactional view is not obsolete; it is still an appropriate way of looking at the process whereby low cost items, for which there are plenty of competing suppliers, might be purchased. However, it is no longer thought to be a suitable basis for most organisational purchasing expenditure (Baily *et al.* 2005). Much more attention has been paid in recent years to the development of 'mutual' supplier–buyer relationships, where the benefits of doing business together arise from ideas of sharing as well as exchanging. In a mutual relationship the emphasis is on building a satisfactory outcome together. Confidence and support are invested by both sides with the intention of adding value, a process not possible with a simple transaction. The organisations involved seek to come closer together and to identify overlapping interests.

Figures 11.2 and 11.3 enable a comparison between the transactional and the mutual relationship. The list of shared benefits in Figure 11.3 is by way of example only and will vary between relationships.

Figure 11.2: The 'Transactional' Relationship

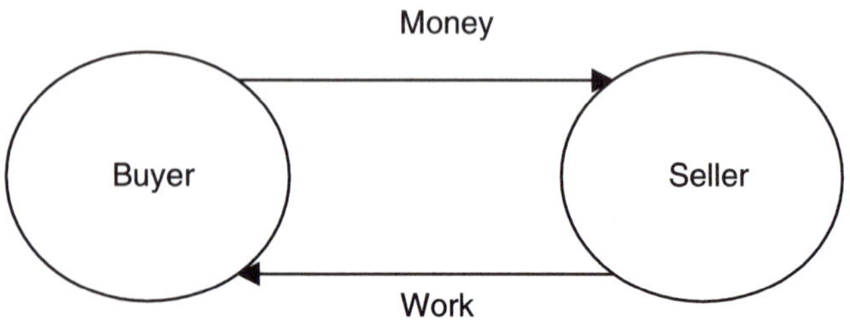

```
                    Money
        Buyer  ───────────────▶  Seller
               ◀───────────────
                     Work
```

THE CHANGING NATURE OF RELATIONSHIPS

Using Pareto's principle, it will generally be found that 80 per cent of expenditure will be with 20 per cent of suppliers, and it is likely that the suppliers with whom large sums of money are spent will be the ones with whom closer relationships are sought. A useful tool in determining those suppliers with whom closer relationships might be sought is the 'Procurement Positioning' matrix based on the work of Kraljic (1983) and illustrated in Figure 11.4.

Figure 11.3: The 'Mutual' Relationship

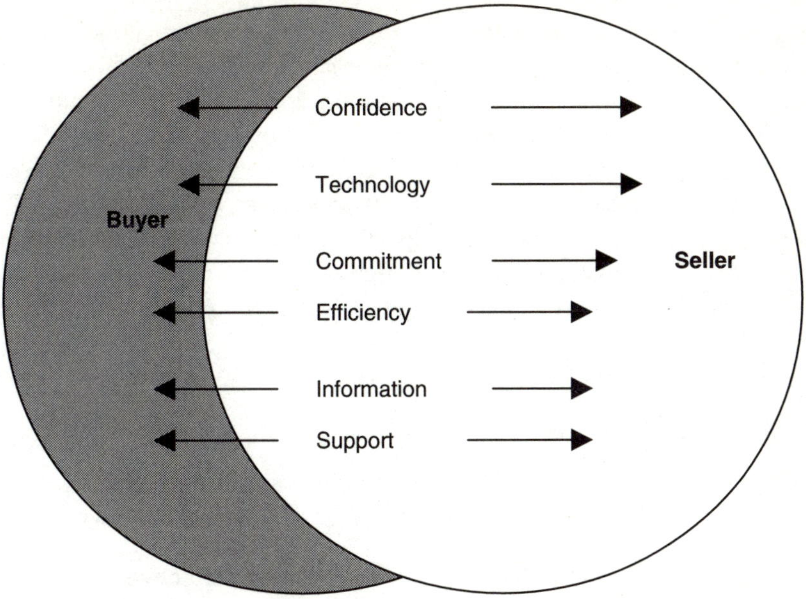

Buyer ←→ Seller

- Confidence
- Technology
- Commitment
- Efficiency
- Information
- Support

Figure 11.4: The 'Procurement Positioning' Tool

Risk ↑

Bottleneck e.g. a proprietary spare part, or a specialised consultancy need	Critical e.g. key sub-assemblies for a car maker, engines for an airline
Routine e.g. common stationery items, commercial grade industrial fasteners	Leverage e.g. paper supplies for a printing firm, common chemicals

→ Profit Potential

Source: Adapted from Kraljic, P. (1983), 'Purchasing Must Become Supply Chain Management', *Harvard Business Review*, September/October.

The vertical axis, labelled 'Risk', is concerned with the degree of difficulty associated with sourcing a product or service, or the vulnerability of the client organisation to a failure of a supply in service. The horizontal axis, 'Profit Potential', is used to indicate the extent of the potential of the supply to contribute to the profitability (or efficiency) of the buying concern. This profit potential might be realised by achieving lower costs, either

Prespectives on Supply Chain Management and Logistics

by paying a lower price for a good or service, or by introducing more efficient buying methods.

There is no single best approach to relationships: a transactional approach might well be seen as appropriate for the *routine* purchases, whereas a strategic approach will be of obvious benefit to a mutual relationship in the *critical* sector. A buyer is likely to be uncomfortable with suppliers of services or goods in the *leverage* sector and may well wish to move the requirements to the routine sector – perhaps by developing in some way to increase the seller's dependence. Where supplies and suppliers are in the leverage category, buyers are likely to feel quite comfortable, though of course it must be expected that vendors will be keen to see their products or services repositioned as critical.

TRADITIONAL APPROACHES TO PURCHASING

Objectives of Purchasing

It might be useful to consider purchasing objectives in the form of a 'hierarchy'. Figure 11.5, as proposed by Baily *et al.* (2005), suggests the way in which

Figure 11.5: Hierarchy of Purchasing Objectives

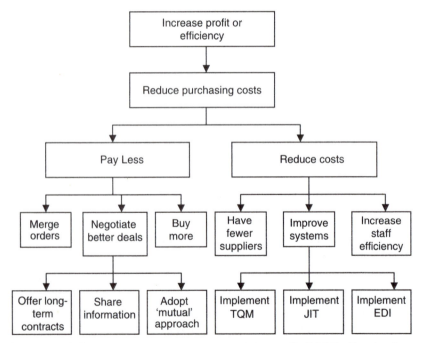

Source: Baily, P., Farmer, D., Jessop, D., and Jones, D. (2005), *Purchasing Principles and Management*, 9th edition, Harlow, England: Pearson Education Limited.

this might be done – of course the chart will differ from one organisation to another. The illustration is given merely to illustrate the principle and is not intended to encompass all possible ideas.

Phases of Traditional Purchasing

Apart from pre-purchase activities, such as participation in the preparation of specification and budget decisions, the purchasing function has traditionally involved three main phases (Killen and Kamauff 1995): the *identification* phase, the *ordering* phase and the *post-ordering* phase, each requiring specific documentation and considerable transactional activity.

Identification Phase

Killen and Kamauff (1995) suggest that notification of the need to purchase is generally in the form of either:

- A requisition issued by the stores, stock control or a potential user.
- A bill of materials (BOM) issued by the drawing office, production control or equivalent.

Ordering Phase

On receipt, the requisition or BOM will be checked by the buyer for accuracy, conformity to specification and purchase records to determine whether the purchase is a 're-buy' or a 'new buy' request. If the item is a standard re-buy request for an item that has been previously purchased from a satisfactory supplier at an acceptable price, a repeat order may be issued. If, however, the item is a new buy, the following steps will typically be involved.

1. Enquiries or requests for quotation (RFQs) will be sent to possible suppliers, accompanied by additional documents, such as drawings, specifications and so on, that will enable them to submit a quotation.
2. Quotations will be received in response to the enquiries and details of price, quality, delivery and so on and terms of business compared.
3. When quantities are substantial and quality and/or delivery of great importance, further negotiation with suppliers – including an evaluation of their capacity to undertake the order – may be required.
4. A purchase order will be issued to the vendor that gave the quotation – amended wherever necessary by subsequent negotiation – that was most acceptable. A copy of the order will be retained in the purchasing

department (sometimes two copies are retained for filing both alphabetically and chronologically). Further copies of the order may be provided for other departments (e.g. the department originating the requisition, accounts etc.).
5. An order acknowledgement should be required from the vendor. On receipt, the acknowledgement should be examined to ensure that the order has been accepted on the terms and conditions defined by the buyer or as subsequently agreed between the parties and then filed.

Post-Ordering Phase

Typically, this phase comprises a number of steps including:

1. It may be necessary to expedite the order to ensure that delivery dates are met or to expedite delivery of overdue orders.
2. An advice note, notifying that the goods have been dispatched or are ready for collection, will be issued by the supplier.
3. On receipt, the goods will be checked for quantity by the stores. Where matters of quality or specification are involved, they may be examined by an inspection department. If satisfactory, a goods received note will be completed and copies sent to the purchasing department. If they are not satisfactory, the purchasing department will be notified so that the complaint can be taken up with the supplier.
4. An invoice for the value of the goods will be received from the supplier. This will be compared with the purchase order and goods received note. Usually, prices will be checked by the purchasing department, paying special attention to the legitimacy of any variations from the quoted price. If satisfactory, the invoice will be passed to the accounts department for payment.
5. On completion, the order will be transferred to a completed orders file.

Purchasing and Supplier Manuals

Purchasing and supplier manuals are often used by organisations as a way of documenting key aspects of the process.

Purchasing Manuals

Richardson (2003) defines a purchasing manual as a medium for communicating information regarding *policies, procedures, instructions* and *regulations*. *Policies* may be general or consequential. General policies state, in broad terms, the objectives and responsibilities of the purchasing function. Consequential policies state, in expanded form, how general policies are applied in specific activities and situations, such as the selection of suppliers. *Procedures* prescribe the sequence of activities by which policies are implemented, such as the receipt of bought-out goods. *Instructions* give detailed knowledge or guidance to those responsible for carrying out the policies or procedures, such as suppliers with whom call-off contracts have been negotiated. *Regulations* are detailed rules regarding the conduct of purchasing and ancillary staff in the various situations arising in the course of their duties, such as concerning the receipt of gifts from suppliers. When drafting a manual, it is useful to keep these distinctions clearly in mind. Appendix A to this chapter outlines some of the advantages and disadvantages of using purchasing manuals, as well as the content of a typical manual.

Supplier Manuals

Supplier manuals provide information for the providers of goods and services. Lysons *et al.* (2006) suggest that such manuals may relate to a specific aspect of supplier relationships, such as quality or delivery requirements and ethical or environmental issues, or be a comprehensive publication covering all aspects of supply.

Lysons *et al.* (2006) further elaborate on the purpose of supplier manuals, suggesting that supplier manuals may achieve the following:

- Set out parameters within which the purchaser is prepared to trade with the supplier. Most supplier manuals contain a statement such as:
    Variation from the requirements/standards prescribed in this manual will only be permitted with the specific written agreement of the supply manager.
- Provide the legal basis for trading. The manual may contain a statement such as:
    Compliance with the requirements of this manual is a requirement of the conditions of purchase that form part of the trading terms and conditions and that suppliers accept when agreeing to supply goods or services. Failure to comply is a breach of contract.
- Provide essential information required by the supplier relating to the purchaser's requirements regarding such issues as packaging, transportation, deliveries, delivery locations, environmental and ethical policies and e-procurement.

Appendix B to this chapter sets out the content of a typical supplier manual.

Inefficiencies of Traditional Approaches

Some of the inefficiencies of typical traditional procedures, as outlined above, have been identified by Heinritz *et al.* (1993) as including:

- A sequence of non-value-adding clerical activities.
- Excessive documentation – for a new buy purchase, a minimum of seven different documents (requisition, enquiry, quotation, order acknowledgement, advice note, goods received note and invoice) will be involved, with expensive copying for purchase department records and information to other departments.
- Excessive time in processing orders, both internally and externally.
- Excessive cost of purely transactional activities. Clearly the act of placing a traditional purchase order will differ from one organisation to another.[1]

It is because of such inefficiencies that many organisations are increasingly recognising that administrative paperwork often serves merely to document a chain of events or to provide a logistical trail. Leading edge purchasing organisations need to transform this administrative function into value-adding processes by reducing, eliminating or combining steps whenever possible. All organisations are therefore being forced to embrace the strategic implications of information and communications technology (ICT) and e-procurement.

E-Commerce, E-Business and E-SCM

E-Commerce

The UK Department of Trade and Industry (DTI 2005) definition of electronic commerce is 'any forms of business transaction carried out electronically over public telephone systems'. While this definition encompasses the whole scope of business activities, e-commerce is usually concerned with buying and selling via the Internet.

E-Business

According to Mukhopadhyay and Sunder (2002), e-commerce relates primarily to transactions – or the buying and selling of products or services – on the

---

[1] In 1993, Heinritz *et al.* noted that the average cost of labour and services for requesting, locating suppliers, order placement, postage, receiving and payment had been variously estimated in the range of €100 to €200.

Internet. It usually refers to a website that has an online storefront or catalogue and the facility for electronic order processing. E-business, however, as Mukhopadhyay and Sunder (2002) suggest, incorporates a wide range of production, customer and internal processes that are only indirectly related to commercial transactions. Production-focused processes include electronic links with suppliers, especially manufacturing resource planning (MRP II), enterprise resource planning (ERP) and advanced planning and scheduling (APS). Customer-focused processes include online customer support and customer relationship management (CRM). Internal or management-focused processes include automated employee services, training, information sharing, video conferencing and recruiting.

There are also many general benefits of e-business, such as (Mukhopadhyay and Sunder 2002):

- Provision of 24 hours a day, seven days a week information access.
- Aggregation of information from several sources.
- Accurate audit trails of transactions, enabling businesses to identify areas offering the greatest potential for efficiency improvements and cost reduction.
- Personalisation and customisation of information.

E-SCM

E-supply chain management (e-SCM) is concerned with streamlining and optimising the whole supply chain by means of internal applications, with the aim of ensuring maximum sales growth at the lowest possible cost (Parker 2001). This includes setting up an internal online purchasing system, joining an industry-wide electronic marketplace and implementing e-SCM across the entire value chain.

Parker (2001) observe that purchasers and suppliers can derive the following benefits from e-SCM:

- The ability to purchase, both directly and indirectly, materials at a lower cost, primarily due to price transparency and competition. So while large purchasers can exert powerful leverage to obtain more substantial price reductions and discounts, small purchasers using such systems can obtain more favourable prices as many suppliers are competing for the business of purchasers via the medium of e-marketplace and trading exchanges.
- Achievements of greater efficiency when purchasing goods and services and ultimately lowering the overall cost of transactions, as business-to-business (B2B) marketplaces often offer smaller purchasers opportunities to discover

lower prices for things that would be prohibitively time-consuming and expensive to discover by human effort alone.
- Purchasers being able to form strong ties with suppliers in forecasting, scheduling and planning production data and sharing data designs to develop supplier collaboration.

In addition, Reason and Evans (2001) have identified that supplier-specific benefits tend to fall into two classes, depending on whether the e-SCM programme emphasises collaboration or commercial opportunities. Supplier benefits include the enhancement of forecasting ability, resulting in the capacity to meet and exceed customers' demands, achieve the right combination of products and services at the right time and align their production schedules, manufacturing capacity and inventory to customers' buying patterns.

E-Procurement

The Chartered Institute of Purchasing and Supply (CIPS) definition of e-procurement is 'using the Internet to operate the transactional aspects of requisitioning, authorising, ordering, receiving and payment processes for the required services or products' (CIPS 1999).

The CIPS statement also points out that e-procurement is typically the focus of local business administrators – one of the key goals of e-procurement is to devolve buying to local users.

The key enabler of all the above is the ability of systems to communicate across organisational boundaries (Stefano 2003). While the technology for e-commerce provides the basic means, the main benefits derive from the resultant changes in business procedures, processes and perspectives. Stefano (2003) maintains that e-commerce is made possible by the open standard of extensible mark-up language (XML) – a structured computer programming language that allows for the easy identification of data types in multiple formats and can be understood across all standard Internet technologies. Adoption of XML will help organisations to integrate applications seamlessly and exchange information with trading partners.[2]

The Evolution of E-Procurement Models

Kalakota and Robinson (2001) have identified seven basic types of e-procurement trading models. These, together with their key differences, are shown in Table 11.2.

---

[2] These issues are discussed elsewhere in this book, notably in Chapters 12 and 14.

Table 11.2: Comparison of Various E-Procurement Models

Trading Method	Characteristics
Electronic Data Interchange (EDI) Networks	• Handful of trading partners and customers • Simple transactional capabilities • Batch processing • Reactive and costly value-added network (VAN) charges
Business-to-employees (B2E) requisition applications	• Make buying fast and hassle free for a company's employees • Automated approvals routing and standardisation of requisition procedures • Provide supplier management tools for the professional buyer
Corporate procurement portals	• Provide improved control over the procurement process and let a company's business rules be implemented with more consistency • Custom, negotiated process posted in a multi-supplier catalogue • Spending analysis and multi-supplier catalogue management
First-generation trading exchanges: community, catalogue and storefronts	• Industry content, job postings and news • Storefronts: new sales channels for distributors and manufacturers • Product content and catalogue aggregation services
Second-generation trading exchanges: transaction-orientated trading exchanges	• Automated requisition process and purchase order transactions • Supplier, price and product/service availability discovery • Catalogue and credit management
Third-generation trading exchanges: collaborative supply chains	• Enable partners to closely synchronise operations and enable real-time fulfilment • Process transparency, resulting in restructuring of demand and the supply chain • Substitute information for inventory
Industry consortia: buyer and supplier led	• The next step in the evolution of corporate procurement portals

Source: Kalakota, R. and Robinson, M. (2001), *E-Business 2.0*, 2nd edition, Boston MA: Addison Wesley.

Table 11.3: 'Hard' and 'Soft' Measures of the Benefits of E-Procurement

Hard measures include:	**Soft measures** include:
Automated purchase to buy process (order processing time and cost of auction)	Freeing up of purchasing staff time, enabling them to focus on more strategic procurement issues
Automated 'P-card' purchasing	Reduction in maverick buying (which is when staff buy from suppliers other than those with whom a purchasing agreement has been negotiated)
Electronic payment of invoices	
Lower prices by means of strategic sourcing	
Average inventory reduction	Improved monitoring of supplier performance
Supply base rationalisation	Improved order tracking
	Improved availability of management information and accounting

The Advantages of E-Procurement

Buy IT (2002) states that the benefits of an investment in e-procurement can be both hard (i.e. directly measurable) and soft (i.e. indirectly measurable). Table 11.3 summarises these benefits.

In addition to the above benefits, intangible benefits include such things as cultural changes consequent on the implementation of e-procurement. These benefits cannot be measured within the business case but may support it. Buy IT (2002) states that, to identify e-procurement cost savings as distinct from those achieved by means of other procurement best practice, the measurement system needs to discriminate between 'business as usual' type savings and those directly attributed to the implementation of the e-procurement systems.

LEGAL ASPECTS OF PURCHASING

Before concluding this chapter, it is important to note that, although purchasing procedures may have changed from manual to electronic methods, all commercial transactions must conform to the relevant legal requirements. A valid contract – a promise or agreement that the law will enforce – is a key element of this. A detailed discussion of contract law is beyond the scope of this chapter. However, Leenders *et al.* (2002) argue that, to be legally enforceable, a contract must satisfy the various essentials set out in Appendix C to this chapter. Furthermore, the typical structure and outline content of a contract is shown in Appendix D.

Conclusion

At one end of the spectrum is an image of the purchasing and supply function which characterises it as involving mainly clerical, order-placing activities and in which personnel tend to adopt a short-term, hand-to-mouth approach, merely reacting to contingencies as they arise. Movement towards the other end of the spectrum opens up possibilities in which a strategic, long-term approach is developed in shaping the direction of sourcing and supply plans, with immediate requirements being controlled in the light of these.

This approach takes a broad, universal or holistic view of supply chains or pipelines and suggests that the purchasing and supply function can exercise significant influence in relation to the creation of product value at various stages along the chain. Indeed, in many cases, suppliers add more value to the final product in their operations than is added in the final stages of the company apparently making it. The purchasing strategies of more powerful companies can influence the structure of the supply chain as well as the behaviour of other participants in the chain.

REFERENCES

Baily, P., Farmer, D., Jessop, D. and Jones, D. (2005), *Purchasing Principles and Management*, 9th edition, Harlow, England: Pearson Education Limited.

Buy IT (2002), E-Procurement Guidelines: 'Measuring the Benefits: What to Measure and How to Measure It', available at: <http://www.buyit-net.org/Best_Practice_Guidelines/e-Procurement/metric.jsp>, accessed April 2007.

CIPS (1999), 'The CIPS E-Procurement Guidelines: E-Invoicing and E-Payment', London: Chartered Institute of Purchasing and Supply Management.

DTI (2005), 'DTI Consultation Document on the Electronic Commerce Directive: The Liability of Hyperlinkers, Location Tool Services and Content Aggregators', London: Department of Trade and Industry.

Heinritz, S., Farrell, P., Giunipero, L. and Kolchin, M. (1993), *Purchasing Principles and Applications*, 8th edition, New Jersey: Prentice Hall.

Leenders, M., Fearon, H., Flynn, A., Johnson, Fraser, P. (2002), *Purchasing and Supply Management*, 12th edition, England: McGraw-Hill Irwin.

Lysons, K. and Farrington, B. (2006), *Purchasing and Supply Chain Management*, 7th edition, Harlow, England: Pearson Education Limited.

Kalakota, R. and Robinson, M. (2001), *E-Business 2.0*, 2nd edition, Boston MA: Addison Wesley.

Killen, K.H. and Kamauff, J.W. (1995), *Managing Purchasing*, England: Irwin.

Kraljic, P. (1983), 'Purchasing Must become Supply Chain Management', *Harvard Business Review*, September/October.

Mukhopadhyay, T. and Sunder, K. (2002), 'Strategic and Operational Benefits of Electronic Integration in B2B Procurement Processes', *Management Science*, 48(10).

Parker, G. (2001), 'Money for Something', *Supply Management*, March.

Reason, M. and Evans, E. (2001), *Implementing E-Procurement*, Cambridge: Hawksmere.

Richardson, T. (2003), 'Guide to Purchasing Cards', supplement in M. Leenders *et al*, *Purchasing and Supply Management*, 11th edition, England: McGraw-Hill Irwin.

Stefano, R. (2003), *The Internet and the Customer Supplier Relationship*, London: Ashgate Publishing.

Appendix A: Advantages, Disadvantages and Typical Content of Purchasing Manuals

Advantages of Purchasing Manuals

Scheuing (1989) claimed that the advantages for purchasing manuals include the following:

- Writing it down helps with precision and clarity.
- The preparation of the manual provides an opportunity for consultation between purchasing and other departments to look critically at existing policies and procedures and, wherever necessary, change them.
- Procedures are prescribed in terms of activities undertaken or controlled by purchasing, thus promoting consistency and reducing the need for detailed supervision of routine tasks.
- A manual is a useful aid in training and guiding staff.
- A manual coordinates policies and procedures, and helps to ensure uniformity and continuity of purchasing principles and practice, as well as providing a point of reference against which such principles and practice can be evaluated.
- A manual may help to enhance the status of purchasing by showing that top management attaches importance to the procurement function.
- Computerisation, which needs detailed and well-documented systems, has given further impetus to the preparation of purchasing manuals.

Disadvantages of Purchasing Manuals

Scheuing (1989) also noted that some disadvantages of manuals are that they:

- Are costly to prepare.
- Tend to foster red tape and bureaucracy and stifle initiative.
- Must be continually updated to show changes in procedures and policy.

Contents of Purchasing Manual

A purchasing manual may consist of three main sections (Scheuing 1989) dealing, respectively, with organisation, policy and procedures.

- Organisation
  - Charts showing the place of purchasing within the undertaking and how it is organised, both centrally and locally.
  - Possibly job descriptions for all posts within the purchasing function, including, where applicable, limitations of remits.

- Teams relating to purchasing and supply chain activities.
  - Administrative information for staff, such as absences, hours of work, travelling expenses and similar patterns.
- Policy
  - Statements of policy, setting out the objectives, responsibilities and authority of the purchasing function.
  - Statements, which can be expanded, of general principles relating to price, quality and delivery.
  - Terms and conditions of purchase.
  - Ethical relationships with suppliers, especially regarding gifts and entertainment.
  - Environmental policies.
  - Supplier appraisal and selection.
  - Employee purchases.
  - Reports to management.
- Procedures
  - Descriptions, accompanied by flow charts, of procedures relating to requisitioning, ordering, expediting, receiving, inspecting, storing and payment of goods with special reference to procurement.
  - Procedures relating to the rejection and return of goods.
  - Procedures regarding the disposal of scrap and obsolete or surplus items.

REFERENCE

Scheuing, E. (1989), *Purchasing Management*, Harlow, England: Prentice Hall.

Appendix B: Typical Content of Supplier Manuals

The following are typical headings for a supplier manual (Lysons *et al*. 2006).

- Introduction
  - The purpose of the manual.
  - Non-variation statement.
  - Compliance with the manual as a condition of purchase.
- Conditions of purchase
  - Definitions, such as the meaning attached to such terms as the 'purchaser', 'the supplier' and 'goods'.
  - Supply of goods.
  - Quality of goods.
  - Remedies for supplier non-compliance.
  - Payment.
  - Intellectual property rights.
  - Termination.
  - General provisions relating to subcontracting, privacy of information, law governing contracts.
- Pre-order requirements
  - Procedures that the supplier must observe before the dispatch of goods.
- Pre-delivery requirements
  - First production samples.
  - Pallet requirements.
  - Configuration of palletised stock.
  - Split deliveries.
- Transportation and delivery requirements
  - Carriers.
  - Timelines and time of deliveries.
  - Documentation.
- Post-delivery requirements
  - Post-delivery procedures.
  - Pallet redemption.
  - Misdeliveries.
  - Goods for return.
- Policies and quality
  - Purchaser's environmental policies.
  - Health and safety policies.
  - Code of conduct for ethical trading.
  - Quality assurance terms and conditions.

- Appendices
  - Glossary of terms.
  - Warehouse addresses, telephone and fax numbers.
- Agreements (to be signed and returned)
  - Purchaser's trading terms and conditions.
  - New supplier account agreement.
- Questionnaire (to be completed and returned)
  - Supplier EDI questionnaire.

Reference

Lysons, K. and Farrington, B. (2006), *Purchasing and Supply Chain Management*, 7th edition, Harlow, England: Pearson Education Limited.

Appendix C: Essentials of a Legally Enforceable Contract

- *Intention*: Both parties must intend to enter into a legal relationship.
- *Agreement*: In a dispute, the court must be satisfied that the contracting parties had reached a firm agreement and were not still negotiating. Agreement will usually be shown by the unconditional acceptance of an offer. It is important to determine who has made the offer, whether the offer is valid and if it has been accepted.
- *Consideration*: English law of contract is concerned with bargains, not mere promises. Thus, if A promises to give something to B, B will have no remedy if A breaks his promise. If, however, B has undertaken to do something in return so that A's promise is dependent on B's, the mutual exchange of promises turns the arrangement into a contract. The consideration must also exist and have some ascertainable value, however slight, otherwise there is no contract.
- *Form*: Certain exceptional types of agreement are only valid if made in a particular way, such as in writing. Thus, conveyances of lands and leases for over three years must be by deed. The absence of written evidence, while not affecting the validity of a contact, may make it unenforceable in the courts. This evidence may be from correspondence or any other documentation made at the time the contract was made, or subsequently. Such written evidence must clearly identify the parties against whom the evidence is to be used or by authorised agent.
- *Definite terms*: There will be no contract if it is not possible to determine what has been agreed between the parties. Where essential terms have yet to be decided, the parties are still in the stage of negotiation. An agreement to concur in the future is not a contract.
- *Legality*: Some agreements, such as contracts to defraud the revenue authorities or immoral contracts, such as agreements to fix prices or regulate supplies, while not illegal, are void under the UK Competition Acts, unless the parties can prove to the Restrictive Practices Court that their agreement is beneficial and in the public interest.

Reference

Leenders, M., Fearon, H., Flynn, A., Johnson, and Fraser, P. (2002), *Purchasing and Supply Management*, 12th edition, England: McGraw-Hill Irwin.

Appendix D: The General Structure of a Contract

The following is a typical structure for a contract (Lysons *et al.* 2006):

- *The agreement*: This names the parties to the contract. In a standard contract, it is only necessary to change the names and any other relevant detail. If the parties sign on the front page, this saves leafing through the whole, but there should be a statement that the parties have read and understood all the terms and conditions appertaining to the contract.
- *The terms and conditions*: These are comprised of the following points.
  — Definitions: These are inserted to avoid ambiguity and avoid the repetition of long sentences. When, in the text, a capital letter is used for a word, it indicates that the word has been defined in the 'definitions' section.
  — General terms: These are the general agreements clause, changes, alterations and variations clause, 'notice' clause – stating how and by what method any notice relating to the contract is to be sent – and a clause stating that the headings and definitions are for information only.
  — The commercial provisions: These set out the rights and obligations of the supplier and, in a separate clause, the rights and obligations of the purchaser. Another separate clause will specify payment terms.
  — Secondary commercial provisions: These deal with such matters as condition, warranties, confidentiality, intellectual property, indemnity and termination.
  — Boilerplate clauses. These are standard clauses that appear in almost all contracts such as the following:
    ➤ Serverability – the right of a court to remove a term or condition that is invalid, void or unenforceable without prejudice to the rest of the contract.
    ➤ Waiver – a statement that failure to enforce a 'right' at a given time will not prevent the exercise of that right later.
    ➤ *Force majeure* – applicable where a 'major force', such as an act of God, war, riots, floods, tempests and so on, prevents or delays the performance of the contract.
    ➤ Law and jurisdiction, the law that governs the contract – the Principles of International Contracts, produced by the International Institute for the Unifications of Private Law (UNIDROIT) in 1994 aim to establish a balanced set of rules designed for use throughout the world, irrespective of the legal traditions and the economic and political conditions of the countries in which they are to be applied.

These principles have no legal force and depend for their acceptance on their perceived authority. When, however, the parties agree, they can become legally binding.

REFERENCE

Lysons, K. and Farrington, B. (2006), *Purchasing and Supply Chain Management*, 7th edition, Harlow, England: Pearson Education Limited.

Section 4
ICT in the Supply Chain

12

The Role of Information and Communications Technology in the Supply Chain[1]

RONAN MCDONNELL, JOHN KENNY AND
EDWARD SWEENEY

ICT HAS TRANSFORMED THE WAY COMPANIES DO THEIR BUSINESS

As noted earlier, the movement of goods along the supply chain is reflected by corresponding movements of information. Indeed, a critical part of *Fundamental Three* of SCM relates to the effective management of information across the supply chain (see Chapter 3). Recent developments in information and communications technology (ICT) have facilitated this and have enabled higher levels of supply chain data and process integration. For example, the moment an item is sold at the supermarket check-out, this information is captured via a bar code reader and can then be read immediately anywhere in the distribution chain. Computers communicate with other computers via local area, national and, in some cases, international networks. However, without properly designed supply chains, and capable people, this will not succeed. This chapter examines the evolving role of ICT in the supply chain and explains some of the underpinning technological concepts.

CATEGORIES OF SCM ICT SOLUTIONS

Recent years have seen rapid developments in the ICT used to facilitate SCM. As noted in Chapter 3, the authors have proposed a taxonomy of

---

[1] In this chapter, references to relevant websites are used extensively. These sites, the addresses of which are provided throughout the text, were mainly accessed by the authors during the early part of 2007.

supply chain ICT solutions which identifies four primary categories as follows (McDonnell *et al.* 2004):

1. **Point solutions**, which are used to support the execution of one link (or point) in the chain (e.g. warehouse management systems or WMS).
2. **'Best of breed' solutions**, where two or more existing stand-alone solutions are integrated, usually using middleware technology.
3. **Enterprise solutions**, which are based on the logic of enterprise resource planning (ERP); these solutions attempt to integrate all departments and functions across a company into a single computer system that can serve all those different departments' particular needs.
4. **Extended enterprise solutions (XES)**, which refer to the collaborative sharing of information and processes between the partners along the supply chain using the technological underpinnings of ERP.

The move away from point towards enterprise solutions in many ways reflects the shift – highlighted in Chapter 3 – from traditional internally oriented to more integrated process oriented SCM models in recent years. Other 'integrative' technologies, in particular electronic data interchange (EDI) and the Internet, have enabled upstream and downstream supply chain partners to use common data. As noted by Christopher (2000), this facilitates supply chain agility as companies can act based on 'real demand, rather than be dependent on the distorted and noisy picture that emerges when orders are transmitted from one step to another in an extended chain'. It also facilitates higher levels of inventory visibility throughout the supply chain, thereby creating the conditions where excessive reliance on stockholding and forecasting can be reduced.

Point Solutions

A large number of point solutions have been developed in recent years. The following sections provide an overview, based on the 'buy-make-store-move-sell' model of the internal supply chain (see Chapter 3).

Buy: There are a variety of purchasing ICT solutions which support a range of both operational and strategic decision-making. In addition to managing what and how much to buy, other systems support vendor selection and management (see Table 12.1), and order processing.

Make: Sophisticated planning systems can be configured to model the production facility in great detail, and can be programmed to optimise the production process based on production volumes, product mix, available

Table 12.1: Example of a 'Buy' Solution

Fragmented buy-side processes, from sourcing and negotiation to procurement, fulfillment, and payment can be integrated into a single seamless process, reducing time-consuming and repetitive manual tasks by implementing supplier relationship management (SRM) applications such as that offered by Perfect Commerce.

Source: Perfect Commerce, <http://www.perfect.com/home/index.html>

capacity and any other constraints that impinge on production planning. Such systems can interface with a stock control system or a warehouse management system to ensure that sufficient materials are, or will be, available. The production planner can also run 'what–if' scenarios to make the best use of resources. Table 12.2 provides an example of such a system.

Table 12.2: Example of a 'Make' Solution

Dynalogics is a suite of expert systems for manufacturing. The system uses artificial intelligence to manage all the phases of manufacturing, from estimating to shop floor control, costing and scheduling. It holds knowledge of each process, method, material and rate, and the capability and constraint of every item of plant on the shop floor.

Source: Dynalogics, <http://www.dynalogics.com.au/index.html>

Manufacturing execution systems (MES) receive orders and dynamically manage resources on the shop floor, from equipment and labour to inventory needed to fill those orders.

Store: The function of a warehouse in the supply chain can be described as a *centre for flexible value-added services and information*. Warehouse operations have been made easier through the introduction of WMS. The basic functions of a WMS (Obal 1998) are receiving, put-away, work planning, picking, inventory-level control and shipping. Also important is a WMS which is able to calculate the exact cost of the warehousing component in an order. Many software companies provide WMS, from tailor-made packages such as EXE Technologies to off-the-shelf systems such as Swisslog's WarehouseManager (see Table 12.3).

Move: A wide range of Transportation Management Systems (TMS) are available, and include the following functionalities:

- Complete support of transportation order management, transport planning and fleet management.

Table 12.3: Example of a 'Store' Solution

Swisslog's WarehouseManager automates key processes from inbound goods arrival and processing through inventory storage to fulfilling outbound shipping orders. Such a system can offer the improved inventory visibility that allows companies maximum throughput with minimum inventory.

Source: Swisslog, <http:// www.swisslog.com>

- Communication with other supply chain participants. Most interfaces are supported by EDI. However, the use of Internet technology has enhanced communication between supply chain participants.
- Open database for execution and administration of transport activities.
- Evaluation of transportation performances (key performance indicators, KPIs).
- Distribution modelling and route optimisation.

A brief description of an example of a route optimisation tool is shown in Table 12.4.

Table 12.4: Example of a 'Move' Solution

Optrak is a vehicle routing tool that allows the user to quickly build distribution routes which are mileage and volume efficient. Users can customise the system to model their own unique distribution network, incorporating any delivery constraints or special requirements.

Source: Optrak, <http://www.optrak.co.uk>

Sell: The use of spreadsheets to monitor key customers' accounts, as well as to track trends in sales has evolved into customer relationship management (CRM). CRM applications are designed to collate as much relevant information as possible about each individual customer. But, the ultimate goal of CRM must be to provide the entire supply chain with as much information as possible about what has happened to maximise customer satisfaction. This involves understanding the customer well enough so as to be able to anticipate their needs, not just forecasting the future by extrapolating the past. A brief description of an example of a 'sell' solution is shown in Table 12.5.

'Best-of-Breed' Solutions

A study published by the Meta Group in 2007[2] found that the average implementation time for an ERP solution was twenty months. The study

---

[2] <http://www.mhmonline.com/nID/2973/MHM/viewStory.asp>

Table 12.5: Example of a 'Sell' Solution

By streamlining processes and providing sales, marketing and service personnel with better, more complete customer information, customer relationship management (CRM) such as that provided by Oracle's Siebel solutions enables organisations to establish and maintain more profitable customer relationships and decrease operating costs.

Source: Oracle, <http://www.oracle.com/applications/crm/siebel/index.html>

also found that it took two and a half years from project initiation to achieve 'any kind of quantifiable benefit from such a system'. Companies very often do not have time to build integrated infrastructures. In addition, in many cases departments within a company might have invested time and money in implementing and developing systems that are robust and ably fit their business processes.

'Middleware' companies have developed data translation that has enabled organisations to integrate 'best-of-breed' solutions. Middleware is a 'software that connects two otherwise separate applications.'[3] It functions as a conversion or translation layer; it is also a consolidator and integrator. Custom-programmed middleware solutions have been developed for decades to enable one application to communicate with another that either runs on a different platform or comes from a different vendor or both. In some cases applications are built on open standards, making the integration easy because all good middleware incorporates those standards. This technology has been facilitated in recent years by the advent of extensible markup language (XML), which allows designers to create customised tags, and share documents between different platforms and computer languages.

The trend towards 'best-of-breed' solutions has also decreased the anticipated role of ERP as a central repository of all business data for manufacturers (Berton Latamore 2000).

Enterprise Resource Planning

The shift from fragmentation, which is a characteristic of many traditional supply chains, to integration is a key goal of SCM (as detailed in *Fundamental Two* of SCM, see Chapter 3). A major disadvantage of point solutions is that they can reinforce barriers between functional parts of the business. Enterprise solutions or ERP represent an attempt to achieve more effective integration across traditional supply chain functions.

---

[3] <http://webopedia.internet.com/TERM/m/middleware.html>

ERP came about in the 1990s because of an organisational shift away from the traditional task-based structures, which had been based on Adam Smith's theory that industrial work should be broken down into its simplest and most basic tasks, to process-based structures. The phrase ERP was first coined by the Gartner group[4] to describe the change in computer systems from the inventory-focused, transaction-centric and reactive nature of ERP's predecessors – MRP (materials requirements planning) and MRP II (manufacturing resource planning) – to systems focused on customer service.

ERP attempts to integrate all departments and functions across a company into a single computer system that can serve all those different departments' particular needs. Traditionally, each department – from finance to human resource management to the warehouse – has had its own computer system, each optimised for the particular ways that the department does its work. But ERP combines them all together into a single, integrated software program that runs off a single database so that the various departments can more easily share information and communicate with each other.

For example, when a customer places an order, that order would typically begin a mostly paper-based journey from in-basket to in-basket around the company, often being keyed and re-keyed into different departments' computer systems along the way. All that time in in-baskets causes delays and lost orders, and all the keying into different computer systems invites errors. Meanwhile, no-one in the company truly knows what the status of the order is at any given point because there is no way for the finance department, for example, to get into the warehouse's computer system to see whether the item has been shipped. Well-known ERP systems include Oracle, PeopleSoft and SAP.

Extended ERP Systems

Traditional ERP is focused internally and does not easily extend beyond the boundaries of the organisation. The supply chain focus, on the other hand, extends to all supplier and customer linkages both within and outside the organisation. This conflict within ERP systems is now being addressed, on a technology level at least, through what has become known as extended ERP.[5] The term extended enterprise solution (XES, see above) has also been used in this context. Essentially, this refers to the collaborative sharing of information and processes between the partners along the supply

---

[4] See <http://www.gartner.com>
[5] ERP II according to Gartner Group.

chain using the technological underpinnings of ERP. Extended enterprise software suites incorporate functionality that was previously limited to 'best-of-breed' applications such as supplier management, procurement and CRM.

Supply Chain Software

ERP vendors have been evolving and extending their products' capabilities to address areas such as SRM and CRM, data mining and business intelligence, and product life-cycle management. Broadly speaking, the extended functionality falls into either supply chain planning or supply chain execution category.

As supply chains become more dynamic and operate in real time, the lines between planning and execution continue to blur. Real-time information from execution systems gives the capability to feed back into and allow the development of continually adjusting optimal plans. The ultimate realisation is perhaps technologies which lead to the adaptive or 'self-healing' supply chain – where a software engine monitors all the numerous events happening supply chain-wide, identifies and escalates exceptions, sends notifications and reacts appropriately (Friese *et al.* 2005).

Web-Based ERP

Internet technology has made it possible for companies to operate their ERP systems in real-time, even across a number of sites. In this way, up-to-date information is always available on-screen. This information may be made available to the necessary parties through the use of intranets[6] and extranets.[7] Web-based ERP facilitates the sharing of information between companies and their suppliers, customers and other trading partners.

Enterprise Application Integration

Whichever application platform is chosen, 'best-of-breed' or ERP, the need is not diminished for integration with diverse software and hardware platforms within and external to the organisation. This need has come more into focus in recent times with tighter ICT budgets and the desire to gain more from existing ICT investments. Extensible Markup Language (XML), along with other standard and open protocols, has given rise to the next

---

[6] A site based on Internet technology but placed on private servers and designed not to allow 'outsiders'.
[7] An intranet that is partially accessible to authorised outsiders.

level of integration tools – web services and the broader concept of Service Oriented Architecture (SOA).

Web services, by virtue of this new level of integration ability, have given rise to a new form of software delivery where applications or functionality within an application is downloaded and used when needed – something like JIT for software. This is referred to as *on-demand business applications*.[8] An organisation essentially leases this software on a per-use basis, a pay-as-you-go style service. This is not the same as the older software delivery concept known as Application Service Providers (ASPs). Unlike the ASPs, which were building massive data centres and basically running rental services for other companys' software, today's web-service companies design their software from the ground up to be delivered over the Internet as a service.

SOA is being used by companies that think seriously about how to assemble their business systems out of common parts. It is an approach to constructing the systems architecture that takes a bit more thought and investment in the beginning, but enables the companies that use it to build systems faster as the inventory of reusable parts grows. With SOA, systems are composed of reusable components, called 'services'. A service is a software building block that performs a distinct function – such as retrieving customer information from a database – through a well-defined interface (an electronic description of how to call the service from other services). Services can be retrieved from a library of services that have been developed in-house or from third-party vendors of such services – called web service providers.

All of these initiatives are leading to better integration capabilities within organisations and the ability to build fully working systems from services or functionalities which are reusable. Furthermore, this enables organisations to change the functionality of applications as fast as the needs of the business changes. This is a different vision to the purchase of a monolithic application system such as an ERP system from a single vendor where new functionality comes with the next release of the software. This model represents a new departure in the software industry's capability in meeting the changing needs of businesses.

New SCM Challenges

All of the technological potential identified in this chapter presents opportunities for companies throughout the supply chain. The necessary ICT is now available to enable a company to provide finished goods just in time

---

[8] Perhaps best typified by <http://www.salesforce.com> who specialise in CRM software.

for delivery, based on an individual unique order received from anywhere in the world; source the optimum materials for the order; and identify the optimum means of shipping it to the customer.

The proliferation of sophisticated technology solutions has led to ICT investment decisions becoming a complex choice between (a) custom or standard solutions and (b) point or enterprise solutions. Even more challenging is the realisation that most ICT solutions are no longer likely to provide strategic advantage, but simply the business basics. The competitive advantage for companies will originate from developing creative information technology strategies and implementing them superbly.[9]

---

[9]The appendix to this chapter provides an overview of guidelines on developing strategy and on the planning and implementation of projects.

REFERENCES[10]

Berton Latamore, G. (2000), 'Integration Software Builds Bridges', *APICS – The Performance Advantage*, 10(11).

Christopher, M. (2000), 'The Agile Supply Chain Competing in Volatile Markets', *Industrial Marketing Management*, 29(1), 37–44.

Friese, T., Muller, J. and Freisleben, B. (2005), 'Self-Healing Execution of Business Processes Based on a Peer-to-Peer Service Architecture', *Systems Aspects in Organic and Pervasive Computing* (ARCS 2005), 108–123.

McDonnell, R., Sweeney, E. and Kenny, J. (2004), 'The Role of Information Technology in the Supply Chain', *Logistics Solutions*, 7(1), 13–16.

Obal, P. (1998), *What to Look for in Warehouse Management System Software*, Tulsa OK: Industrial Information & Data Inc.

---

[10]In this chapter, references to relevant websites are used extensively. These sites, the addresses of which are provided throughout the text, were mainly accessed by the authors during the early part of 2007.

Appendix: Effective Adoption of ICT in the Supply Chain – Guidelines on Developing Strategy and on the Planning and Implementation of Projects

Introduction

As noted in this chapter, the recent rapid rate of development in ICT has created the potential for technology to be a key enabler in the supply chain integration process. For this potential to be turned into reality the ICT planning and implementation process needs to be:

(i) Driven by a clear ICT strategy.
(ii) Carried out in a logical and systematic manner.

The former is essential to ensuring that ICT investments are in line with overall company and supply chain objectives and strategies. The latter recognises that attention to detail is imperative, if ICT projects are to meet specified targets and to yield significant benefits. This appendix provides some guidance on each of the above. However, it must be recognised that all companies and projects are different and what follows provides no more than a checklist. The exact nature of any ICT strategy, and associated planning and implementation processes, need to be thought through carefully.

ICT Strategy

Why does an enterprise need an ICT strategy? There are two overriding reasons. Firstly, the rapid rate of development in ICT in recent years has resulted in decision-making in this area involving many complex and often inter-related choices (between, for example, point and enterprise solutions and between customised and standard solutions). The sheer volume of applications which have been developed in the general area of SCM means that simply getting to grips with what is available in terms of scope and functionality is itself quite difficult. Secondly, the business environments in which companies and supply chains operate have also become more complex. This results from increasing levels of competition, more sophisticated markets, more discerning customers and shortened product life-cycles.

Developing an ICT strategy for the supply chain involves the following steps:

- **Assessment of the capabilities required to meet market demand**: This sets the priorities and helps in identifying the gaps as part of overall corporate strategy development.

- **Assessment of the role and impact of ICT**: This involves assessing the ability of current ICT resources and capabilities in addressing market requirements. It goes on to assess the potential role of ICT in addressing evolving market requirements. This sets the priorities and helps in identifying the gaps as part of an enterprise's ICT strategy.
- **Assessment of corporate investment opportunities**: An examination of competing investment priorities sets the level of funding available for ICT and other corporate investments. For most organisations, ICT is one of the most significant areas of capital investment.
- **Assessment of ICT costs and investments**: This involves assessing current ICT spend and identifying areas where reallocation of capital spend could be achieved to build the capabilities required. This, in turn, sets the overall available level of ICT spend.

The ICT strategy and available levels of funding then set the parameters for the detailed planning and implementation of appropriate solutions.

ICT Planning and Implementation Process

- **Project initiation**: Based on the ICT strategy, those areas of the business which have the potential to be improved using ICT are identified. An initial evaluation of the technical options is carried out.
- **Create project planning team**: A multi-functional project team is established. Its members include technical as well as non-technical staff. The latter should represent the main user groups across the supply chain (typically for an ERP project this will include purchasing, production, warehousing, distribution, logistics and customer service personnel).
- **Construct a User Requirement Specification (URS)**: The project team develops this spec through consultation with as wide a group of users as possible. With developments in XES this consultation process increasingly needs to extend beyond the boundaries of an individual company into customers, suppliers and other trading and joint-venture partners.
- **Development of an Invitation to Tender (ITT)**: It is important that any trade-off between the requirements of different user groups are identified prior to the ITT being issued. Potential vendors are requested to submit cost and functionality information.
- **Shortlist vendors and select preferred vendor**: Vendors will be scored and ranked based on a range of cost and non-cost factors. The non-cost factors include, but are not limited to, system flexibility, scalability, connectivity with existing systems, ability and ease of upgrading functionality, timing and implementation issues, after-sales service support and sector experience

(by use of reference sites where possible). The overall completeness and clarity of the quotation should also be considered.
- **Construct a Functional Requirement Specification (FRS)**: The functionality required from the system needs to be agreed and detailed. Any bespoke programming changes required, where the FRS does not meet the URS, are identified. Business benefits should also be validated against costs at this stage in light of the overall ICT strategy. The FRS is signed off with the vendor as the agreed document to deliver against.
- **Detailed implementation**: The detail of this stage will vary enormously from project to project (e.g. point solutions versus enterprise solutions). Typical key stages and issues will include: extensive testing through all stages in the process; ongoing consultation and briefing of user groups and other stakeholders; documentation of work instructions; agreement of software and hardware service contracts; and training of all affected personnel.
- **Post-implementation evaluation**: This involves ongoing evaluation of system performance against required functionality. It should also embrace 'post-audit' evaluation of the actual financial benefits versus those estimated in the original business plan.

Concluding Comments

For any ICT implementation to achieve its true potential, an organisation must decide what to do and then do it properly. The former is based on the development of an ICT strategy, while the latter require a logical and systematic planning and implementation process. This appendix provides a template for both stages.

13

Information and Communications Technology (ICT) Applications in Transportation and Logistics

PIETRO EVANGELISTA

INTRODUCTION

As the enabling role of information and communications technology (ICT) applications in the wider supply chain context has been examined in Chapter 12, the main objective of this chapter is to focus on technology applications and tools supporting transportation and logistics (i.e. mainly at the 'move' and 'store' links in the supply chain, see Chapter 3). ICT plays a key role in every stage of the transport and logistics decision-making process, enabling managers to make decisions on the basis of accurate data and information. The chapter is organised into two parts. The first part gives an overview of the main information systems and applications supporting the management of logistics activities. To this end a matrix, based on a segmentation of information systems, is introduced. This matrix provides an understanding of where each system should be applied and the type of problem it is able to solve. The second part of the chapter provides an outline of the impact of ICT on the third-party logistics (3PL) industry. Starting from the recent evolution of the logistics service provision industry, the main trends associated with the widespread dissemination of new technologies in the sector are analysed.

MAPPING ICT APPLICATIONS IN TRANSPORTATION AND LOGISTICS

The rapid changes that have affected the evolution of SCM – and especially logistics – concepts in recent decades have been accompanied by a parallel development in ICT systems and applications. The use of ICT in the field of logistics has evolved over the past 30 years, delivering significant benefits in terms of enabling management to make decisions which have a significant impact on the company's performance. The successful application of ICT in logistics depends on the objectives and type of technology being deployed. Considering the significant range of technology tools and options available, with complex and varying levels of functionality, it is important to have a picture that facilitates an understanding of the roles of the various technologies that are used in different logistics functions. To this end a matrix is proposed in Figure 13.1. It mainly covers applications focused on the four fundamental logistics functions: order and fulfilment, inventory, warehousing and transportation.

It has been built on two dimensions: the scope of the logistics function covered by the information system (horizontal) and the decision-making level in which the system is used (vertical). The horizontal dimension defines the scope of the information and communication system – cross-functional information systems have also been considered, as there are many systems on the market that are able to integrate in one single software package the different applications used at the functional level. The vertical dimension describes the decision phase within the logistics decision-making process for which an information system is adopted. Under this dimension, four different types of information systems have been identified – strategic, planning, control and execution – according to the different types of problems they are able to solve. Each level has a different time-frame ranging from short-term to long-term decisions. For example, ICT supporting transportation optimisation and network facilities configuration provides the basis for logistics planning decisions on an approximately monthly basis. On the other hand, ICT applications used in the logistics execution phase have to provide real-time information about order, inventory, warehouse and transportation management.

The first level at the top of the matrix is referred to the *supply chain design and planning systems* level. It refers to strategic decisions that go beyond the scope of logistics management to embrace the entire supply chain configuration and planning. The time-frame of decisions in this level spans many years. At this level, managers need to define the customer target, the type of product to manufacture, the number of production sites to be involved and their location, the type of distribution system to be adopted and decisions about vertical integration and outsourcing. ICT used at this level is highly analytical as it is focused on analysing rather than gathering information. The main characteristics of ICT adopted at this level have been outlined in Chapter 12 – the so-called enterprise solutions – and they include: collaborative planning, forecasting and replenishment (CPFR), extended enterprise resource planning (EERP), enterprise integration applications (EIA), advanced planning systems (APS) and various decision

Figure 13.1: A Matrix of ICT Systems and Applications in Logistics Management

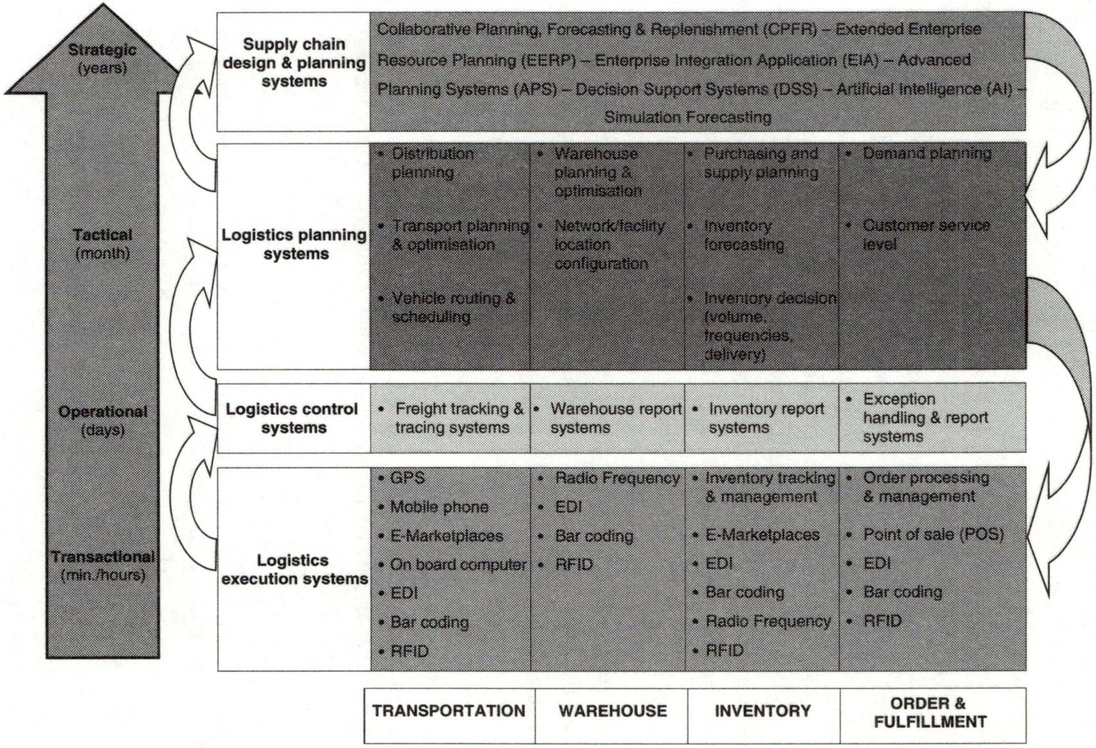

	TRANSPORTATION	WAREHOUSE	INVENTORY	ORDER & FULFILLMENT
Supply chain design & planning systems	Collaborative Planning, Forecasting & Replenishment (CPFR) – Extended Enterprise Resource Planning (EERP) – Enterprise Integration Application (EIA) – Advanced Planning Systems (APS) – Decision Support Systems (DSS) – Artificial Intelligence (AI) – Simulation Forecasting			
Logistics planning systems	• Distribution planning • Transport planning & optimisation • Vehicle routing & scheduling	• Warehouse planning & optimisation • Network/facility location configuration	• Purchasing and supply planning • Inventory forecasting • Inventory decision (volume, frequencies, delivery)	• Demand planning • Customer service level
Logistics control systems	• Freight tracking & tracing systems	• Warehouse report systems	• Inventory report systems	• Exception handling & report systems
Logistics execution systems	• GPS • Mobile phone • E-Marketplaces • On board computer • EDI • Bar coding • RFID	• Radio Frequency • EDI • Bar coding • RFID	• Inventory tracking & management • E-Marketplaces • EDI • Bar coding • Radio Frequency • RFID	• Order processing & management • Point of sale (POS) • EDI • Bar coding • RFID

Strategic (years) → Tactical (month) → Operational (days) → Transactional (min./hours) support systems (DSS), some of which make use of artificial intelligence (AI), simulation and forecasting.

The *logistics planning systems* level focuses on information support to develop and refine the logistics activities within a company. Such systems enable accurate planning of each logistics activity. The main objective is to allocate available resources among the different logistics activities. This level is of particular importance as it provides a critical link between the supply chain decision level and decisions affecting a company's logistics functions. Typical planning decisions involve time frames of several months to a year. Information requirements at this level include costs, capacities and demand to assist managers in identifying, evaluating and comparing tactical logistics alternatives. Typical analyses include transport planning/optimisation, vehicle routing and scheduling, warehouse planning/optimisation, network/facility location configuration, purchasing and supply planning, and inventory forecasting. Planning decisions also focus on analysing rather than gathering information.

The *logistics control systems* level is focused on performance measurement and management reporting for each logistics function. Here it is important to identify exceptions that allow the solution for problems related to specific customers or orders. Logistics control systems are focused on both gathering and analysing information.

Logistics execution systems initiate and record individual logistics activities. Such systems aim to execute what has been planned in the earlier levels and deal with time frames of typically minutes or hours. At this level information systems execute and record transactions that include: order entry, inventory assignment, order selection, transportation, pricing, invoicing and customer inquiry. This level is information-intensive as it requires that information be available for every transaction executed. Logistics execution systems are characterised by formalised rules and a large volume of transactions. For this reason, the emphasis is on system efficiency that means faster processing or higher transaction volume with fewer resources. The typical example in this field is electronic data interchange (EDI), which has become the transaction system messaging standard in many industries. Systems based on radio frequency identification (RFID) technology and global positioning systems (GPS) are also becoming more prevalent.

Point solutions and functionally focused applications in transport and logistics link planning and control activities together. Such applications, often based on sophisticated algorithms (e.g. linear programming, mixed integer programming, genetic algorithms and the theory of constraints), include transportation management systems (TMS) and warehouse management systems (WMS).

The aim of a TMS is to optimise the management of product shipping. The following five functionalities are typically incorporated in this application: freight payment auditing, transportation planning, carrier performance, trailer loading and vehicle/fleet management. The main benefit associated with the use of a TMS is the capacity of the company to increase the speed of order processing with a high service level without incurring additional operating costs. Furthermore, a TMS allows the automation of the above activities, thus allowing a company's transportation function to manage, instead of reacting to, transportation events and opportunities.

A WMS is a software package that enables maximisation of the use of space, equipment and labour. It enables the execution of inventory planning commands, inventory and location control and the management of the flow of warehouse orders and processes on a day-to-day basis. The main benefits relate to reductions in order fulfilment lead time and inventory management. These include improved customer service and quicker turnover of inventory, resulting in substantial potential savings in warehousing operational costs.

The Use of ICT in the 3PL Industry

To understand the role that ICT can play in the 3PL service provider industry it is worth answering the following question: *To what extent can technology help transportation and logistics operations?* It has been calculated that the value of all logistics services in international trade was $1 trillion in 1999 (Frankel 1999). This included $128 billion on shipping, $196 billion on road, rail and river transport, $300 billion for port, warehousing and associated infrastructure, and $388 billion for information, transaction and associated management costs (see Figure 13.2).

Through the effective use of the Internet and other new technologies, carriers and 3PLs could reduce these costs by 50 per cent with a 15 to 25 per cent reduction in transportation costs. Furthermore, 45 per cent of the door-to-door delivery cost of products is wasted time and money for documentation. This waste could be largely reduced by effective use of ICT that allows for much tighter real-time movement and operational control. From this point of view, ICT is seen as a key factor that will affect the growth and development of the 3PL industry.

There is little doubt that the logistics service industry is undergoing a major transition. In the last few years a series of major changes have occurred which have profoundly affected the logistics service industry at an

Figure 13.2: Breakdown of Value of Logistics Services in International Trade

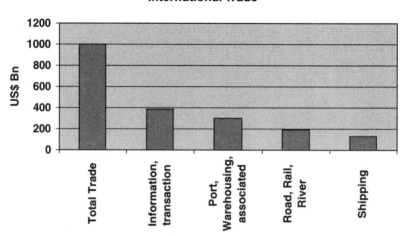

Source: Frankel, E.G. (1999), 'The Economics of Total Trans-ocean Supply Chain Management', International Journal of Maritime Economics, 1(1), 61–69.

international level. One of the main driving forces is the widespread adoption of the SCM concept by manufacturers and retailers in managing their businesses. This has resulted in the delivery system becoming an integral part of their product, to the extent that transportation and logistics have become as important as the product itself (Sheffi 1990). In the context of evolving SCM adoption, manufacturers and retailers are pursuing two complementary strategies. On the one hand, such companies have increased the outsourcing of significant parts of their logistics activities (McKinnon 1999) and have reduced the number of logistics providers with which to establish long-term relationships for the supply of 'tailor-made' transportation and logistics services (Razzaque and Sheng 1998). On the other hand, they are demanding a higher degree of integration from all supply chain participants. As noted in Chapter 3, the shift from traditional supply chain configurations, often characterised by fragmentation, to more coordinated and integrated approaches is central to SCM. This emphasis on integration gives ICT an increasingly important role within contemporary SCM strategy.

Accordingly, 3PLs have started to transform the scope and characteristics of their services to improve customer service levels (Daugherty *et al.* 1992). As a result, 3PLs play a more important role than in the past insofar as they are entrusted with the task of integrating and accelerating physical and information flows along multiple levels of the supply chain (Cooper *et al.* 1998). This has given 3PLs a new potential role in customising supply chains as they assume responsibility for a growing number of activities beyond transportation and warehousing. For example, the practice of postponement of product finishing to downstream stages of supply chains means that 3PLs have the opportunity to offer services such as final assembly and customisation of products. Offering these services gives 3PLs the opportunity to penetrate segments of supply chains with higher added-value services compared to traditional transportation and warehousing services. The supplementary customised services can give a differentiation edge, while raising added value in services can improve margins, as well as deepen the relationships with customers.

In this scenario, the major challenges for 3PLs include meeting demands for global sourcing, supply chain integration, 'one-stop' solutions and flexibility in service offerings. With more companies opting to outsource distribution and logistics activities to 3PLs, the ability to differentiate becomes critical. Logistics service providers are under constant pressure to enhance their customer relationships and continually expand the range of services offered. Core service offerings are being commoditised, while value-added services and technological capabilities are considered points of differentiation (Evangelista 2004). While the primary driving forces in the 3PL sector previously were to reduce cost and release capital for alternative purposes, the driving forces today have more strategic influences in terms of market coverage, improving the level of service or increasing flexibility in view of the changing requirements of customers (Ojala 2003). This has given 3PLs a new potential role in customising the supply chain, as a growing number of activities beyond transportation and warehousing can be carried out by logistics service providers (Cooper *et al.* 1998). For example, by providing solutions that include value-adding services, such as final assembly, packaging and quality control, 3PLs can improve their competitive position through increasing the level of customisation of the service offered (Skjoett-Larsen 2000).

The growing need for businesses to diversify and delegate as their supply chains become broader and more complex has validated the role of 3PLs in every aspect of logistics. After gaining acceptance in logistics operations and growing with notable speed over the past few years, 3PL providers are settling into their roles as integral parts of their customers' business plans. This has fuelled the transition from the traditional 'arms length' approach to the supply of integrated logistics services packages on a 'one-stop shopping' basis and has further facilitated the migration of companies from asset-based to information and knowledge-based, and value-added logistics service enterprises. Accordingly, the 3PL market is moving towards a tiered system, as shown in Figure 13.3.

Three different evolving stages can be identified during the past three decades. In each stage different types of companies entered the logistics

Figure 13.3: Evolving Role of Logistics Service Providers in Logistics Outsourcing

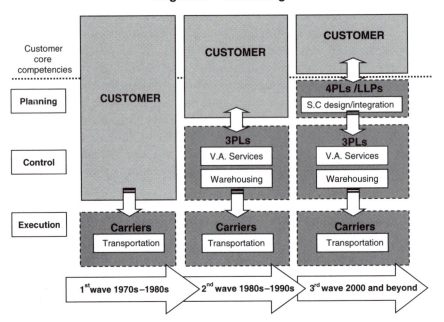

service market according to the different levels of customer logistics outsourcing. During the first wave (1970s to 1980s) commodity providers (carriers) operated in the market as transportation was the main outsourced activity. The competitive weapons of these companies were mainly based on operational efficiency and a resulting low cost base. In the second wave (1980s to 1990s) 3PL companies appeared in the market. The competitive abilities of these companies mainly relied on integrated transport and warehousing services provided in combination with a range of customised value-added logistics services. Such companies often outsourced basic and low margin services (such as transportation) to carriers which worked as tier suppliers in the system.

The most recent wave (2000 and beyond) has been characterised by the entry of a new type of company (fourth-party logistics (4PL) service providers) offering integrated strategic supply chain orchestration. 4PLs typically handle all aspects of the supply chain, from procurement through to inventory control, final delivery and invoicing. In this context, 4PLs are able to supply highly customised and specialised services through the control of strategic functions such as supply chain design and integration on a global scale, while value-added services and other logistics activities are outsourced to local 3PLs that act as sub-contractors.

Logistics service companies now have the opportunity to evolve from playing their traditional tactical roles (first wave) to become adaptive supply chain providers (third wave). The key challenge is to decide which of these three tiers they are going to concentrate on and then to build an organisation to support this strategy. These tiers mirror those within the automotive sector with the first tier taking full responsibility for the coordination of their customers' supply chains (with a strong emphasis on introducing innovation), as well as managing a second tier of companies.

It is evident that, in the evolving landscape of the logistics outsourcing market, ICT is playing an increasingly important role posing new strategic challenges and opportunities to logistics service providers. In today's turbulent supply chain environment characterised by time compression and the need for agility, ICT capabilities become both a critical variable for logistics service differentiation (Sauvage 2003) and a significant tool to cut costs and effectively serve clients through a better customisation of the service provided (Van Hoeck 2002).

The widespread use of ICT is reinforced by the trend towards the outsourcing of shippers' information applications. According to a survey by Lieb and Schwarz (2002), many users of 3PL services rely on their 3PL providers for ICT support as shown in Table 13.1. Users were asked to identify the information-based services they have outsourced to their 3PLs. The information-based services most frequently outsourced to 3PL providers are freight payment services (45 per cent), transportation planning/optimisation (45 per cent), warehouse management systems (27 per cent), shipment tracking (18 per cent) and international documentation (18 per cent).

The supply of information-based services (such as real-time tracking and tracing of shipments) is a great challenge for 3PLs, particularly for small- and

Table 13.1: The Information-Based Services Most Frequently Outsourced to 3PLs

Applications	Percentage of Respondents
Freight payment/accounting	45%
Transportation planning/optimisation	45%
Warehouse management systems	27%
Shipment tracking	18%
International documentation	18%
Supply chain planning/scheduling	6%
Order management	6%

Source: Lieb, R., and Schwarz, B. (2002), 'The Use of Third Party Logistics Services by Large American Manufacturers: The 2001 Survey', paper presented at the Annual Conference of the Council for Logistics Management, October, San Francisco CA. Courtesy of the Council of Supply Chain Management Professionals.

medium-sized logistics service providers. Such companies have more difficulties in using ICT due to reluctance to change and insufficient human and financial resources. ICT is often perceived as an added cost involving company re-organisation and the skills development associated with technology investments. The result is that small 3PLs generally underestimate the potential of ICT as a tool for increasing cost-efficiency and improving customer service simultaneously (Evangelista and Sweeney 2006).

The increasing role of ICT has contributed to the evolution of the competitive scenario in the international 3PL industry. It has allowed the entry of new players in the market from unexpected industries and has led to changes in the way 3PLs conduct their business (Regan and Song 2001). The following three trends emerge as a result of the impact of ICT and web technologies on the 3PL industry (Evangelista 2003).

New E-Services

One of the first visible effects is the integration of traditional services with information services facilitated by the dissemination of the Internet. Although transport firms have used telecommunication systems and networks for some time,[1] the sector as a whole may not be considered a leader in the field of technological innovation (Tilanus 1997). However, over the past few years firms operating in the sector have made significant progress in their adoption of new technologies, particularly those linked to the Internet and e-business. Low-cost access to the web and the dissemination of e-business technologies (see Chapter 14) have provided these firms with the tools to satisfy customer demand by using traditional services in conjunction with growing information-based services. Today, the main transport and logistics service firms are in a position to provide a variety of information via the Internet and to secure transactions online with customers. However, the range of initiatives online appears to be somewhat diversified. There are firms that initially used their own websites as e-service catalogues. Some firms offer limited functionality (such as tracking and booking services). In other cases, customised portals have been developed to provide a wide range of online e-service and capabilities to support the company's competitive advantage. For example, the shipping line OOCL provides a full range of e-services through its website. Such services include: sailing schedule; tariff and rates; e-forms; EDI; track and trace;

---

[1] The first applications were in the air transport sector at the beginning of the 1960s. Later, their use was extended first to maritime transport and then, in the 1980s, to other transport modes.

booking request; shipping instructions and shipment details; milestone notifications and exception alerts; bill of lading; document management; and invoicing and payment. However, the rapid development of e-business is expected to give rise to a gradual increase in the functionality of websites.

New Functions

The dissemination of ICT has opened up opportunities for the development of new roles and functions in the supply chain, the so-called infomediaries or on-line transportation e-marketplaces. The purpose of these web-based intermediaries is to give added value to the transport and logistics business through greater efficiency and information transparency. Their work is based on running Internet transport portals which bring together buyers and sellers of transport services, provide the buyer with information and make communication between the two faster and more direct. As for their services, whilst on the one hand there is a strong similarity between the services of different portals, on the other hand there are significant differences in the scope and objectives of these portals (UNCTAD 2000). There is also a variety of infomediary typologies operating on the Internet and the dividing lines between them are somewhat blurred. Regan and Song (2001) have identified the following five different categories:

1. **Spot Freight Markets** (NTE, DATconnect) allow shippers and carriers to post available loads or capacity on the web.
2. **Auction and Request for Quote (RFQ) markets** (Logistics.com, Celarix) provide automated RFQ and auction capability.
3. **Exchanges** (3PLEX, Nistevo, Leanlogistics, Trantislink) may provide spot market and auction capabilities but must also provide creative e-business solutions for shippers, carriers and 3PLs.
4. **Applications Service Providers (ASPs)** (Manugistics, i2, Accuship, GoShip, Intershipper) are primarily developing web-enabling and e-business enabling technology for the logistics industry.
5. **Purchasing Consolidation Markets** (TruckersB2B, Transplace) provide an opportunity for member companies (typically small carriers) to purchase equipment and supplies at bulk rates over the Internet.

The development of on-line transportation e-marketplaces tends to alter the role of traditional transport intermediaries and relations between these firms and other actors in the logistics chain. There is little doubt that the development of the Internet and e-business have led to far more information being made available to all actors along the supply chain. This may pose a threat to operators such as agents and freight forwarders, who have based their business on information asymmetries between those requiring and providing transport and logistics services. Some intermediary functions risk becoming redundant, to be subsequently replaced by the phenomenon of disintermediation.[2] The pressure of this threat has induced some intermediaries to form alliances with other transport operators, as in the case of the alliance between AEI, a freight forwarding company, and the shipping line P&O. They set up a strategic alliance to send standard EDI shipping instructions and bookings and receive tracking information in return. At the same time the development of infomediaries may provide traditional intermediaries with an opportunity to extend and differentiate their own businesses. For example, in the case of freight forwarders they can become truly global and multimodal logistics service providers, focusing on the entire chain process rather than on the narrow region of origin or destination under the traditional approach. Consequently, their key competencies are shifting from traditional agency-based freight forwarding services (e.g. freight documentation, customs clearance) to optimising the total transport and logistics needs of shippers. In the maritime transport industry, a similar process is affecting shipping agents.

In reality, the use of web transport portals by 3PLs is difficult to assess due to the lack of consistent data on the overall volume of services sold. It appears that a small number of traditional intermediaries are using online exchanges to help their shipper clients match with carriers. A study carried out by KPMG and Benchmarking Partners on the way in which carriers use the Internet would appear to confirm the above findings (Logistics Management and Distribution Report 2000). Providers do not foresee that infomediaries will have a significant effect on their business, while only 50 per cent of the shippers interviewed replied that they might use infomediaries in the near future.

New Alliances

Another trend emerging alongside the Internet and e-business is the creation of a new category of service provider called fourth-party logistics (4PL) provision. According to Bade *et al.* (1999), a 4PL is a supply chain integrator who assembles and manages the resources, capabilities and technology of its organisation with those of complementary service providers

---

[2]Stough (2001) defines the disintermediation process as '... the bypassing of intermediaries between buyer and seller by introducing a middle man'.

to deliver a comprehensive supply chain solution. In brief, the emergence of these providers derives from the fact that many manufacturers and retailers operating at an international level find it increasingly difficult to satisfy the growing expectations of their customers, mainly because of the widespread use of the Internet and web-based solutions and that of enterprise integration technologies. Pressures from customers are therefore forcing these firms to re-engineer their supply chains, especially in terms of strategy, operations and technology. To improve their skills, some 3PLs have started to secure alliances with complementary service providers (Rockwell 1999). The relationship between UPS Logistics Group and Alcatel is a good example of a 4PL relationship. Alcatel is one of the world's major players in the areas of telecommunications and the Internet, building next generation networks and delivering integrated end-to-end voice and data networking solutions to telecommunications carriers, enterprises and consumers. UPS Logistics Group has been providing fourth-party SCM services for Alcatel eND (eBusiness Networking Division). Alcatel eND is a leader in both the French and European markets with a 50 per cent and 24 per cent share, respectively. UPS Logistics acts as the sole point of contact for the operational, ICT and financial aspects of Alcatel eND's supply chain.

The emergence of 4PLs enables manufacturers to outsource to a single organisation the entire re-engineering of their supply chain processes, beginning with the design stage through to implementation, and ending with the execution of comprehensive supply chain solutions. Beyond the emergence of 4PLs, there is an ongoing trend in the transport and logistics service sector to form alliances with other firms operating in complementary sectors (Eyefortransport 2001).

Conclusion

The need to serve customers in an innovative and flexible manner is putting companies under pressure to continuously refocus their strategies and to respond quickly to change. This requires appropriate investment in information systems for integrating logistics functions within the company and with other supply chain members. There has been a strong proliferation of tools and applications in the area of logistics activities in recent years. This situation can result in mistakes in selecting the right ICT applications for supporting a particular logistics function. Understanding the role of different ICT solutions is of great importance for managers in optimising logistics decisions. Furthermore, it is very important that managers include the future state of the business in the decision process and make sure that their technology choices take these trends into account. This is particularly evident in the context of today's logistics service industry scenario where ICT has the undeniable role of a catalyst in changing business models. The availability of capable ICT-based services is becoming an expected element of 3PL service supply. The cost of entry into the 3PL arena now includes technology and implementation capabilities for warehouse management, transportation management and web-enabled communications to the extent that logistics providers compete in two separate yet closely linked markets: firstly, the *marketplace*, where goods are physically exchanged and where traditional transport and logistics services are required for the shipment of goods; secondly, the *marketspace*, in other words the virtual market of e-business where information is the main transactional element. In the future, the success of 3PLs will depend increasingly on their ability to deliver an integrated, end-to-end solution that provides significant improvements in financial and operational performance. Consequently, 3PLs need to focus on a number of key issues, including the development and implementation of appropriate ICT strategies, instituting effective relationship management processes, integrating services and technologies globally, and delivering comprehensive solutions that create value for the users and their supply chains. Considering that customer demands for performance and sophistication are accelerating, improving these areas is a key imperative for 3PLs.

REFERENCES

Bade, D., Mueller, J. and Youd, B. (1999), 'Technology in the Next Level of Supply Chain Outsourcing: Leveraging the Capabilities of Fourth Party Logistics', available at: <http://www.ascet.com/documents.asp?d_ID=229>, accessed April 2007.

Cooper, M.C., Lambert, D.M. and Pagh, J.D. (1998), 'What Should Be the Transportation Provider's Role in Supply Chain Management?', paper presented at the 8th World Conference on Transport Research, 12–17 July, Antwerp, Belgium.

Daugherty, P.J., Sabath, R.E. and Rogers, D.S. (1992), 'Competitive Advantage through Customer Responsiveness', *The Logistics and Transportation Review*, 28(3), 257–272.

Evangelista P. (2003), 'A Framework for Assessing the Impact of Information and Communication Technologies on Logistics and Supply Chain Management', *Logistics Solutions*, 3, 9–13.

Evangelista, P. (2004), 'Leveraging Technology Capabilities in the 3PL Industry', *Logistics Solutions*, 1, 24–29.

Evangelista, P. and Sweeney, E. (2006), 'Technology Usage in the Supply Chain: The Case of Small 3PLs', *International Journal of Logistics Management*, 17(1), 55–74.

Eyefortransport (2001), *Digital Logistics – Value Creation in the Freight Transport Industry*, Eyefortransport – First Conference Ltd., available at: <http://www.eyefortransport.com/report/index_first.shtml>, accessed April 2007.

Frankel, E.G. (1999), 'The Economics of Total Trans-Ocean Supply Chain Management', *International Journal of Maritime Economics*, 1(1), 61–69.

Lieb, R. and Schwarz, B. (2002), 'The Use of Third Party Logistics Services by Large American Manufacturers: The 2001 Survey', paper presented at the Annual Conference of the Council for Logistics Management, October, San Francisco CA.

KPMG and Benchmarking Partners (2000), 'Study Looks at how Carriers Use the Web', *Logistics Management and Distribution Report*, 1 April.

McKinnon, A. (1999), 'The Outsourcing of Logistical Activities', in D. Waters (ed.), *Global Logistics and Distribution Planning*, London: Kogan Page, 215–234.

Ojala, L. (2003), 'Estimating the Size of the Finnish TPL Market', in D. Andersson, H. Dreyer *et al.* (eds.), *Third Party Logistics – A Nordic Research Approach*, Finland: Turku School of Economics and Business Administration, 50.

Razzaque, M.R. and Sheng, C.C. (1998), 'Outsourcing of Logistics Functions: A Literature Survey', *International Journal of Physical Distribution and Logistics Management*, 28(2), 89–107.

Regan, A.C. and Song, J. (2001), 'An Industry in Transition: Third Party Logistics in the Information Age', proceedings of the Transportation Research Board, 80th Annual Meeting, January, Washington DC, USA.

Rockwell, B. (1999), 'Seamless Global Logistics and the Internet', paper presented at the Electronic Commerce for Freight Transportation Conference, 3 June, New Orleans, USA.

Sheffi, Y. (1990), 'Third Party Logistics: Present and Future Prospects', *Journal of Business Logistics*, 2, 27.

Sauvage, T. (2003), 'The Relationship between Technology and Logistics Third-Party Providers', *International Journal of Physical Distribution and Logistical Management*, 33(3), 236–253.

Skjoett-Larsen, T. (2000), 'TPL from an Interorganisational Point of View', *International Journal of Physical Distribution and Logistics Management*, 30(2), 112–127.

Stough, R.R. (2001), 'New Technologies in Logistics Management', in Brewer et al. (eds.), *Handbook of Logistics and Supply Chain Management*, UK: Pergamon, 517.

Tilanus, B. (1997), *Information Systems in Logistics and Transportation*, Oxford: Elsevier Science Ltd.

UNCTAD (2000), *Review of Maritime Transport,* Geneva: United Nations.

Van Hoeck, R. (2002), 'Using Information Technology to Leverage Transport and Logistics Service Operations in the Supply Chain: An Empirical Assessment of the Interrelation between Technology and Operation Management', *International Journal of Information Technology and Management*, 1(1), 115–130.

14

E-Business and Supply Chain Management

BERND HUBER AND CLAUDIA WAGNER

INTRODUCTION

As outlined in Chapter 3, the constituent parts of a supply chain are linked together via the flow of information and therefore the proper implementation and integration of information and communications technology (ICT) is vital for supply chain management (SCM). Globalisation forces multinational enterprises (MNEs) as well as small- and medium-sized enterprises (SMEs) to reduce costs and increase efficiency. SCM is increasingly recognised as a strategic weapon, by which business operations can be streamlined and overall competitiveness enhanced. Supply chain integration is defined as the extent to which all activities within an organisation, and the activities of its suppliers, customers and other supply chain members are integrated together (Narasimhan and Jayaram 1998).

EVOLUTION OF INTER-ORGANISATIONAL SYSTEMS

Integrated SCM has generated much interest dating back to the 1960s (e.g. Forrester 1961) because actions taken by one member in the supply chain can influence the profitability of all other members. However, the lack of ICT hindered the implementation of a more 'systems-oriented' approach in the starting phase. Inter-organisational systems (IOS) such as electronic data interchange (EDI) have been used since the 1970s to link one or more organisations to their suppliers or customers through private value-added networks. IOS are automated information systems shared by two or more companies and differ from internal information systems by allowing information to be sent across organisational boundaries. However, entities within a supply chain often have different and conflicting objectives and interests and, therefore, complex interactions take place

(Gregor and Johnston 2000). As noted by Riggins and Mukhopadhyay (1999):

> IOS projects are inherently more risky than traditional internal IT projects because there is less control due to the uncertainty of external trading-partner actions. Additionally, since inter-organisational systems often have interdependent benefits, the way in which a trading partner implements a system may affect the benefits realised by the other party.

EDI, in its traditional form, is partially ineffective for allowing multiple enterprises to make use of common data and process models of the whole supply chain. It offers limited functionality and is problematic because it has not been standardised world-wide. EDI data is usually exchanged in batch fashion, which makes it complicated to handle exceptions. Process-level integration between multiple enterprises is, therefore, complex to implement because the data produced by one organisation's EDI applications is frequently processed by dissimilar application sets in the receiving organisation. Although EDI can help to decrease transaction costs, it is rather inflexible and limited to the establishment of bilateral relationships typically for manufacturers that could afford their implementation at high cost per contact. That is why, for example, despite years of pressure from MNEs, only an estimated five per cent of the automotive value chain is connected to EDI to date (Roland Berger Consulting and Deutsche Bank 2001).

Advent of E-Business

Therefore, traditional EDI provided only limited success in the context of supply chain integration. The advent of more advanced ICT, most notably the Internet, promises to move beyond the limited EDI transaction sets to automate the data flows across the supply chain, make a contribution to a more multilateral information exchange and foster market-based exchanges in all transaction phases. Replacing expensive EDI solutions governed by only one buyer in a closed system, low entry costs, fast return on investment and protection of existing EDI investment, recent developments in XML-programming[1] are all reasons for the transformation of the supply chain into a network by Internet technologies (Richmond et al. 1998).

---

[1] XML (Extensible Markup Language) is a vendor-neutral data exchange language for passing not just data, but information. The World Wide Web Consortium created XML in early 1998; XML is becoming a *de facto* standard for B2B applications and transactions in many industries. The authors of XML planned to develop a meta-language that would overcome the complexity of HTML but also allow for the encapsulation of intelligent description of the language.

One of the first industry players to have used the concept 'e-business' was IBM in 1997. E-business has generally been pioneered by computing companies, where demand is constantly changing and products have to have a very short delivery time as a result. E-business is defined by Amor (1999) as follows:

> A secured, flexible and integrated approach in order to offer various companies values through the combination of systems and procedures and so being able to manage the core business procedures with the simplicity and penetration of Internet technology.

Prior to the evolution of the Internet, transactions would have been mostly completed in more traditional ways: telephone, postal mail, facsimile or face-to-face contact. E-commerce is a subset of e-business and is the term used to describe Internet-based electronic transactions. In this respect, business-to-business (B2B) differs from business-to-consumer (B2C) e-commerce. In B2B, relationships between customers and suppliers are much more complex, often contractual, long-term and involve larger order amounts than B2C.[2] E-procurement is the use of ICT (especially the Internet) in the purchasing process (Boer *et al.* 2002).

MacDuffie and Helper (2000) explain that the Internet is a powerful tool for promoting fast, asynchronous communication among large groups of people, without a need to invest in a specific asset. As noted by the Federal Trade Commission (2000), 'the aggregating power of the Internet can overcome circumstances where otherwise the cost of information gathering outweighs the value of the surplus.'

For example, e-business can be observed in the electronics industry, which is challenged by a combination of mass customisation, shrinking product life-cycles, rapid inventory depreciation, complex multi-sourced supply chains and rising expectations of retailers and consumers. Leon (2000) argues that the electronics industry is way ahead of other sectors in experimenting with e-business. The availability of advanced ICT was one of the key enablers of accelerating the process of outsourcing non-core activities and of evolving the electronics industry from its traditional vertically integrated structure to a variety of multi-stage supply chain configurations. Organisations increasingly form part of a network in which they collaborate with other organisations dynamically to fulfil market demand. The requirement for a more responsive and integrated supply chain emphasises that e-business plays a key role in the electronics value chain due to the amount and complexity of required data and information.

---

[2]Another approach is Business-to-Government (B2G) e-commerce.

BENEFITS AND SERVICES PROVIDED BY E-BUSINESS

The emergence of e-business can help organisations to address issues of a higher degree of complexity and volatility. For example, Raisch (2001) points out some elements where Internet-based systems replace traditional trust systems (see Table 14.1).

Overall, e-business solutions in general are seeking to enhance supply chain effectiveness and efficiency through the automation of business processes. The adoption of e-business can result in benefits such as more transparency, help to reduce transaction, manufacturing and other costs, check unmonitored corporate spending (also known as maverick or rogue purchasing)[3] and centralise purchasing spend or coordinate efficient collaborations for such projects as joint product design. E-business may also:

- Facilitate collaboration and supply chain information sharing, such as order forecasts and inventory planning.
- Automate requisition and purchase order creation, integrate payment processes.
- Help organisations develop plans for managing sourcing and logistics.

However, Knudsen (2002) points out that there are still some uncertainties as to how the overall company performance can be improved by e-business. Solutions and tools are still remarkably diverse. The concept has

Table 14.1: Traditional versus Internet-Based Value Trust Systems

Traditional	Internet-Based
Paper-based documents	Electronic documents
Photo ID	Authentication
Handwritten signature	Digital signature
Handshake	Email acknowledgement
Physical meetings	Videoconferencing
Qualification	Digital certificate
Authorisation	Rule-based access, public key infrastructure
Business card	Signature file
Key	Password
Fingerprint	Biometrics

Source: Raisch, W. (2001), *The E-Marketplace: Strategies for Success in B2B E-Commerce,* New York: McGraw-Hill.

---

[3]Maverick buying takes place when purchases are out of compliance with master contracts and when there is not a consolidated record of the total effect of such purchases. The National Association of Purchasing Managers (NAPM) estimates that one-third of all corporate purchases are out of compliance with purchase agreements. On average, maverick buyers pay 18 to 27 per cent more than the actual pre-negotiated price.

many different meanings, ranging from shopping on the web via online auctions to collaborative initiatives taking place in virtual meetings, among others. Boer *et al.* (2002) note in that respect that the potential merit of various e-business forms, such as electronic catalogue systems and software, intelligent agent applications and e-marketplaces, seems largely undisputed. However, given the wide range of solutions available, many organisations struggle with assessing the suitability of the different solutions for their specific commodities and portfolio of business requirements. To provide an overview of the available e-business tools, Gebauer and Zagler (2000) have developed a framework that helps to position available B2B solutions (see Figure 14.1).

For example, while purchasing managers have traditionally covered the entire range of purchasing operations and activities, recent trends show a transition of short-term-oriented operational activities towards end-user requisitioners. E-business can enable them to order products such as maintenance, repair and operations (MRO) in online catalogues or desktop purchasing systems, whereby the requisitioner's authorisation is electronically checked. The order information can pass electronically through various checking procedures, for example authorisation by the relevant managers or directors. Once cleared, the order can be aggregated with others to the same destination and issued electronically to the supplier. This process flow

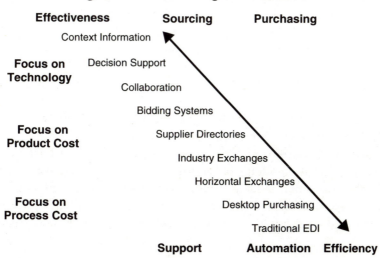

Figure 14.1: Positioning B2B Solutions

Source: Similar to Gebauer, J. and Zagler, M. (2000), 'Assessing the Status Quo and Future of B2B E-Commerce', Fisher Center for IT and Marketplace Transformation, Haas School of Business, University of California, Berkeley, available at: <http://www.zagler.ch/data/StatusQuoandFutureECommerce_RevueInternationalledelAchat.pdf>, accessed 23 February 2007.

may reduce operational costs, improve process efficiency, deliver greater centralised control over purchasing and may increase negotiating power with suppliers through order consolidation.

Boer et al. (2002) have also identified other forms of e-business. E-informing does not involve transactions, but instead it handles gathering and dissemination of relevant information across the supply chain. E-sourcing is the process of finding new potential suppliers using ICT with the aim of decreasing the search costs. Identifying new sources of supply increases the competitive forces during the tendering process. E-Tendering is the process of sending RFx (see below) to suppliers and receiving the responses by the use of ICT systems.

The three types of RFx commonly used for sourcing include RFI (Request for Information), RFP (Request for Proposal), and RFQ (Request for Quotation). RFIs typically involve a potential buyer asking a seller to provide additional information on a product or process. RFQs involve a potential buyer requesting a specific price for a given items, while RFPs tend to include both a quote and a qualitative description of the work to be done.

Thereby, organisations can also take advantage of electronic purchasing consortia (EPC) to electronically conduct tasks that are necessary for the management of demand aggregation between two or more legal entities. EPC can exploit the potential of economies of scale and scope without the diseconomies of increased transaction and communication costs (Corsten and Zagler 1999) and result in average net reductions in purchasing costs of over five per cent and a return on investment of over 70 per cent (Huber et al. 2004). However, there can also be some conflict with EPC due to anti-trust limitations, cultural and structural impediments (e.g. overcapacity, vertical integration) and technical factors (e.g. high level of modularised assembly).

On the other hand, EPC can deliver the required volume (especially for SMEs) to carry out reverse auctions. An electronic reverse auction is a buyer-initiated quotation process, where purchasers post an RFQ for a product, while suppliers electronically bid against each other in a progressive way and compete in an online bidding event to achieve a sale for the requested product. Reverse auctions are based on game theory and are dynamic price applications used to streamline the RFx process. Only pre-qualified suppliers

---

[4]A variety of parameters such as the level of suppliers' quality, warranty or customer service are typically pre-qualified by purchasers and integrated into reverse auctions by multimode codings. When competition in reverse auctions would be based on purchasing price alone, suppliers are traditionally anxious about decreased profit margins or lack of opportunity to provide value-added services.

might be allowed to bid electronically for a specific demand.[4] Reverse auctions may make a contribution to the EPC sourcing process when:

- The addressed markets are fragmented.
- A critical mass and global sourcing expertise is needed.
- Standardisation of products is desired.
- Transactions costs are high.

However, implementation of reverse auctions has not been without controversy, because they can be contradictory to the long-term benefits associated with collaborative buyer–supplier alliances. This perceived conflict is primarily caused by the emphasis of reverse auctions on awarding business based on aggressive price competition and increased supplier transparency instead of long-term total cost of ownership (TCO) considerations.

Electronic linkages in the supply chain can change the nature of inter-organisational relationships. However, they should ideally enable the sharing of resources and core competencies and the synchronisation of working processes between external partners in virtual network organisations, although there is a wide diversity of e-business tools and services and the above-mentioned should be regarded as a condensed list. Van Weele and Rozemeijer (1996) claim that network structures and their respective electronic implementation may well be one of the most central elements of business strategy in the next decade.

Efficiencies in e-business can be achieved by disintermediation strategies (Lucking-Reiley and Spulber 2000), which is the potential elimination of 'middlemen' by supplanting presumably costly intermediaries with direct transactions and the realisation of lower transaction costs by ICT. However, lower transaction costs and less expensive intermediation do not necessarily result in fewer third-party organisations in e-business. New technology providers such as e-marketplaces can facilitate electronic structures in business processes and were created as mediators to help to develop Internet solutions as regards business communications and management.

The Role of E-Marketplaces

An e-marketplace is an Internet-based solution that links businesses interested in buying and selling related goods or services from one to another (Lipis *et al.* 2000). E-Marketplaces can create value as they can, for example, facilitate the search and choice of trading partners, increase visibility and transparency in terms of product information, availability or price, aggregate trade volumes for the generation of scale/scope economies and reduce transaction costs, resulting in more efficient, networked markets (see Figure 14.2).

Figure 14.2: Networked E-Marketplace Model

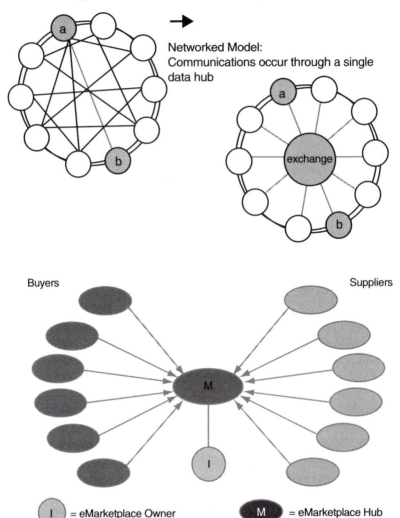

Source: Better Business Wales (Holdings) Ltd. (2007), *E-Commerce and Your Business*, online guide, available at: <http://www.opportunitywales.co.uk/2-5-2d.htm>, accessed May 2007

E-marketplaces can perform a variety of services that are often complex, inconvenient or costly for the buyers and sellers to undertake. As a result, adaptation of intermediary roles or reintermediation has been more common than disintermediation (Clarke 2001).

E-marketplaces can focus vertically (operating in only one specific industry), but also focus horizontally (across various industries). Horizontal e-marketplaces are often well suited to buy indirect inputs such as MRO, which tend not to be industry specific. Vertical e-marketplaces, by contrast, are well suited to buy direct or strategic goods that are incorporated into the final product.

Another classification of e-marketplaces can be done into buy-side, open or sell-side systems. Open e-marketplaces can be distinguished from a buy-side system insofar as it must be a neutral community not only to buyers, but also to sellers, thereby considering the interests of both purchasers and sellers. Buy-side solutions are governed by one organisation (private e-business solution) or several firms (consortia-led solution) and are set up to support the purchasing processes. A sell-side solution is typically composed of a supplier and multiple buyer market hierarchy and is initiated by suppliers and distributors to support their sales processes. Sell-side solutions can be direct ordering on supplier websites or seller-led e-marketplaces. Baldi and Borgman (2001) also identify 'meta' e-marketplaces that are formed by a group of independent market providers who collaborate and exchange requests and offers by interconnecting their e-marketplaces to increase liquidity.

In the automotive industry, for example, the large consortia-led e-marketplace 'Covisint' was formed by several OEMs, while other manufacturers rather pursued separate, private initiatives. Therefore, there are several automotive B2B e-marketplaces, when most suppliers would probably have preferred a unified structure. However, arguments for private e-marketplaces include that they can offer more control and design opportunities, which potentially can result in benefits such as a quicker integration of legacy systems, as compromises with other OEMs are not required. With this constellation of various OEM e-marketplaces, the automotive supplier market was confronted with multiple platform interfaces. In response to this development, even more tier 1-driven e-marketplaces have been formed to establish common standards for exchange of communication and transactions between tier 1 and tier 2 suppliers, as complementary approaches to the OEM initiatives. There are also a number of after-market sites serving the wider automotive industry and other e-marketplaces devoted to trade in products such as new and used tyres. Despite a significant consolidation of e-marketplaces in recent years, the panorama is still complicated if the interactions with other related horizontal e-marketplaces are considered.

Given the wide diversity and variety of e-marketplaces, integration, harmonisation and standardisation are the major issues[5] and companies have to

---

[5]One initiative was, therefore, the creation of a collaboration and unification platform on standards among sixteen European automotive manufacturers and four national automotive associations.

carefully consider whether to develop or use buy-side, neutral or sell-side e-business solutions. According to the research firm e-marketer, which is cited by Memishi (2001), it appeared from press releases that consortium-centric and neutral e-marketplaces have been implemented more widely than independent efforts governed by single organisations. However, e-marketer estimated that more than 93 per cent of B2B e-commerce is being transacted through private e-business exchanges.[6]

So far, however, we are still in the first stages of increasing the recognition of e-business. Most organisations still lack an effective ICT infrastructure, which may organise, support and facilitate the highly complex and often rapidly changing interfaces among the organisational entities and disciplines involved in business processes (van Weele 2000).

Uptake of E-Business among SMEs

Although there are benefits to be gained, the diffusion of e-business has been rather low particularly among SMEs to date. SMEs are often short of resources, which directly affects their capability to improve competitiveness. SMEs have more difficulties than large organisations to bear the risk of new technology adoption. Implementation of IOS is subject to substantial uncertainty in terms of return on investment (ROI) and adoption is, therefore, a likely problem for SMEs. Fear of the unknown, change and technology have also been posited as reasons why the uptake of technology is lower for SMEs (Lewis 2002).

For example, organisations often also remain uncertain about the security of transacting by ICT or in which way sensitive information may be used or disclosed to third parties or competitors. Security risks make businesses reluctant to use the Internet or participate in online transactions and therefore could prevent them from obtaining the benefits promised by online commerce (Federal Trade Commission 2000). Trust in the technology is a significant factor that affects the intention to adopt e-business. This is especially obvious in the SME sector, as small companies tend to have a lower level of technological competence and are in many cases unaware of e-procurement (Chan and Lee 2003).

That is why SMEs are still trying to understand their many options in e-business or are holding back until more is known about this quickly changing area. Most SMEs use the Internet as a basic communications

---

[6]The figure includes e-business software and private e-marketplaces and is based on findings from 2001.

facility, but only a minority reap significant benefits from the Internet. They still heavily rely on traditional tools (e.g. phone, facsimile, face-to-face) and are still in the beginner's level of e-business adoption (e.g. Chan and Lee 2003). SMEs are still waiting for the existence of a critical mass of e-business adopters and require some role models to follow in carrying out successful e-business.

Concomitantly, the media has also created an additional barrier for adoption of e-business initiatives with saturation coverage of 'dot.com' business consolidation since 2001 (Walker et al. 2003). The decline of activity in the ICT stock market has further increased the practice of most companies adopting a 'wait and see' approach to many aspects of e-business. Lack of skills and human inertia also appear to be significant barriers. A lot of SMEs are not e-business ready and are in need of further information and assistance. Walker et al. (2003) found that a lot of SMEs acknowledge that they did need to up-skill, but that time was the critical issue.

Critical Factors for the Future

E-business has not only to deal with technology, but also a range of important human and organisational issues. Studies of ICT-based systems in organisations consistently demonstrate that insufficient consideration of a system's social environment and the relationships between people and technologies has been a major reason why investments have often been assessed as being a failure, or only a partial success (e.g. Nathan et al. 2003). The social and technical aspects (i.e. 'hard' and 'soft' wiring) of e-business need to be designed and optimised concurrently. Without top management support, e-business is difficult to implement successfully. At the SME level, in particular, where resources and ICT/IOS sophistication are limited, the lack of financial resources, managerial and technological skills and system integration can inhibit e-business adoption.

More adequate training and education in e-business and change management is a critical factor for the future, as companies tend to express hesitancies about using e-business. These barriers in e-business are related to the human factors (e.g. insufficient leadership, unwillingness to cooperate, resistance to change, inertia, lack of trust, personal insecurity, fear of losing jobs, threat of being by-passed by technology, lack of motivation and professionalism, communications problems and difficulties in aligning the processes and cultures of partner companies); others are related to structures, processes and systems (e.g. lack of resources, plethora of different standards, lack of services provided by e-marketplaces).

Many organisations have focused on a few key e-business services to date, but are not considering potential benefits across the whole range of services available and across the supply chain (Huber *et al.* 2004). Currently available e-business solutions are still some way from covering the entire spectrum of business requirements and relatively few options are readily available to support or automate complex activities. They have the potential to evolve from a matchmaking or transaction support focus to knowledge and trust networks, where common workflows can enable SCM on a more widespread basis in future. The introduction of e-business might serve as a 'Trojan Horse' to enforce necessary changes in organisational structures and processes (e.g. part standardisation or use of a single coding system). E-business can drive new organisational forms (such as virtual organisations), fulfil certain tasks in the inter-firm context and allow firms to improve supply chain processes. Therefore, e-business has a vital role to play in integrated SCM.

REFERENCES

Amor, D. (2000), *The E-Business (R)evolution*, Dedham MA: Galileo Press.

Baldi, S. and Borgman, H.P. (2001), 'Consortium-Based B2B E-Marketplaces – A Case Study in the Automotive Industry', *14th Bled Electronic Commerce Conference*, 25–25 June, Bled, Slovenia, , available at: <http://domino.fov.uni-mb.si/proceedings.nsf>, accessed February 2007.

Better Business Wales (Holdings) Ltd (2007), *E-Commerce and your Business*, online guide, available at: <http://www.opportunitywales.co.uk/2-5-2d.htm>, accessed May 2007.

Chan, J. and Lee, M. (2002), 'SME E-Procurement Adoption in Hong Kong – The Roles of Power, Trust and Value', *Proceedings of the 36th Hawaii International Conference on System Sciences*, available at: <http://csdl2.computer.org/comp/proceedings/hicss/2003/1874/07/187470179c.pdf>, accessed November 2006.

Clarke, R. (2001), 'Towards a Taxonomy of B2B E-Commerce Schemes', 14th International EC Conference, Bled, Slovenia, June, available at: <http://www.anu.edu.au/people/Roger.Clarke/EC/Bled01.html>, accessed October 2006.

Corsten, D. and Zagler, M. (1999), 'Purchasing Consortia and Internet Technology' in A. Erridge (ed.) *Perspectives on Purchasing and Supply for the Millennium, 8th International Annual IPSERA Conference*, 28–31 March, Belfast: University of Ulster, 139–147.

de Boer, L., Harink, J. and Heijboer, G. (2002), 'A Conceptual Model for Assessing the Impact of Electronic Procurement Forms', *European Journal of Purchasing and Supply Management*, 8(1), 25–33.

Federal Trade Commission (2000), *Entering the 21st Century: Competition Policy in the World of B2B Electronic Marketplaces: A Report by Federal Trade Commission Staff*, Washington DC, available at: <http://www.ftc.gov/os/2000/10/b2breport.pdf> accessed January 2007.

Forrester, J. W. (1961), *Industrial Dynamics*, Cambridge MA: Productivity Press.

Gebauer, J. and Zagler, M. (2000), 'Assessing the *Status Quo* and Future of B2B E-Commerce', Fisher Center for IT and Marketplace Transformation, Haas School of Business, University of California, Berkley, available at: <http://www.zagler.ch/data/StatusQuoandFutureECommerce_Revue InternationaledelAchat.pdf>, accessed 23 February 2007.

Gregor, S. and Johnston, R.B. (2000), 'Developing an Understanding of Inter-Organizational Systems: Arguments for Multi-level Analysis and Structuration Theory', in Hansen, H.R., Bichler, M. and Mahrer, H.

(eds.), *Proceedings of the 8th European Conference on Information Systems*, 1, 3–5 July, Vienna: Vienna University of Economics and Business Administration, 567–574.

Huber, B., Sweeney, E. and Smyth, A. (2004), 'Purchasing Consortia and Electronic Markets – A Procurement Direction in Integrated Supply Chain Management', *International Journal of Electronic Markets*, 14(4), 284–294.

Knudsen, D. (2002), *Uncovering the Strategic Domain of E-Procurement*, available at: <http://www.tlog.lth.se/documents/publications/Knudsen_2002_IPSERA.pdf>, accessed February 2006.

Leon, M. (2000), *Electronics Exchanges Signal B-to-B Change*, available at: <http://archive.infoworld.com/articles/hn/xml/00/09/11/000911hnetrend.xml>, accessed October 2006.

Lewis, S. (2002), 'Fear of the Unknown', *Asian Business*, February, 41.

Lipis, L., Villars, R., Turner, V. and Byron, D. (2000), 'Putting Markets into Place: An E-Marketplace Definition and Forecast', IDC, Document #22501, June, Framingham MA.

Lucking-Reiley, D. and Spulber, D.F. (2000), 'Business-to-Business Electronic Commerce', paper available at: <http://www.econ.jhu.edu/People/Harrington/375/ls00.pdf>, accessed January 2007.

MacDuffie, J.P. and Helper, S. (2000), *E-volving the Auto Industry: E-Commerce Effects on Consumer and Supplier Relationships*, The Fisher Center of the Strategic Use of Information Technology, Haas Scholl of Business, UC Berkeley, 12 September.

Memishi, R. (2001), 'B2B Exchanges Survival Guide', *Internet World Magazine*, 1 January, available at: <http://www.iw.com/magazine.php?inc=010101/01.01.01feature1.html>, accessed January 2007.

Narasimhan, R. and Jayaram, J. (1998), 'Causal Linkage in Supply Chain Management: an Exploratory Study of North American Manufacturing Firms', *Decision Science*, 29(3), 579–605.

Nathan, M., Carpenter, G. and Roberts, S. (2003), *Getting by, Not Getting on: Technology in UK Workplaces*, London: The Work Foundation and Society.

Raisch, W. (2001), *The e-Marketplace: Strategies for Success in B2B E-Commerce*, New York: McGraw-Hill.

Richmond, C., Power, T. and O'Sullivan, D. (1998), *E-Business in the Supply Chain: Creating Value in a Networked Market Place*, London: Financial Times Retail and Consumer.

Riggins, F.J. and Mukhopadhyay, T. (1999), 'Overcoming EDI Adoption and Implementation Risks, *International Journal of Electronic Commerce*, 3(4), 103–123.

Roland Berger Consulting, Deutsche Bank (2001), *Automotive E-Commerce: A (Virtual) Reality Check*, available at: <http://www.touchbriefings.com/pdf/977/transport2.pdf>, accessed March 2007.

van Weele, A.J. (2000), 'Purchasing and the Information Age: Towards a Virtual Purchasing Organisation?', paper available at: <http://www.nijenrode.nl/download/cscm/art_avweele2.pdf>, accessed December 2006.

van Weele, A.J. and Rozemeijer, F.A. (1996), 'Revolution in Purchasing: Building Competitive Power through Pro-active Purchasing', paper available at: <http://www.tm.tue.nl/ipsd/research/articles/rip.pdf>, accessed March 2007.

Walker, B., Bode, S., Burn, J. and Webster, B. (2003), 'Small Business and the Use of Technology: Why the Low Uptake?', 16th Annual Conference of Small Enterprise Association of Australia and New Zealand, 28 September–10 October, Ballarat, available at: <http://www.cric.com.au/seaanz/conference_papers.php?list_type=author>, accessed February 2007.

SECTION 5

THE FUTURE OF SCM: MAKING CHANGE HAPPEN

15

Supply Chain Benchmarking and Performance Measurement: Towards the Learning Supply Chain

EDWARD SWEENEY

INTRODUCTION

As pointed out in Chapter 3, the overall objectives of supply chain management (SCM) are to:

- Optimise total supply chain costs and investment.
- Deliver appropriate levels of customer service in targeted market segments.

When introducing supply chain improvement projects within companies, two broad aspects need to be measured in line with these overall objectives:

- The impact of the improvement on the performance of the local area.
- The impact of the improvement on overall supply chain performance.

Examining both aspects ensures that a holistic (top-down) approach is combined with a detailed (bottom-up) perspective. This is important if all measurement is to be carried out in an integrated manner whilst simultaneously ensuring that requisite attention is paid to detailed issues (after all the devil is often in the detail!) at each link in the chain.

Supply chain improvement projects are so diverse that this chapter could not hope to cover all methods of measuring individual initiatives and so the aim is to examine the measurement of overall supply chain performance from both an external and internal perspective.

Traditionally companies, and management accounting systems, measure two key aspects of performance, namely effectiveness and efficiency. *Effectiveness* is the degree to which a predetermined objective or target is met. *Efficiency,* on the other hand, is the degree to which inputs are used in relation to a given level of outputs. Colloquially, effectiveness is concerned with *doing the right things*, while efficiency is concerned with *doing the things right*. Customer service measures are examples of the former while many cost-based measures are aimed at the latter. It is possible to achieve one of these aspects without the other but obviously both efficiency and effectiveness are required simultaneously (i.e. one would ideally like to be *doing the right things right!*). The inability of traditional management accounting and performance measurement systems to both encourage and measure both the areas has become a major issue in both academic and industrial circles. Furthermore, there is evidence that there is serious room for improvement in the approaches adopted by companies in relation to performance measurement generally, and to supply chain performance measurement specifically.[1]

This chapter addresses:

- External performance measurement and how external information on other companies can be used as a basis for benchmarking.
- Internal performance measurement and the establishment of integrated approaches.
- The concept of the *learning supply chain*.

External Measurement

External performance measurement information is required by two main groups. Shareholders and potential investors use this data to inform investment decisions. Managers (including supply chain managers) use it as a basis for strategic and tactical decision-making. The primary source of this information for shareholders and investors is the company's published financial accounts. Interpretation of published financial accounts involves a number of techniques, which can be applied to measure financial performance based on the information contained within a company's annual, or interim, report. A detailed discussion of these techniques is beyond the scope of this chapter. They include:

- **Trend analysis** techniques where a series of figures are compared over time (e.g. stock turnover).

---

[1] In Ireland, for example, a minority of companies recently surveyed measure customer service and, of these, most adopt quite an informal and incomplete approach (NITL 2005).

- **Common size statements** where outside factors such as inflation are removed (e.g. stock as a proportion of total assets).
- **Financial ratio** analysis.

The latter area is very well developed and financial ratios typically used include:

- **Performance ratios** which measure profitability (e.g. return on net assets or capital employed or *ROCE*).
- **Financial status ratios** which measure financial liquidity (e.g. current or working capital ratio and the acid test or liquid ratio).
- **Investor ratios** which assess investment attractiveness (e.g. earnings per share or EPS and the price to earnings, or *P/E*, ratio).

Since many of the ratios are interrelated, it is common to use a pyramid of ratios to assess a company's performance across a number of areas.

The focus thus far has been on the use of financial reports by stockholders and investors, but there is a growing need for companies to review their own performance with respect to their competitors and to the world's best companies. This practice has existed for many years but has become more formalised in recent years under the banner of *benchmarking*.

The Role of Benchmarking

In very simple terms, to benchmark is to compare yourself with someone else to measure how effective and/or efficient you are. In athletics events, for example, the benchmark might be the current world record and individuals get the opportunity to compete openly with one another at events such as the World Championships. Even within sport athletes will not necessarily know the details of an opponent's training schedule, diet or use of drugs. Companies compete in world markets and, just like the athlete, firms would like to identify specifically why they are failing to win orders with respect to the competition or where they need to improve.

The following are definitions of terminology associated with benchmarking (based on Spendolini 1992).

- **Benchmarking**: A continuous systematic process for evaluating the products, services and work of organisations that are recognised as representing best practices for the purpose of organisational improvement.

- **Best (or appropriate) practices**:[2] The methods used in work processes, the outputs of which best (or most appropriately) meet customer requirements.
- **Benchmarks**: Performance measurement standards derived from definition of best practices.

The Benchmarking Process

The most obvious and simple form of benchmarking is to buy your competitor's product or service. Many companies have used this technique, also known as reverse engineering, in design and manufacturing where they strip down the competitor's product to examine the design, manufacturing methods, sources of component supply and other relevant factors. However, Xerox is usually credited as being the first to see the real potential for benchmarking. They started in 1979 by stripping down products but went on to experiment with the concept in other areas. There are now several different ways to carry out benchmarking comparisons (based on Ahmed and Rafiq 1998):

Internal benchmarking: This is where operations within one company are compared. For instance, in a large group several strategic business units (SBUs) might make similar products or use similar processes. Benchmarking of performance between country operations in multinational companies is also an example of this.

Competitive benchmarking: The next step might involve going outside the company to direct competitors. There are many aspects of supply chain performance which can be usefully benchmarked in this way. Access to appropriate data can be a problem between direct competitors but there are ways of overcoming this obstacle.[3]

Functional benchmarking: Comparisons are still made within the same broad industry using similar functions. The classic example of this involves printed circuit board (PCB) assembly. Many industries assemble PCBs, so rather than making a comparison with a direct competitor, a company in another market (or making a different product but with the same technology) is chosen. Naturally, non-competitors are more likely to be a fertile source of useful information.

Generic benchmarking: Here comparisons are made with totally unrelated industries. For instance, it is said that the founder of just-in-time (JIT),

---

[2] As noted earlier, it is for this reason that the author is more comfortable with the concept of 'appropriate practice', as opposed to 'best practice'. The latter implies that there is one superior approach, irrespective of the nature of the company and its environment.

[3] For example, NITL runs a number of supply chain benchmarking clubs where data supplied by a club's membership is generally confidential to the club members.

Taitchi Ohno of Toyota, based his thinking on supermarket operations in the USA. The relatively low levels of stock in these operations provided the foundation for the JIT pull system.

Through benchmarking, a company is continually looking for new ideas, methods, practices and processes which can be adapted to suit the company. The basic philosophy involves the following stages:[4]

(i) **Identify *what*?** This involves identifying the critical success factors (CSFs) which the benchmarking exercise will focus on.
(ii) **Identify *who*?** This is concerned with deciding on the form of benchmarking to be used (e.g. internal, competitive, etc.) and on the SBU, company or companies to work with.
(iii) **Plan *how*?** This stage involves planning the detail of the exercise. Ensuring that the required data is collected efficiently is a key consideration.
(iv) **Analyse:** At this stage the data collected is analysed with specific reference to the identification of appropriate supply chain best practices and benchmarks.
(v) **Use:** This is when the information generated is actually used to develop new and innovative practices. It must be emphasised that, as all companies are unique, it is imperative that the appropriateness and applicability of any practice to one's specific operation is considered in detail. Benchmarking is not about copying other companys' approaches; rather it is about learning and *adapting* appropriate practices so that they can be usefully *adopted* in an effort to improve efficiency and/or effectiveness (*adapt* before *adopt*ing!).

The author's experience suggests that companies do not need to be the world's best at everything. All companies have finite resources and benchmarking can help to identify where these resources should be targeted.

Internal Measurement

Having looked briefly at measurement based on information available externally, the focus now moves on to examine a critical area of interest for supply chain managers: internal performance measurement.

---

[4]Based on Watson (1993) and the Xerox methodology (see Camp 1989). A more detailed supply chain benchmarking methodology, developed by the author (Sweeney 2003), is contained in the Appendix to this chapter.

Robust performance measurement systems need to be designed to measure and encourage the key overall supply chain objectives of customer service and cost/investment in a manner consistent with the company's overall strategic direction. It is not intended to examine in great depth the psychological implication of performance measurement, but merely to recognise that the introduction of performance measurement will cause people to alter their behaviour (*what gets measured gets done* or *you get what you measure*). Obviously the objective of a performance measurement system will be to provide information which will both enable people to identify where improvements are needed and to motivate them to make these improvements. However, most people can recall examples of where performance measurement has encouraged behaviour which was inconsistent with an organisation's overall goals. For example, in manufacturing the measurement of utilisation can encourage managers to keep their staff busy making products which are not needed and end up in stock, increasing inventory-holding costs and tying up resources. Most businesses are complex and measurements in many different areas will be needed to accurately establish the level of operational effectiveness and efficiency.

A key objective of SCM is concerned with activity integration. Traditionally, many companies have measured, and have therefore managed, the various supply chain functions (e.g. purchasing, manufacturing, distribution, etc.) very much in isolation from each other. It is vital that an integrated approach to supply chain performance measurement is adopted if the move away from this form of fragmentation, towards a more integrated approach, is to be achieved.

ESTABLISHING A SUPPLY CHAIN PERFORMANCE MEASUREMENT SYSTEM

One approach to the establishment of integrated systems of performance measurement involves the use of the performance pyramid originally proposed by Lynch and Cross (1991). This pyramid (see Figure 15.1) shows the translation of corporate vision into business unit objectives with respect to financial and market targets. These are then broken down into goals for each area of the business in three areas: customer satisfaction, flexibility and productivity. These are finally translated into day-to-day measures for individual teams. The pyramid also indicates that objectives are cascaded down the organisation while measures are communicated back upwards.

Figure 15.1: Performance Pyramid

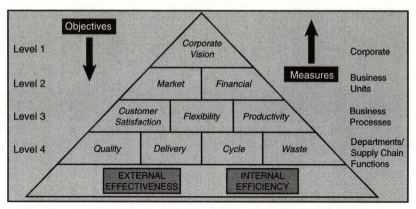

Source: Adapted from Lynch, R.L. and Cross, K.F. (1991), *Measure up! Yardsticks for Continuous Improvement*, Cambridge, MA: Blackwell.

Applying this approach to the development of a supply chain performance measurement system involves:

- Understanding the role of customer service (***market*** objectives and measures in the pyramid) and supply chain costs and investment (***financial*** objectives and measures in the pyramid) in the context of the overall ***corporate vision*** (Levels 1 and 2).
- Identification of the key elements of customer service in each targeted market segment and setting objectives in relation to each element. A similar process is carried out in relation to supply chain costs and investment. For example, all supply chain cost drivers need to be identified and objectives set in relation to each one (Level 2).
- By a process of stepwise decomposition these objectives are broken down into specific goals for each link in the supply chain. In line with the pyramid, goals are established in relation to ***customer satisfaction***, ***flexibility*** and ***productivity*** (Level 3).
- Finally, these goals are translated into detailed key performance indicators (KPIs) of, for example, ***quality***, ***delivery***, ***cycle time*** and ***waste***. This is done for each supply chain link: for example, purchasing and procurement, production, warehousing, transportation and customer service (Level 4).

The overall objective of this approach is to ensure that an integrated system of supply chain performance measurement is put into place, thus avoiding the scenario where individual functions are measured, and therefore managed, in isolation from each other. This facilitates the transition from the traditional, highly fragmented approach to a more holistic and integrated one.

Performance Measurement in World-Class Companies

In designing robust and integrated supply chain performance measurement systems it is important to study and learn from organisations that are regarded as exemplars of best practice. Based on the work of Dixon *et al.* (1990) and Maskell (1992), and on the author's experience, the following are some of the features which tend to be incorporated into the performance measurement systems of successful companies:

- Measures should relate directly to company and business unit strategy.
- An integrated approach should be adopted across the company and the supply chain in line with the performance pyramid approach.
- Within this integrated overall approach detailed measures will vary from area to area.
- Measures should change over time to reflect changing imperatives and priorities.
- Measures should be as simple and easy to use as possible.
- Measures should give fast feedback to staff.
- Measures should be acted upon (otherwise they become somewhat futile).
- Excessive numbers of measures should be avoided (if you try to measure too many things you may end up effectively measuring nothing!).
- Measures should aim to 'teach' staff about their sphere of operation and as a basis for continuous improvement, rather than being purely for monitoring and control purposes.

Conclusion: The *Learning Supply Chain*

The need for continuous innovation and improvement in all aspects of a company's supply chain has long been recognised – successful companies practice this Kaizen approach. Standing still means falling behind in today's increasingly competitive marketplaces. Effective performance measurement provides companies with the only rational basis for continuous improvement. As world-class companies have experienced, external and internal performance measurement is the primary mechanism for organisational learning at all levels. Furthermore, supply chain learning – based on firm-to-firm exchange of knowledge – is about leveraging the supply chain as a mechanism to enable learning and competence development (Bessant *et al.* 2003; Sweeney *et al.* 2005). A *learning organisation* is an organisation that recognises the importance of this type of learning, and has developed practices which reflect this. Similarly, a *learning supply chain* is a supply chain that takes learning seriously at all levels and which bases its learning initiatives on its performance measurement system. The successful supply chains of the future will be those that are agile. A key ingredient of agility is the ability to learn and to respond quickly to changing markets and other requirements. The organisational learning that effective supply chain performance measurement delivers will become even more important. In short, the successful supply chains of the future will be the *learning supply chains* that:

- Learn world-class best practice through benchmarking;
- Develop and implement robust and integrated performance measurement systems;
- Base improvement initiatives on the learning derived from these systems.

REFERENCES

Ahmed, P.K. and Rafiq, M. (1998), 'Integrated Benchmarking: A Holistic Examination of Select Techniques for Benchmarking Analysis', *Benchmarking for Quality Management and Technology*, 5(3), 225–242.

Bessant, J., Kaplinsky, R. and Lamming, R. (2003), 'Putting Supply Chain Learning Into Practice', *International Journal of Operations and Production Management*, 23(2), 167–184.

Camp, R.C. (1989), *Benchmarking – The Search for Industry's Best Practices That Lead to Superior Performance*, Milwaukee: Quality Resources.

Cross, K.F., Lynch, R.L. and McNair, C.J. (1990), 'Do Financial and Non-financial Measures Have to Agree?', *Management Accounting USA*, November, 28–36.

Dixon, J.R., Nanni, A.J. and Vollmann, T.E. (1990), *The New Performance Challenge: Measuring Operations for World Class Competition*, Homewood: Dow Jones/Irwin.

Lynch, R.L. and Cross, K.F. (1991), *Measure Up! Yardsticks for Continuous Improvement*, Cambridge, MA: Blackwell.

Maskel, B.H. (1992), *Performance Measurement for World Class Manufacturing, A Model for American Companies*, Cambridge, MA: Productivity Press.

National Institute for Transport and Logistics (2005), *Competitive Challenges: Chain Reactions*, Dublin: NITL.

Spendolini, M.J. (1992), *The Benchmarking Book*, New York: Amacon.

Sweeney, E., (2003) 'The Benchmarking Process', *Technical Focus in Logistics Solutions*, 6(6), 34.

Sweeney, E., Evangelista, P. and Passaro, R. (2005), 'Putting Supply Chain Learning Theory into Practice: Lessons from an Irish Case', *International Journal of Knowledge and Learning*, 1(4), 357–372.

Watson, G.H. (1993), *Strategic Benchmarking: How to Rate Your Company's Performance against the World's Best*, New York: Wiley.

Appendix: The Benchmarking Process

As indicated in this chapter, benchmarking is a process through which a company is continually looking for new ideas, methods, practices and processes which can be usefully employed as part of the overall continuous improvement process. Over the years several benchmarking methodologies have been developed, each of which provides a checklist of the main steps required. These methodologies aim to ensure that the process is carried out in a logical and systematic manner. The following is a five-step approach which summarises the main tasks typically followed in the benchmarking process:

(i) **Identify *what*?** This involves identifying the critical success factors (CSFs) which the benchmarking exercise will focus on. This is an important step as any useful benchmarking exercise needs to set priorities in relation to what is being studied. The objective is to narrow the scope of the study sufficiently so that unrealistic objectives are not established, whilst simultaneously allowing the exercise to remain flexible. Ideally, the focus should be on those aspects of the supply chain which are regarded as critical to the achievement of strategic objectives (usually in terms of optimising total supply chain costs and investment and delivering appropriate levels of customer service to targeted market segments).

(ii) **Identify *who*?** This is concerned with deciding on the form of benchmarking to be used. This usually involves choosing between the main forms of benchmarking (i.e. competitive, internal, generic, functional or customer). In reality, the ideal partner may not be available. For example, direct competitors may be unwilling to share information which is considered commercially confidential or it may be logistically impossible to initiate an exercise with the ideal company/SBU/division. The key is to choose a partner from whom real learning can be derived and who is willing and available to participate in the exercise. Successful benchmarking exercises involve the development of a 'win–win' approach. There needs to be 'give and take' (i.e. teaching and learning) on both sides. In the case of benchmarking clubs, all parties should ideally be contributing as well as learning.

(iii) **Plan *how*?** This stage involves planning the detail of the exercise. Like any project, benchmarking needs to be planned and managed effectively. If the project is to achieve its potential, then paying the required attention to detailed issues at the planning stage is imperative. Ensuring that the required data is collected efficiently is a key consideration as part of this planning. As much as possible, the work should be carried out in advance of site visits and/or partner meetings. This is often done through the use of questionnaires and other research devices. The actual data gathering is also part of this stage. Data collection is a time-consuming activity and only data which is relevant to the priority issues identified in Step (i) should be collected. Often some initial analysis (or at least summarising) of data is conducted at this stage.

(iv) **Analyse:** At this stage the data collected is analysed with specific reference to the identification of *appropriate supply chain best practices* and the *benchmarks* themselves. Identifying performance gaps is the first stage in this process. Once performance gaps have been identified then associated process gaps can be identified. The key principle here is that benchmarking is not just about process outputs – it is also about understanding the processes and practices that result in these outputs. The former may provide useful inputs when developing performance measurement standards (i.e. *benchmarks*); the latter is central to the identification of *appropriate supply chain best practices*. There are a range of analytical techniques which can be used as part of the process. These include, but are not limited to, statistical techniques (e.g. analysis of variance), graphical techniques (e.g. process mapping) and a range of other approaches (e.g. cause and effect analysis).

(v) **Use:** This is when the information generated is actually used to develop new and innovative practices. In terms of the well-known Deming cycle it is the final stage – Plan, Do, Check, *Act* (PDCA). It must be emphasised that, as all companies are unique, it is imperative that the appropriateness and applicability of any practice to one's specific operation is considered in detail. Benchmarking is not about copying other companys' approaches; rather it is about learning and *adapting* appropriate practices so that they can be usefully *adopted* in an effort to improve efficiency and/or effectiveness (*adapt* before *adopt*ing!). Finally, the overall objective of any benchmarking exercise is improvement. The only real test of the value of benchmarking is in the process improvement to which it directly contributes.

16

Re-engineering the Supply Chain: Making SCM Work for You

EDWARD SWEENEY

INTRODUCTION

The changing business environment has sharpened the focus on the need for robust approaches to supply chain improvement. This chapter sets out the key elements of traditional re-engineering processes. It goes on to outline some of the key characteristics of SCM excellence, based on the author's experience and on documented evidence in the literature. Based on the performance of firms in relation to these key characteristics, a number of critical success factors (CSFs) for effective supply chain re-engineering are identified and the key elements of a roadmap are proposed. Finally, a number of research and managerial conclusions are drawn.

ORGANISATIONAL RE-ENGINEERING

Companies have long realised the need for company-wide approaches to organisational design and redesign. The development of systems engineering approaches to manufacturing system redesign in the 1970s and 1980s (Hitomi 1996) was followed by the focus on organisational re-engineering, often based on business processes, in the 1980s and 1990s (Macdonald 1995). A common feature of all of these approaches is a recognition that 'the whole is greater than the sum of the parts'. In other words, optimising subsystems (whether those subsystems are functional departments, production sites or individual processes in the manufacturing cycle) can result in a sub-optimised total system. Lack of efficiency and/or effectiveness is often a result of the poorly designed interfaces between subsystems rather than any inherent subsystem weaknesses. There are numerous examples of companies who have generated significant improvements in competitive advantage as a result of the application of this 'total systems' thinking.

As noted in Chapter 3, it must be recognised that a product is delivered to the ultimate customer through a complex interaction of several companies on the way. The supplier's ability to give the customer what they want, when they want it, at the price and quality that they want is not just determined by the efficiency and effectiveness of the supplier's own operation. Inefficiencies anywhere in the supply chain will reduce the chances of the supplier competing successfully. Without a proper focus on 'total' (i.e. integrated) SCM, therefore, a company will never achieve its true competitive potential (Christopher 1992). The increasingly international nature of markets and companies has resulted in many companies becoming part of large and complex global supply chains. In addition, the potential benefits associated with emerging ICT solutions provide the opportunity to simultaneously improve customer service levels and to reduce supply chain costs. These factors have sharpened the focus on the need for improvements in all aspects of supply chain performance.

CHARACTERISTICS OF SCM EXCELLENCE

Identifying some of the characteristics in evidence in companies that might be regarded as world class provides a useful strating point for this discussion. 'World class' in this context means companies that have been successful in tough, competitive international markets over a sustained period of time. It is impossible to develop an exhaustive list of the characteristics of SCM excellence but the following four elements appear to be of critical importance for most companies in most sectors:

1. Identification and measurement of customer service *because* customer service 'sets the spec' for supply chain design.
2. Integration of supply chain activities and information *because* many supply chain NVAs are caused by fragmented supply chain configurations.
3. SCM is a senior management function *because* SCM is a strategic activity.
4. Establishment and measurement of supply chain key performance indicators (KPIs) *because* what gets measured gets done!

This is based on documented evidence of SCM 'best practice' and allies with the author's experience. These characteristics will be returned to later in the context of development of a roadmap for effective supply chain re-engineering. However, firstly it is worth exploring the performance of companies in Ireland in relation to these issues.

How Do Companies Measure Up?

The foregoing raises fundamental questions about the extent to which companies understand and implement SCM concepts and practices. In Ireland, for example, research aimed at assessing the supply chain capability of companies is being carried out on an ongoing basis. NITL (2005) is a comprehensive study which covers a wide range of SCM activities based on over 1,000 companies, representing both the Republic of Ireland and Northern Ireland. A number of interesting facts emerge in relation to the four key characteristics of SCM excellence outlined in the previous section:

1. Approximately 50 per cent measure customer service formally and those have very limited measurements.
2. Companies score low in relation to having the latest supply chain information and communications technology (ICT) and having them integrated across the supply chain.
3. Less than 10 per cent have any formal SCM position.
4. Few companies had clearly defined SCM KPIs.

Overall, initial analysis of the survey findings appears to indicate that, whilst pockets of excellence undoubtedly do exist, there is significant room for improvement in these key areas. It is important, therefore, that any robust approach to supply chain improvement and re-engineering at least addresses these areas meaningfully. The next section explores these areas in the context of a systematic and holistic approach to supply chain re-engineering. A number of possible barriers to SCM excellence have been identified and will be explored as part of the ongoing research and associated analysis:

- Inefficiencies are often built into the supply chain.
- Communication structures are ineffective and exchange of information poor.
- Culture is inappropriate.
- There is an excessive reliance on forecasting and stockholding.
- Problems are often managed, rather than their causes eliminated.

These characteristics are in line with the prerequisites for effective SCM implementation and the *Four Fundamentals* as introduced in Chapter 3.

Supply Chain Re-engineering

Improving supply chain performance through re-engineering involves: analysis of internal and external parameters using relevant data which has been collected; the identification and evaluation of possible alternative improvements and their detailed planning; and the implementation of planned improvements including the associated change management. In short,

Re-engineering = Analysis + Planning + Implementation

It is important to bear in mind that, in supply chain re-engineering, no panacea or 'magic solution' exists. Furthermore, as every company and every supply chain is unique in some respect, it is inappropriate to attempt to copy or imitate companies regarded as being exponents of good practice.[1] The uniqueness could be with respect to products or services supplied, processes, customer expectations, people and cultural issues, systems or any one of a number of other factors.

However, there is a logical and systematic way of addressing the re-engineering challenge. The *Systems Approach* is an example of such an approach. The following section identifies some of the key elements of such an approach, based on the characteristics of supply chain re-engineering discussed earlier.

Elements of a Systematic Approach to Supply Chain Re-engineering

Understanding Customer Service

As pointed out earlier, customer service 'sets the spec' for supply chain design. In other words, as shown in Figure 16.1 a market-driven customer service strategy provides the performance specification for integrated SCM.

In short, understanding customer service requirements in targeted market segments forms the basis for any effective supply chain re-engineering and change process.

Supply Chain Organisation

In many traditionally managed supply chains, individual supply chain functions (e.g. purchasing, production, transport and warehousing) are measured

---

[1] As noted in Chapter 15, it is for this reason that the author is more comfortable with the concept of 'appropriate practice', as opposed to 'best practice'.

Figure 16.1: Customer Service 'Sets the Spec' for Integrated SCM

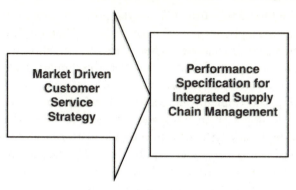

and managed in isolation from each other. The net result is that the overall supply chain fails to achieve its true competitive potential as the constituent elements operate at cross purposes. A key SCM objective relates to the replacement of this traditional, often highly fragmented, supply chain organisation with structures which are characterised by higher levels of integration. This has serious implications for approaches used to more effectively structure organisations. For example, it is the author's contention that future organisational structures are more likely to be described in terms of processes and networks (both internal and external) rather than functions and hierarchy. Figure 16.2 shows a possible future organisational shape based on internal and external networks, as well as shared services. In such structures, the boundaries between supply chain companies and between internal processes become more seamless. The focus is on organising around value-adding processes rather than on creating fragmented structures (often developed chiefly for internal administrative convenience). The latter often results in 'pseudo' efficiency, but poor levels of overall performance. The former focuses on customer value and effectiveness, and is more likely to lead to real efficiency.

Figure 16.2: The Organisational Shape of the Future

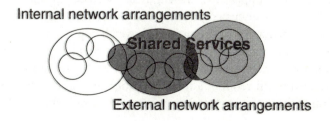

Technology: The Great Enabler?

There can be little doubt that ICT has the potential to have a serious positive impact on supply chain performance (see Chapter 12). This is largely due to its potential to facilitate higher levels of integration of supply chain activities and supply chain data. However, this potential has often been unfulfilled for a variety of reasons. These include a piecemeal approach to ICT planning and implementation, and tactical (as opposed to strategic) approaches to supply chain integration. These problems have often been exacerbated by legacy systems with multiple platforms and standards both internally and across the wider supply chain. The key to success in ICT terms is no longer likely to derive from the technology itself – most solutions are becoming essential order qualifiers and, in any case, are imitable and therefore unlikely to be a source of sustainable competitive advantage. In future, competitive advantage is more likely to originate from the development and implementation of creative ICT strategies. The focus needs to shift away from systems and hardware, and move towards processes (which add value) and people.

Supply Chain KPIs in World-Class Companies

In designing robust and integrated supply chain performance measurement systems, it is important to study and learn from organisations which are regarded as exemplars of best practice. Some of the features which tend to be incorporated into the performance measurement systems of successful companies were identified in Chapter 15.

The importance of performance measurement and KPIs in the re-engineering process cannot be overstated. It provides companies with a rational basis for continuous improvement. It is important that an integrated system of KPIs is designed as part of the process and that the measures become an integral part of the supply chain.

TOWARDS A SUPPLY CHAIN RE-ENGINEERING ROADMAP

A comprehensive supply chain re-engineering roadmap must incorporate the four key issues discussed in the previous section. Figure 16.3 shows a graphical representation of the proposed overall approach.

It starts with a market-driven customer service strategy which provides the performance specification for integrated SCM. In relation to supply chain organisation it requires a focus on processes and effectiveness, with a strong emphasis on network arrangements and shared services. ICT has the

Figure 16.3: Elements of a Roadmap for Supply Chain Re-engineering

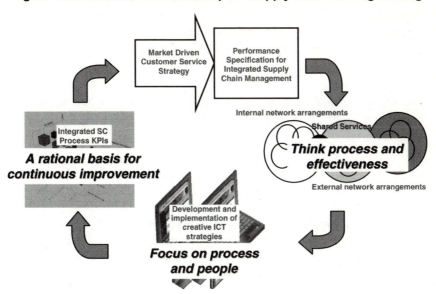

potential to facilitate integration between supply chain processes. However, for this potential to be realised, creative ICT strategies need to be developed and implemented. Again the focus needs to be on (value-adding) processes and on the people dimension. Finally, the integrated supply chain process KPIs provide organisations with a rational basis for continuous improvement. These measures feed back into the development of the customer service strategy, thus closing the loop. This roadmap provides the basis for logical and systematic approaches to supply chain re-engineering. The *Systems Approach* is one such approach.

ELEMENTS OF THE *SYSTEMS APPROACH*

The systems approach to analysing supply chains and improving their performance recognises that the process of re-engineering supply chains needs to be carried out in a logical and systematic manner. The approach has been developed based on the experiences of a range of companies in a range of different business sectors. There are at least four distinct constituent elements of this systems approach. The principles summarise the underlying thinking and concepts. If the supply chain under consideration is regarded as the system then the environment is the business environment in which that supply chain operates. The business strategy of firms is concerned with the interaction between supply chain companies and their business environment

(Porter 1980). Essentially, the strategy formulation process defines the nature of this interaction (see Chapter 4). The methodology is the series of steps to be followed in analysing and improving a typical supply chain. The methodology helps to identify the most suitable solution for a particular supply chain, but there are approaches which appear to exist in the majority of world-class companies (Schonberger 1996). The guidelines on good practice summarise the main relevant elements of world-class operating practice. Finally, the tools and techniques support the implementation of the methodology.[2]

Concluding Comments

Re-engineering is, first and foremost, about change. The development of a supply chain change management capability is of paramount importance if the re-engineering process is to result in real change and sustainable performance improvement. The reality in today's competitive world is that standing still effectively means falling behind. Innovation in all aspects of SCM is the key to survival and success. It is also worth noting that, in reality, most innovations are a series of small incremental steps in line with the Japanese Kaizen principle. The approach to re-engineering outlined in this chapter focuses on the four key aspects of service delivery based on clearly understood market requirements, integration of supply chain activities and data, supply chain organisation and the measurement of performance. The systems approach (to analysing supply chains and improving their performance) provides a basis for achieving world-class standards for supply chains operating in all types of industry. The approach involves considering the whole supply chain and avoiding a situation where subsystems are optimised but the whole supply chain is sub-optimal. Finally, the author's experience indicates that the real CSFs in any re-engineering or change process relate to the people dimension, and specifically to the need for enhanced levels of knowledge and skills through supply chain learning.

---

[2]Some guidelines for managing supply chain improvement projects are contained in the Appendix to this chapter.

REFERENCES

Christopher, M. (1992), *Logistics and Supply Chain Management: Strategies for Reducing Costs and Improving Service*, London: Pitman.

Hitomi, K. (1996), *Manufacturing Systems Engineering: A Unified Approach to Manufacturing Technology and Production Management*, 2nd edition, London: Taylor and Francis.

Macdonald, J. (1995), *Understanding Business Process Re-engineering in a Week*, London: Headway.

National Institute for Transport and Logistics (2005), *Competitive Challenges: Chain Reactions*, Dublin: NITL.

Porter, M. (1985), *Competitive Strategy*, New York: Free Press.

Schonberger, R. (1996), *World Class Manufacturing – The next Decade: Building Power, Strength, and Value*, New York: Free Press.

APPENDIX: MANAGING SCM IMPROVEMENT PROGRAMMES

Introduction

Competition is more intense than ever. Customers no longer just want product at a competitive price. Now they want a better product at a lower price, and they want it faster. That means beating the competition not just on the basis of quality or price or customer service, but all three at once.

Satisfying customers profitably in today's market comes down to how companies buy, make, store, move and sell their product: in other words, how they manage their supply chain. This requires managers who are willing to:

- step back and reassess the fundamentals of how they are operating their business;
- challenge established business practices;
- redraw lines of cooperation;
- replace the hard assets with good information.

In other words, it requires SCM professionals who are prepared to re-engineer their operations.

Re-engineering the supply chain is easy to say. The opportunities may even be easy to identify but they may be more difficult to implement. A comprehensive approach to implementing change within the organisation is an essential part of any re-engineering exercise. Below is a three-step process to the business of managing improvement programmes in SCM.

Step 1: Making the Case for Change

Senior management have a key role in first making the case for change. They need to communicate a powerful message to the organisation, based on the overall mission, strategy and corporate objectives. At the same time, through broad participation, the rest of the organisation should buy into the need for change. Employees from all parts of the company should be used to identify opportunities for cost and service improvements, for brainstorming options for achieving these improvements, and for prioritising implementation actions on the basis of the expected return. Involving staff throughout the organisation means that the company can educate their employees, gain buy-in and make the case for implementation before true implementation before ever starts.

Step 2: The Implementation Process

To progress implementation, it is helpful to form cross-functional teams to plan and execute implementation. Team leader selection is crucial to the success of the project. Ironically, some of the most reluctant team leaders – leaders who did not buy into opportunities for supply chain improvement immediately – can turn out to be the best leaders when it comes to implementation. Once the reluctant leaders are convinced that the opportunities exist, they will send a strong message throughout the organisation that supply chain opportunities are real. They become the key influencers who are able to reach out to employees at all levels. Of course, being a cross-functional team leader is not a trivial task, especially in an organisation that has never before undertaken such initiatives. Team leaders need to be trained in how to lead meetings, how to set realistic but challenging goals, and how to communicate progress upwards, laterally and downwards.

Like the process in Step 1, this implementation step could be condensed. Senior managers could just dictate all the necessary change from above. Broad participation at all levels, however, will help to ensure that the change is a lasting one, and not just the fad of the year.

Step 3: Institutionalising Change: Making Change Stick

There are number of steps which can be taken to institutionalise change. First the CEO and other senior managers can help to motivate the team leaders by encouraging those responsible for making change happen. The impact of congratulating someone for a job well done should not be underestimated. Second, and more important, is the need to align the organisation so that there is a focus on total supply chain costs, not just manufacturing costs, or just transport costs, or just procurement costs, etc. Finally there is a need to redefine roles, responsibilities and incentives so that all managers clearly understand how they can contribute to the initiative. For example, some tasks which were previously centralised might now be given to each functional division. Other strategic responsibilities will remain centralised. There is also need to design new measurements so that the managers in all areas pay as much attention to total supply chain costs as they do to, for example, manufacturing costs.

Lessons Learned

There are five lessons to be learned from using the alignment process outlined above:

1. **Sound Analysis:** Change is best driven by sound analysis of customer needs and alternative strategies. Efforts directed at thoroughly understanding critical supply chain issues and devising effective solutions will be more than repaid as the implementation process proceeds along

clearly defined paths. Specific improvement objectives and tools will allow the steady harvesting of opportunities.
2. **Broad Participation:** Implementation takes time. Striking the right balance between rapid and measurable change and patiently waiting for employees to buy in to the change is the key. There is a need to take time to educate employees about the change. This investment in time will pay off in results that are more genuine and lasting. Once the employees have been given the tools, it is surprising how they will often come up with savings opportunities that far exceed initial expectations.
3. **Team Leadership:** When selecting team leaders, the path of least resistance is not necessarily the best path. Selecting team leaders is an important issue, and team leaders should be key influencers among their peers. They will not necessarily be the quickest to buy into the proposed changes, but when they do, their colleagues will follow.
4. **Organisational Change:** The timing of reorganisation is crucial. Often we consider reorganisation first when we think of implementing change. However, reorganisation roles, responsibilities and incentives should come fairly late in the implementation game. If a company reorganises too early, then there is too much unnecessary turmoil and no clear understanding of what is happening or why. Since every organisation is different, the timing of reorganisation needs to be well thought out.
5. **Management Communication:** Small actions by senior management can have a major impact. Recognising success goes a long way to motivating team members. The three-step alignment process – making the case for change, implementing change and making change stick – will help a company to internalise the need to achieve supply chain excellence. As the company continues to implement supply chain improvements, employees will identify even more opportunities. By managing change properly, continuous supply chain improvement will become a way of life in the organisation.

Acknowledgements

This appendix is based on the work of Dr Stefan Bungart and is, at least in part, inspired by the positive impact of the work of Dr John Gattorna on the author's understanding of the supply chain change process.

17

Supply Chain Management: The Business Model of the 21st Century

EDWARD SWEENEY AND
RANDAL FAULKNER

INTRODUCTION

This final chapter looks to the future and outlines some of the likely challenges set to emerge over the coming years and examines some possible innovative supply chain architectures aimed at meeting these challenges. The future by its very nature can never be forecasted with accuracy. However, emerging trends in relation to the economic and business environment, the strategic role of SCM, technology (in particular ICT) and operational good practice are combining to enable possible future scenarios to be envisioned. This chapter does not in any sense purport to provide an exhaustive guide to these scenarios; rather it is based on the work of the authors both in research ('laboratory') and consultancy ('real-world') environments.

BACKGROUND: THE CHANGING BUSINESS ENVIRONMENT

As noted in Chapter 2, recent years have witnessed significant changes in the global business and economic environment. The growth of trade blocs, particularly in Europe, North America and Asia, has resulted in an increasingly integrated world economy. Increased levels of inward investment have accentuated this trend.[1] Reductions in the barriers to the movement of goods and services, capital and people have all contributed to this fundamental shift. The evolving role of the World Trade Organisation (WTO), currently with over 150 member countries and judicial powers to resolve trade disputes, is central to these structural changes in the world economic order.

---

[1] As noted in Chapter 2, this has been particularly significant in the recent development of the Irish economy.

All of these changes have resulted in substantial shifts in competitiveness, particularly in manufacturing industry. In developed countries, service industries, rather than manufacturing, have become ever more important in terms of economic growth and employment. Developing countries have increased their industrial capability and have, in many sectors and geographical regions, gained a significant foothold in major market segments. This, combined with the outsourcing of many heavily labour-intensive activities to lower-cost locations, has had a major impact on global economic structures and trade patterns.

From an SCM perspective, these changes have brought with them many new challenges. This 'International Challenge' brings with it both opportunities and threats. The opportunities relate mainly to access to markets in rapidly developing new economies and also access to apparently unlimited low cost production capacity. The threats derive mainly from competition from new geographical sources. The former requires organisations to build international logistical and supply chain capability. The latter requires organisations to adopt a strategic view of the role of SCM to minimise the impact of the potential threat.

Customer Service as a Key Order-Winning Criterion

The traditional view of business competitiveness has been based on winning market share based on product quality, price and customer service. In the 1970s and 1980s product quality was regarded in many markets as the critical success factor (CSF). This recognition resulted in the adoption of quality management initiatives by companies in a range of sectors. This was driven by the need to supply products which consistently conformed to customer requirements in terms of functionality and reliability. Whilst this is still of vital importance it has become more of an order qualifier than an order winner in most markets. In other words, product quality has become a 'given' and, as a result, the other success factors have become more important. In relation to price, markets have generally become more competitive with market dynamics, based on supply and demand, determining pricing levels. The room for manoeuvre in this area is therefore limited for many companies. The quest for price leadership and profitability improvement is based on the identification and minimisation of non-value-adding activities (NVAs) in operations. In this new environment, customer service excellence has become the key order-winning criterion for more and more companies.

SCM is fundamentally concerned with the enhancement of customer service. Indeed, as noted earlier, an understanding of customer service level requirements in targeted market segments sets the specification for the design of the supply chain. With customer service excellence playing such an important role in the achievement of competitive advantage, it is no surprise that SCM has become increasingly central to corporate strategy. The overall objectives of SCM are to enhance customer service and to optimise total supply chain costs and investments. The importance of the former has already been discussed; the latter has the potential to eliminate waste, thereby enhancing cost competitiveness and profitability. For these and other reasons, SCM has become a key strategic issue in most world-class companies – those companies which compete effectively in genuinely competitive international markets over a sustained period of time. The ability of companies to think about SCM strategically, and to put appropriate supply chain capability into place in advance of the need in a pro-active manner, has become recognised as an increasingly important determinant of business success. Companies who fail to do this tend to deal with logistical and supply chain issues in a very reactive way, often spending inordinate amounts of time 'firefighting' in their factories, warehouses and transport operations. SCM is not the only factor which determines the competitiveness of businesses but it has become more important.

VALUE AND BUSINESS PROCESSES

As noted in Chapter 3, the concept of *value* has long been an important one in SCM. In essence, a product or service is of value to a customer if that customer is prepared to pay for it. A key element of SCM is concerned with the identification of non-value-adding activities or NVAs. An NVA is an activity which adds cost (or time) to a supply chain without necessarily adding value from a customer perspective. The identification of these activities is an important dimension of SCM. In addition, organisational structures are increasingly being designed based on the concept of value. A business process is a collection of activities which add value. One approach to the achievement of significant improvements in organisations and supply chains is based on the radical re-appraisal and re-design of these processes – this is known as business process re-engineering (BPR).

BPR is 'the fundamental rethinking and radical redesign of business processes to achieve dramatic improvements in critical, contemporary measures of business performance' (Hamer 1995). There are a number of important words and phrases in this definition. Firstly, BPR requires companies to think about their businesses in a *fundamental* way. Fundamental strategic questions about a company's markets, products and organisations need to be asked and answered in an objective manner. *Radical re-design* requires companies

Figure 17.1: The Organisational Shape of the Future[2]

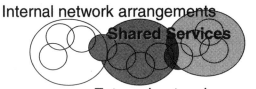

to address the root causes of their problems and to design organisational structures which reflect customer value rather than structures which are primarily focused on internal operating or administrative efficiency. As noted in Chapter 16, the result is supply chains which organise around business processes rather than around traditional functions. These processes often contain skills and resources which traditionally resided in functional departments. In addition, key skills and resources are often shared between business processes in internal network arrangements. External customers and suppliers often form part of these processes in external network arrangements. The latter is particularly true of companies who have moved towards increasingly virtual supply chains as a result of key supply chain activities being outsourced. Figure 17.1 shows a representation of the organisational shape of the future based on internal and external network arrangements with shared services.

The definition of BPR refers to *dramatic* improvements in performance. This is a reflection of the fact that sustaining competitiveness for many companies in the new globalised environment means step change for many companies if they are to become genuinely world class, as they increasingly need to be in their chosen markets.

WHAT ARE THE KEY PROCESSES?

There is no simple answer to this key question. However, in manufacturing-based companies (i.e. companies who primarily supply products rather than services) there are at least three processes which are fundamental.

Firstly, there is the process of new product introduction (NPI), a fundamental element of which is concerned with product research and development (R&D). Successful companies have to get new products into the market in a timely manner. The ability to do so is clearly a major source of competitive

---

[2] As noted in Chapter 16 (see Figure 16.2) in the context of supply chain re-engineering.

advantage. Effective NPI involves designers, manufacturing specialists, logistics professionals, purchasing staff and key suppliers, as well as sales and marketing staff and key customers. This approach is based on the well-established concepts and principles of simultaneous or concurrent engineering. It is based on the use of multi-disciplined teams and contrasts with the traditional sequential approach based on functional departments. The major benefit is reduced time-to-market for new products but there are numerous other benefits in terms of cost, quality and customer service (Finn and Sweeney 2004).

Secondly, there is the process of marketing. As noted in Chapter 6, marketing is concerned with the identification and anticipation of customer requirements. This knowledge is a key input to the NPI process. Marketing is also concerned with market and brand development and management. Brand equity is the additional amount a customer is willing to pay for a product as a direct result of the brand. Developing and sustaining brand equity is, therefore, a key activity in companies. It contributes directly to the value a customer associates with the product (i.e. of itself it adds value).

Good products with a strong brand have the potential to improve competitiveness. However, this is only true if the product can be supplied in a timely and cost-effective manner. In other words, it depends on the third key process, namely effective SCM.

THE ROLE OF SCM

In the words of the time-honoured slogan, SCM is concerned with ensuring that the right goods or services are delivered in the right quality and quantity, at the right time and at the right cost. As set out in *Fundamental One* (see Chapter 3), the overall objectives of SCM are to enhance customer service and to optimise total supply chain cost and investment. The philosophy which underpins SCM is based on the logic that a supply chain is only as strong as its weakest link (*Fundamental Two*, see Chapter 3). It requires companies to manage the major supply chain functions of buy, make, move, store and sell in an integrated and holistic manner. To do so requires that material, information and money flows in the chain are managed in an integrated and holistic manner (*Fundamental Three*, see Chapter 3). To achieve the overall objectives and to put the philosophy into practice often requires a radical reappraisal of both internal and external customer/supplier relationships, as incorporated into *Fundamental Four* (see Chapter 3). This view of SCM demonstrates its centrality as a key business process for most companies.

Figure 17.2: The Role of SCM in the New Business Model

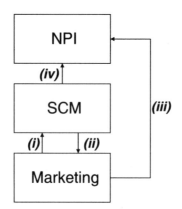

Figure 17.2 shows a conceptual representation of the new business model and the role of SCM as part of it (as proposed by Sweeney and Faulkner 2001). SCM is based on enhancing customer service levels. Understanding service level requirements in different market segments is based on market intelligence, which is generated through market research (a fundamental tool in identifying and anticipating customer requirements). Thus the marketing process is a key input into the SCM process (*i*). Equally, the key supply chain customer service performance indicators act as an input back into the marketing process (*ii*). The marketing process generates information about customer requirements which is an input into the NPI process (*iii*). No total product package is complete without information concerning the service requirements of customers. The SCM process feeds information into the NPI process concerning evolving customer service requirements (*iv*).

It should also be noted that the representation in Figure 17.2 shows the key business processes as quite discrete and independent entities for ease of illustration. However, as noted throughout this book, the lines between these processes are becoming more blurred as companies focus on the development of organisational structures based on integrated value-adding activities. The internal and external network arrangements depicted in Figure 17.1 more accurately represent this approach. In other words, in reality the key processes are becoming more *integrated* and *interdependent* (rather than *discrete* and *independent*).

This model has implications in terms of the organisational structures adopted by companies. Companies who adopt SCM philosophy have often based their organisational structures around the three key business processes, often augmented by 'support' functions such as finance, information technology (IT) and human resources (HR). These 'support' functions are essentially concerned with the management of the enabling resources of money, information and people. In this way, the most senior levels of management in companies are based on genuinely value-adding business processes and have a strong focus on customers as a result.

New Challenges for SCM in the 21st Century

Supply chains have become more global as a direct result of structural changes in the world economy. In addition, they have become more virtual as companies outsource key supply chain functions. These two factors have resulted in SCM becoming a more important determinant of competitive advantage than ever before. They have also made SCM more complex than ever before. In developed economies, the continuing shift in emphasis away from manufacturing and towards the provision of high-value services will have a major impact on the essence of SCM in the coming years and decades.[3] In this context, there is a need to think of SCM in a radically different way. In short, SCM will need to move up the value-adding hierarchy. It will become less concerned with the physical movement of material and more with the management of information and knowledge. This shift has profound implications for the knowledge and skill base of logisticians and supply chain professionals. It also has implications in terms of IT and communications infrastructure.

Supply Chain Virtual Hub Architectures

If the opportunities presented by the new business model, and the central role of SCM as part of it, are to be turned into sustainable competitive advantage there is an urgent need for the key players to begin to put the necessary capability into place. One way to achieve this – as proposed in an Irish context in Sweeney (2002) – is through the creation of a working logistics/SCM centre of excellence or virtual 'hub'. This is based on the concept of clustering and is a model which has been used by many sectors.[4] There are a number of key principles guiding the design of such architectures.

---

[3]Ireland will be particularly affected by this trend due to the open nature of the economy and the high proportion of imports and exports as a percentage of GDP (see Chapter 2).
[4]For example, the successful International Financial Services Centre (IFSC) in Dublin.

Focus on Value

The guiding principle of the proposed hub has to be value creation and addition. Value can only be added or created if there is a strong focus on customers' needs and on the ways in which customer service requirements are changing in key strategic market segments. The focus is on business processes which cross traditional functional barriers, create value and facilitate the shift from fragmentation to integration in organisations.

Information Management as a Key Integrator

Excellence in the management of information is a critical success factor (CSF) for the proposed configuration. This means that the hub has to have extensive knowledge and skills in relation to supply chain ICT as its kernel. If genuine decoupling of material flow from information flow is to be achieved, the effective and efficient management of supply chain information is of paramount importance.

Management of Partnerships and Alliances

In line with the theme of the previous chapters and with *Fundamental Four* in particular (see Chapter 3), the effective management of partnerships and alliances will have to be an underpinning principle of the proposed hub. This is vital as supply chain functions are increasingly outsourced, and as supply chains become more virtual as a direct result.

HUB CONCEPTUAL DESIGN

The virtual hub is based on the 'SCM Village' concept. A conceptual design proposal is shown in Figure 17.3.

The design has SCM learning and research at its core. This supplies the highly trained and educated professionals for the village (and elsewhere). The positioning of this activity at the centre of the village also enhances the learning process itself by providing an active learning environment – the village becomes the SCM campus. Research is carried out here also with the twin objectives of providing village companies with access to leading supply chain thinking and of ensuring that all learning processes are genuinely based on world-class best practice. All learning and research activities are carried out in partnership with village companies.

Around this central activity sit the logistics service provision (LSP) companies. These provide a range of integrated third-party (3PL) and

Figure 17.3: Hub or SCM Village Conceptual Design

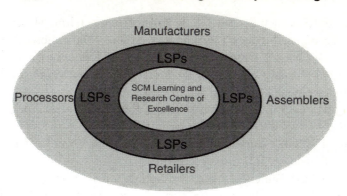

fourth-party (4PL) value-adding logistics services and supply chain solutions to village clients.

Finally, the client companies of the LSPs are clustered in the village, working in close collaboration with the learning and research activities and the LSPs. These companies represent a range of players from different industry sectors and different parts of the supply chain (i.e. processors, manufacturers, assemblers and retailers).

SOME CONCLUDING COMMENTS

The future by its very nature cannot be predicted with absolute certainty. In the SCM and logistics environment, change is pervasive. The international environment continues to change at a rapid rate. The markets in which companies are competing are changing. Customers are becoming more discerning and markets more complex and sophisticated as a result. Technology, in particular ICT, continues to develop at a brisk pace. This has implications in terms of products and processes. Product life-cycles continue to shorten. Success in the future will be predicated on the ability of organisations to design robust and agile supply chain architectures. The focus will be on strategic SCM – based on building supply chain capability in advance of the requirement in a pro-active manner. The effective adoption of contemporary approaches to SCM, such as those introduced in this book, will be central to the building of this capability.

REFERENCES

Finn, C. and Sweeney, E. (2004), 'The Role of Supply Chain Management in Irish Enterprise Strategy Development. A Three-Dimensional Approach', *Enhancing Competitive Advantage through Supply Chain Innovation, Proceedings of the 9th Annual Conference of the Logistics Research Network (LRN2004)*, 9–10 September, Dublin: NITL, 183–187.

Hamer, M. (1995), *The Re-engineering Revolution*, New York: Harper Brothers.

Sweeney, E. (2002), 'Supply Chain Management in Ireland – The Future', *Logistics Solutions*, 5(3), 14–16.

Sweeney, E. and Faulkner, R. (2001), 'Supply Chain Management and the Business Model of the 21st Century', *Logistics Solutions*, 4(5), 8–12.

Glossary

3PL	Third Party Logistics
4PL	Fourth Party Logistics
ABC	Activity Based Costing
AI	Artificial Intelligence
APS	Advanced Planning and Scheduling
ASN	Advance Shipping Notice
ASP	Application Service Provider
B2B	Business-to-Business
B2C	Business-to-Consumer
BOM	Bill of Materials
BPO	Business Process Outsourcing
BPR	Business Process Re-engineering
CEO	Chief Executive Officer
COD	Cash on Delivery
CPFR	Collaborative Planning, Forecasting and Replenishment
CR	Continuous Replenishment
CRM	Customer Relationship Management
CSCMP	Council of Supply Chain Management Professionals
CSF	Critical Success Factor
DPP	Direct Product Profitability
DSS	Decision Support System
DTI	Department of Trade and Industry (UK)
ECR	Efficient Consumer Response
EDI	Electronic Data Interchange
EERP	Extended Enterprise Resource Planning
EFT	Electronic Funds Transfer
EIA	Enterprise Integration Application
EMS	Electronic Manufacturing Services
e-ND	e-business Networking Division
EOL	End of Life

EPC	Electronic Purchasing Consortia
ERP	Enterprise Resource Planning
e-SCM	e-Supply Chain Management
EU	European Union
FDI	Foreign Direct Investment
FMCG	Fast Moving Consumer Goods
FMS	Flexible Manufacturing System
FRS	Functional Requirement Specification
FVI	Fully Vertically (or Virtually) Integrated
GDP	Gross Domestic Product
GPS	Global Positioning System
HR	Human Resource
HRM	Human Resource Management
ICT	Information and Communications Technology
IOS	Inter-Organisational System
IPR	Intellectual Property Rights
IT	Information Technology
ITO	Information Technology Outsourcing
ITT	Invitation to Tender
JIT	Just in Time
KPI	Key Performance Indicator
LSP	Logistics Service Provider
MBO	Management by Objectives
MC	Mass Customisation
MES	Manufacturing Execution System
MNE	Multi-National Enterprise
MRO	Maintenance, Repair and Operations
MRP	Materials Requirements Planning
MRP (II)	Manufacturing Resource Planning
NAPM	National Association of Purchasing Managers
NITL	National Institute for Transport and Logistics
NPD	New Product Development
NPI	New Product Introduction
NVA	Non-Value-Adding Activity
OEM	Original Equipment Manufacturer
PC	Personal Computer
PCB	Printed Circuit Board
PDCA	Plan, Do, Check, Act
PDP	Product Delivery Process
QR	Quick Response

R&D	Research and Development
RFI	Request for Information
RFID	Radio Frequency Identification
RFP	Request for Proposal
RFQ	Request for Quotation
RFx:	Request for x
ROCE	Return on Capital Employed
ROI	Return on Investment
SCC	Supply Chain Council
SCD	Supply Chain Design
SCM	Supply Chain Management
SCO	Supply Chain Orientation
SCOR	Supply Chain Operations Reference
SLA	Service Level Agreement
SMART	**S**pecific, **M**easurable, **A**ligned, **R**ealistic & **T**ime-based (objectives)
SME	Small or Medium Sized Enterprise
SOA	Service Oriented Architecture
TCO	Total Cost of Ownership
TCP	Time Compression Programme
TMS	Transportation Management System
TPS	Toyota Production System
UN	United Nations
UNCTAD	United Nations Conference on Trade & Development
URS	User Requirement Specification
VBM	Value Based Management
VIM	Vendor Managed Inventory
VNC	Virtual Network Consortia
WIP	Work in Progress (or Process)
WMS	Warehouse Management System
WTO	World Trade Organisation
XES	Extended Enterprise Solution
XML	Extensible Mark-up Language

Index

activity based costing (ABC) 44–5, 103–6
  limitations 103–5
  time-driven 105–6
advanced planning systems (APS) 219, 250
AEI 260
agility 30, 75, 79–80, 83, 89–90, 125–6, 291
Airbus 76–7
Alcatel 261
Alignment 304–6
Alliances 125–6
Amazon.com 116
application service provider (ASP) 242, 259
artificial intelligence (AI) 252
Asia 74
auction and RFQ markets 259
automotive sector 8, 266, 273

benchmarking 285–7, 293–4
best of breed solutions 238–9, 241
Boeing 76–7
branding 115, 117, 120–21, 311
BSC Group 128
business process re-engineering (BPR) 32, 35, 180, 309–10
business strategy 73–4, 84, 89–90

Business-to-Business (B2B) 267–9
Business-to-Consumer (B2C) 267
Business-to-Government (B2G) 267

cash-to-cash cycle time 54–5
Celestica 10
change management 304–6
channel masters 100
Chartered Institute of Purchasing and Supply (CIPS) 220
China (People's Republic of) 8–9, 128
collaborative planning, forecasting and replenishment (CPFR) 250
common size statements 285
communal coordination 147
competencies 80
  see also core competency
competitive advantage 141, 161
concentration 78, 81, 90
contracts 150–7, 229, 230–31
core competency 9, 57–8, 171, 173–4, 195
co-sourcing 174
cost analysis 12, 135
cost/benefit analysis 135
cost leadership 12

321

creditor days 97, 98, 101
critical success factor (CSF) 287, 293, 302, 308, 314
customer
  categorisation 131, 137
  profitability 131, 134–7
  segmentation 133–4, 165–6
customer relationship management (CRM) 119, 140, 146–8, 159–66, 219, 239
customer service 41–3, 131–48, 298, 300
  as an order winner 12–13, 43, 137, 308–9
  definition 132
  elements of 42, 47, 132, 162–4
  surveys 160, 161, 164–5
  10 Commandments 133

debtor days 97, 98, 101
de-capitalisation 201–2
decision support system (DSS) 250–52
Dell 89–90, 100, 116
differentiated business model 90
differentiation 12, 78, 81, 115, 116, 120–21
direct product profitability (DPP) 44
disintermediation 260

earnings per share (EPS) 285
Eastern Europe 8
e-Business 218–19, 258–9, 261–2, 265–76
  SME sector 274–5
e-Commerce 218–19
economic and business environment
  Ireland 20–1
effectiveness and efficiency 283

efficient consumer response (ECR) 31–2, 44, 194–5, 201
electronic data interchange (EDI) 56, 221, 238, 252, 265–6
electronic purchasing
  consortia (EPC) 270
  systems 192
electronics industry 267
e-marketplace 271–4
enterprise integration application (EIA) 250
enterprise resource planning (ERP) 55, 219, 236, 238–41, 246
e-Procurement 220–22, 267
e-Supply Chain Management (e-SCM) 219–20
evolving integration 116
exchanges 259
extended enterprise resource planning (EERP) 240–41, 250
extended enterprise solution (XES) 55, 236, 240, 246
extensible mark-up language (XML) 220, 239, 241, 266
external measurement 284–7

financial management 81–3, 93–107
financial status ratios 285
financial supply chain 200–01, 253
Five Forces Analysis 84–6
fixed assets 94–5, 96–7, 102
flexible manufacturing systems (FMS) 30
Flextronics 10
focus strategy 12, 13
Ford 211
  Model T 126
foreign direct investment (FDI) 8, 20

fourth-party logistics (4PL) 202, 256, 260–61, 315
Foxconn 10
fully vertically integrated (FVI) 58
functional requirements specification (FRS) 247

General Electric 80
global positioning system (GPS) 252
glocalisation 9

Hewlett-Packard 211
horizontal e-marketplace 271–4

IBM 211
India 9, 102
infomediaries 259–60
information and communications technology (ICT) 55–6, 235–43
  future 275–6
  logistics 249–62
  planning and implementation process 246–7
  role in SCM 55–6, 235–43, 245–7, 314
  strategy 245–7, 300
  trends 258–61
information
  flows 32, 55–6
  management 314
insourcing 175
integral coordination 148
integrated financial model 95–7
internal measurement 286, 287–8
internationalisation 7–9
inter-organisational system (IOS) 265–6
intersectionist perspective 61
invitation to tender (ITT) 246

Ireland 20–21, 297, 313
  external trade figures 23–5

just in time (JIT) 12, 47, 194, 197, 198, 201, 286–7

Kaizen 290, 302
key performance indicator (KPI) 289, 300–01

leagility 31
lean manufacture 79–80
learning supply chain 290–91
lifetime profitability 134
logistics 29, 60–62
  control systems 252
  execution systems 252
  integrated 29
  management 200
  outsourcing 175–6
  planning systems 252
  service provider (LSP) 314–15

maintenance, repair and operations (MRO) 269, 273
management by objectives (MBO) 41
manufacturing execution system (MES) 237
manufacturing resource planning (MRPII) 219, 240
market
  research 118–19
  saturation 115
  segmentation 119–22, 133–4
marketing 111–29, 311
  definition 111–13
  4Ps 112–13, 122
  mix 116–17, 118, 122–3, 159–60

marketing (cont.)
  orientation 113–16
  7Ps 123–6
  strategy 119–22
mass customisation (MC) 30–1, 43, 117, 120, 126–7, 267
materials management 53–4
materials requirements planning (MRP) 240
MG Rover 77–8
middleware 239
money flow 54–5
muda 12, 29, 47

National Institute for Transport and Logistics (NITL) 2, 297
network economy model 11
new market entry 127–8
new product development (NPD) 122, 142–3, 197
new product introduction (NPI) 196–7, 310–12
Nissan 211
non-value-adding activity (NVA) 12, 29, 96, 308

offshoring 7, 171–2
  see also outsourcing
on-demand business applications 242
OOCL 258–9
order cycle time 162–3
order qualifying criteria 12–13, 30, 138–40
order winning criteria 12, 30, 137–40
organisation structures 125, 299, 310
organisational re-engineering 50, 295–6

original equipment manufacturer (OEM) 10, 273
outsourcing 8, 9–10, 58, 171–84, 187–9
  business process 177
  decapitalisation 201–2
  drivers 180–81
  electronics 176–7
  Ireland 21
  IT 176–7, 181
  levels 174
  logistics 175–6, 206, 257
    see also third party logistics; fourth party logistics
  methodology 187–9
  reasons for 172–3, 178–80
  risk 172, 181–3
  selective 174
  total 174
  transport 177
  vs. subcontracting 201

P&O 260
partnership 56, 125
people 123–4, 302
perfect order 144
performance measurement 283–91
performance metrics 143–5, 153–6
performance pyramid 289
performance/capability continuum 33–4
PEST (Political, Economic, Social, Technological) analysis 84–6
plan, do, check, act (PDCA) 294
point solutions 236–9, 252
Porter model 84–5
postponement 99, 126–7
price to earnings (P/E) ratio 285
price erosion 80

Index

pricing 122–3
process 122
procurement
   models 220–22
   see also e-procurement; purchasing
product
   availability 162
   delivery process (PDP) 46–7
   life cycle 122, 141, 196–9
   supply chain 75, 76–81
production orientation 113–14
profitability 134–7
purchasing 191–203, 209–23
   consortium 10
   legal aspects 222
   logistics 199–200
   manuals 216–17, 225–6
   new product introduction 196–7
   phases 215–16
   process chain 210
   product lifecycle 198–9
   traditional 215–19
   transactional 212–14
purchasing consolidation markets 259

quick response (QR) 31–2, 194–5, 201

radio frequency identification (RFID) 252
re-labelling 61
request for information (RFI) 270
request for proposal (RFP) 205–6, 270
request for quotation (RFQ) 215, 259, 270
request for x (RFx) 270
return on capital employed (ROCE) 93

reverse auction 270–71
reverse engineering 286
reverse logistics 53, 116
Roca 128

sales orientation 114
serial coordination 147
service level agreement (SLA) 145–8, 150–57, 188, 206
service oriented architecture (SOA) 242
service/cost conundrum 46–7
shareholder value 13
Singapore 82
SMART objectives 144, 205
Social Responsibility Orientation 116
spider diagram 87
spot freight markets 259
strategic
   alignment model 13–14
   management 12–14, 74
   partnering 58–9
   procurement management 195–6
supplier manuals 217, 227–8
supply chain
   audit 42–3
   competition 36, 51, 77, 78, 138
   costs 12, 44–7, 82–3, 93, 101–05, 127
   design 141–3, 165–6
   external 49, 51–2, 128
   financial 75, 81–3, 200–01
   ICT 55–6, 235–43, 245–7
   improvement 297–8, 304–6
   information 75, 83–9
   integration 48–52, 116, 254–6, 296
   internal 49–51, 127

Index

supply chain (*cont.*)
  learning 290–1
  models 8–9, 11
  organisation 298–9
  orientation (SCO) 38, 50
  product 75, 76–81
  re-engineering 298–302, 304–6
  software 241–2
  vulnerability 196
Supply Chain Council (SCC) 32
supply chain management (SCM) 140
  agility 89–90
  definitions 27, 34–9, 59, 71–2
  excellence 296–7
  flow management 53–6, 60, 116, 253
  Four Fundamentals 40–59, 311
  goals/objectives 41–8
  historical evolution 27–34, 38–9, 254, 265
  integration 48–52, 116, 161, 288, 290
  logistics 60–2
  performance measurement 288–90
  philosophy 34–5, 48–52, 312
  relationships 56–9, 83, 193
  village 314–15
supply chain operations reference (SCOR) model 32–3, 69, 70
supply management 194, 195, 199
supply structures 80
symbiotic coordination 147–8
systems approach 301–2

third party logistics (3PL) 9, 10–11, 61, 200, 205–7, 253–8, 314–15
time compression 47, 78–9

time-based SCM 47
time-driven ABC 105–6
total cost of ownership (TCO) 45, 271
Total Integration 28, 116
total systems thinking 51, 295
Toyota 192, 287
  production system (TPS) 12
track and trace 257–8
trade
  blocs 307
  figures 8
trade-offs 45
traditionalist 61
transport 199–200
  costs 21
Transportation Management System (TMS) 237, 253
trend analysis 284

unionist perspective 61–2
UPS 261
user requirements specification (URS) 246

value based management (VBM) 13
value chain 36–8, 77, 195, 313
  positioning 195
vendor managed inventory (VMI) 160
vertical disintegration 11, 57–8
vertical e-Marketplace 272–3
virtual corporation 95
virtual hub 313–14
virtual network consortia (VNC) 34, 58

warehouse management system (WMS) 49, 55, 236, 237, 253
waste 12, 29, 47

web-based ERP 241–2
work in progress (or process) (WIP) 98–9
working capital 95–7
  cycle 54–5, 97–8, 101
  optimisation 98–101

World Trade Organisation (WTO) 8, 74, 307

Xerox 286, 287

Zara 126